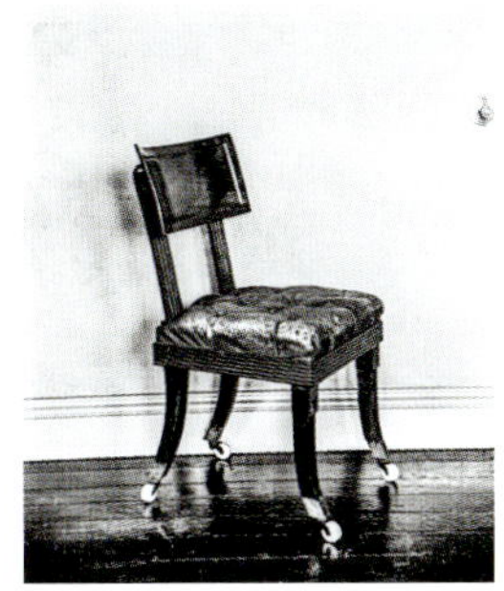

A VANISHING WORLD

The Irish Country House Photographs of Father Browne

Edited by Robert O'Byrne

Published by Messenger Publications, 2024

ISBN: 9781 78812 7073

Designed by Brendan McCarthy
Typeset in Trajan and Adobe Garamond Pro
Printed by GPS Colour Graphics

Messenger MJP Publications

Messenger Publications,
37 Leeson Place, Dublin
D02 E5VO
www.messenger.ie

CONTENTS

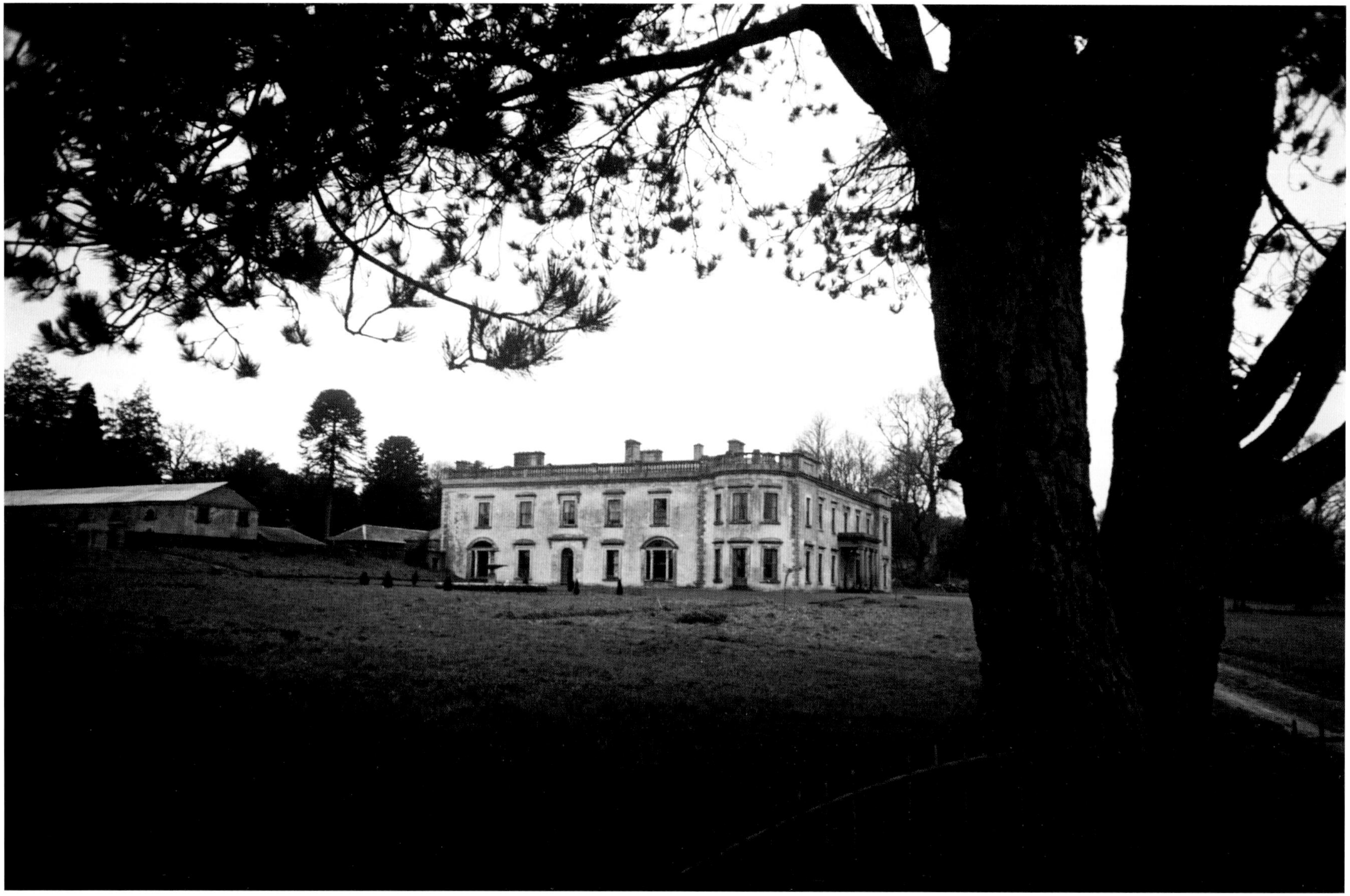

Lamberton, County Laois, photographed 1st January 1944, demolished later that year

Introduction

The youngest of eight children, Francis Patrick Mary Browne was born in Cork city in January 1880. His parents belonged to the country's newly affluent Catholic bourgeoisie. Within a week of being born, he lost his mother to puerperal fever. After primary school, Francis attended the Jesuit Belvedere College, Dublin, as a day pupil, and then boarded with the Vincentian Fathers at Castleknock College also in Dublin. His first photographic attempts were made in 1897 when, accompanied by an older brother, he travelled through France, Italy, Switzerland and Germany. The pictures he took on this trip are those of a tourist, but already there is evidence of the eye for composition that would later be refined.

On returning to Ireland, Francis entered the Society of Jesus novitiate in Tullabeg, County Offaly, aged seventeen. On arrival, he was required to hand over his camera since it was regarded as a 'superfluity' and a distraction from his preparation for the priesthood. Even though he subsequently moved to Dublin to study at University College, several more years would pass before he was permitted to take photographs again. This occurred in 1902 when he was sent to the Jesuit house in the Italian town of Chieri, south-west of Turin. During the summer months of this period, he was able to travel around the country, staying in properties belonging to the order and improving his skills with a camera, which was not difficult in such a photogenic part of the world. He also had an opportunity to visit many museums and art galleries, absorbing ideas on composition from the old masters.

Back in Ireland in 1905, Frank Browne was sent to teach in Belvedere College, and spent the next five years there. During the first of these he put his photographic abilities to use by founding a camera club (as well as a cycling club and a college annual, *The Belvederian*, in which some of his pictures were published). For the next stage of his training, he moved to another Jesuit house, Milltown Park, on the outskirts of Dublin.

It was while here that he received a gift from his uncle Robert Browne, Bishop of Cloyne: a ticket to travel on the first two legs of the maiden voyage of a new liner, the *Titanic*. He boarded the vessel at Southampton on 10 April 1912 and sailed first to Cherbourg, where more passengers were collected, and then to Queenstown (now Cobh), County Cork, the *Titanic's* last stop before crossing the Atlantic. While on board, Frank Browne had become friendly with an American family who offered to pay his fare for the remaining part of the voyage, and a message was sent to the Provincial Superior of the Jesuits in Ireland asking if this might be allowed. On arrival at Queenstown, a reply awaited. It read 'GET OFF THAT SHIP – PROVINCIAL.'

The young man dutifully disembarked, with his camera, and the *Titanic* sailed to its doom. After the vessel sank on 15 April, the photographs he had taken while on board were much in demand, and were published in newspapers around the world. They remain invaluable historical documents and have helped to secure his lasting fame. Had he intended to become a professional photographer the *Titanic* pictures would have been of considerable help in advancing his career. But Frank Browne was intent on becoming a Jesuit priest, finally realising this ambition in July 1915. The following February he became a chaplain to the First Battalion of the Irish Guards, serving in that capacity first on the front line in France and Flanders until November 1918 and then in Germany for another eighteen months. Although gassed once and injured five times (on one occasion needing to have his jaw wired up), he survived this gruelling period, continuing to take photographs which, like those of the *Titanic*, are today of immense historic interest.

Nothing during the second half of his long life brought Father Browne to the centre of global events again, but it was nevertheless filled with activities that were of importance to him. Having once more spent time teaching in Belvedere College, he became Superior of St Francis Xavier's Church on nearby Gardiner Street, where he became renowned as a preacher. In 1928 he was assigned to the mission and retreat staff of the Jesuit order, a position he held for the next thirty years. While based at Emo Court, a late eighteenth-century country house in County Laois that the Jesuits had just acquired, he was required to travel throughout Ireland, and often to England, giving parish missions and leading retreats for nuns, priests and children.

Much of his work took place in the evenings, leaving him time during the day to explore – and photograph – his immediate surroundings. Father Browne took full advantage of these opportunities and, as his substantial archive reveals, little escapes his attention. The camera was an extension of himself and reflects his own curious eye. Everything was of interest to him, and everything deserved to be recorded. This is what makes the collection he left behind so valuable: it documents all aspects of daily life across some fifty years, although, as has been noted by other commentators, one notable lacuna can be found in this visual narrative: there are no pictures of public house interiors.

In 1957, three years before his death, Father Browne was transferred from Emo Court, his home for the previous three decades, back to Milltown Park, Dublin. While there, he catalogued his immense catalogue of photographs, by now running to some 42,000 negatives, providing names and dates for them all, documentation that has proven invaluable when compiling books of his work such as this one. He died aged eighty in July 1960.

This brief summary of Father Frank Browne's life is necessary in order to emphasise that its main focus was always his religious faith and work as a Jesuit priest. Although today recognised as Ireland's finest photographer during the first half of the last century, he perceived the medium that has brought him posthumous fame primarily as just a hobby, to be fitted in – and sometimes set aside – as and when required by his superiors in the order. This is not to ignore his passionate interest in photography. Having already founded a camera club while teaching at Belvedere College, he later became a member of both the Photographic Society of Ireland and the Dublin Camera Club (the two organisations were amalgamated in the early 1930s). The Dublin Camera Club had been established by William Harding, journalist and editor of a magazine called *The Camera*. In June 1927 he proposed to a group of like-minded friends, including Father Browne, that they hold an exhibition of their work: the first Irish Salon

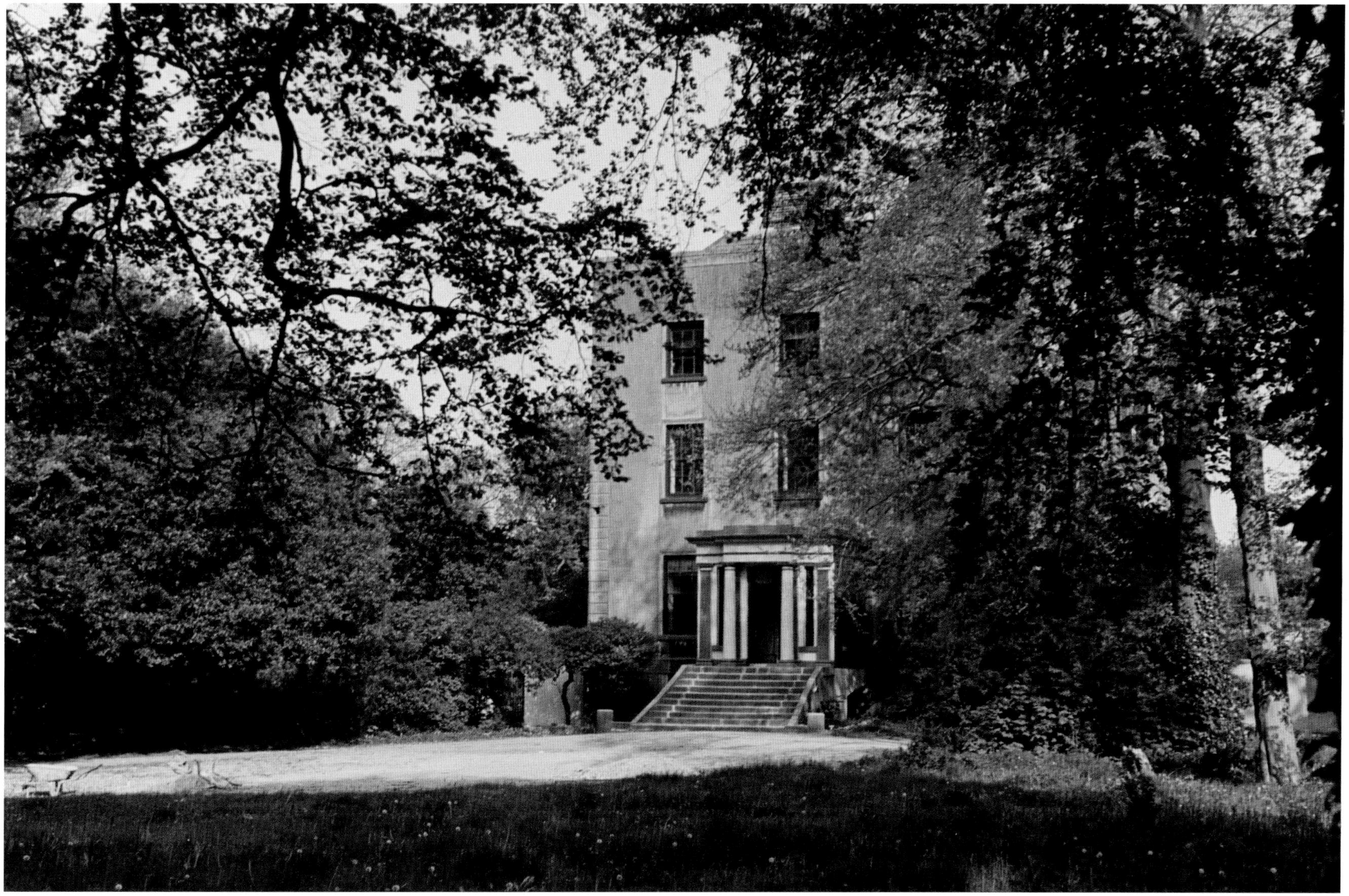

Mespil House, Dublin, photographed 16th October 1943, demolished 1951

of Photography was held later that year and became a biennial event until the outbreak of the Second World War. Father Browne acted as vice-president of the show and exhibited his own work, for which he was awarded many prizes.

However, photography always remained an extra-curricular activity. This makes his achievement in the medium all the more impressive. One way or another, it had to be accommodated within the pre-ordained structure of Jesuit life. Only when other obligations permitted could time be given to this interest. Browne the photographer deserves comparison with Andrea Pozzo, the seventeenth-century Jesuit brother who was also a highly talented painter and architect. Fra Pozzo could have had a successful secular career as an artist, but instead chose to devote himself to the Catholic Church and, in particular, to the Jesuit order, for which he executed his greatest works. Not the least of these is the astonishing illusory perspective ceiling in the Church of Sant'Ignazio in Rome – no doubt Father Browne would have seen this on one of his visits to the city.

He would have known of Fra Pozzo and, like him, have understood the obligation to follow instructions rather than his own personal wishes. Where and when he went was decided for him, and so therefore were the places he had an opportunity to photograph. The handful of letters written by him to his provincial superior that survive demonstrate this point. In June 1944, for example, he explained that he would be leading diocesan retreats in Ennis, County Clare, for a fortnight and therefore asked whether he might be allowed to take a day or two to photograph the monastic ruins at Inis Cealtra. 'Would your Reverence,' he enquired, 'give me permission to spend a night – or if necessary two nights – in the hotel there, so as to have time to get the photos?' Even in his seventies, still obeying the vows he had taken as a young man, he had to submit a request to use his camera while away from his place of residence. His humility is apparent in a letter written in 1945 in which he thanks the provincial superior for 'all the kindness you have shown me on this & other occasions when I have become a burden on the Society. No one has ever been so great a liability – & it is really & truly one of my greatest mortifications to realise it.'

Resisting the urge to follow his own wishes must always have been challenging, particularly during the 1940s and '50s when he received many commissions for pictures. The requests came from a wide variety of individuals and organisations, including the Office of Public Works, the Irish Sugar Company and Bord na Móna. Inevitably his services were regularly called upon by the Irish Tourism Association (a precursor of Fáilte Ireland). Even before this period, he had already achieved sufficient renown that in 1933 Kodak offered to provide him with free film for the rest of his life (one wonders whether the company expected him to live quite so long!).

These commercial assignments indicate that Father Browne could have made a living as a photographer, but chose not to do so. Furthermore, he was not allowed to retain any of the financial compensation received for his work – and during certain busy periods the amounts must have been substantial: the money was immediately forwarded to the provincial treasurer of the Jesuit order. At least he could derive some consolation from the knowledge that the funds were, at his own suggestion, used to assist in the education of Jesuit students by providing what he nicknamed 'Brownie Burses'. In June 1947 he was able to tell his provincial superior that thanks to his latest commissions, the bursary's value currently stood at £1,010.

Nevertheless, Father Browne remained consistently aware that he was a Jesuit priest first and a photographer second. In late October 1944, he received a note from the provincial superior's office noting that his travelling expenses were unusually high, and while there was no desire 'to stint any of our good Fathers, above all those who work so hard and so effectively as our missioners', there was a concern 'to guard against the danger of extravagance, or expenditure unbecoming our religious poverty'. In an apologetic response Father Browne explained that of late, when sent on long journeys he had taken to travelling first class on trains, after suffering a series of lumbago attacks from getting cold while on journeys around the country. In future, he now promised, he would not travel in such a manner.

Before long, however, he found himself taking more trips around the country, and not just to lead retreats or other religious services. In 1947 he received the first of a series of commissions from the *Irish Tatler & Sketch*, which described itself as 'Ireland's Premier Social & Sporting Monthly'. It was first published in 1890 as *The Lady of the House* before changing its title in 1924. From around the time it first engaged with Father Browne until 1961 the magazine carried a series of illustrated articles on Irish country houses. Many of these pieces featured not only photographs by Father Browne but also text that he had written. Unfortunately, only one letter between him and the publication appears to have survived. Dated 5 January 1949, it concerns pictures of Dromoland Castle, County Clare, then still home to the O'Brien family. Father Browne had produced a large number of photographs of both the building and its surrounding gardens, and the editor, N.C. Hartnell, had decided to split them into two articles, to run in the February and March issues.

No information has been found to explain how the *Irish Tatler & Sketch* initiated contact with Father Browne, but by the mid-1940s, thanks to his work with the various organisations mentioned above, he was well known as a photographer of exceptional ability. Furthermore, he had already been taking pictures of historic houses for several years, since at the time quite a number of them were occupied by Catholic religious orders. His earliest images of Rathfarnham Castle, for example, date from 1920, just seven years after the building had been bought by the Jesuit order. Similarly, he often photographed Emo Court in the years after it was acquired by the same order, for many of which he lived in the building. Other such properties in the hands of various religious bodies that he visited to photograph included Ballyfin, County Laois, Moore Abbey, County Kildare, and Dundrum, County Tipperary. He also took pictures of houses still in secular hands. The earliest of the buildings featured in the present volume, Herbertstown in County Meath, was also the most recently constructed; it dates from 1916, just twenty-one years before Father Browne photographed the place. Once again, no correspondence or other archival material seems to survive to explain why he should have visited this property at that date.

By the mid-1940s, therefore, when Father Browne came to take pictures of country houses for publication, he was well used to using them as subjects. Although he had long been in the habit of photographing everywhere and everything, buildings of this type now seem to have piqued a particular interest. In April 1945, in a letter to his provincial superior, he explained that earlier that year, while in Portlaw, County Waterford, to give a triduum (a Catholic religious observance lasting three days), he had received permission to visit nearby Curraghmore, home to the de la Poer Beresfords, Marquises of Waterford. 'I did so,' he elaborated, 'because I am collecting a set of Georgian Houses, & Curraghmore was on the list given me by the Georgian Society.' It is unclear what organisation he means, since the original Georgian Society had come to an end in 1913 and its eventual successor, the Irish Georgian Society, was not established until 1958; it may be that he was using the fifth volume of the *Georgian Society Records* (published 1913), which contained a catalogue of important country houses throughout the country, or else perhaps another work, *Georgian Mansions in Ireland*, by Thomas Sadleir and Page L. Dickinson, which appeared in 1915 and devoted several pages to Curraghmore.

In the same letter of April 1945, he informs the provincial superior that during his visit to the house he had learnt from Mrs Lindsay, mother of the widowed Lady Waterford, that her other two daughters had both converted to Catholicism, 'and she herself quite unexpectedly spoke to me about her own feelings on the subject'. Both Mrs Lindsay and Lady Waterford subsequently wrote to Father Browne encouraging him to visit again, and the latter sent him a donation 'for any charity in which I was interested'. He was clearly welcomed at Curraghmore, and, it would appear, at a great many other such properties, even though not all of their owners would necessarily have felt the same sympathy towards the Catholic faith. It says a great deal about Father Browne's character and is a reflection of his personal charm that he was able to gain access to so many houses at a time when they were still in private hands and not open to the public.

The first of them to appear in the *Irish Tatler & Sketch* was Shelton Abbey, County Wicklow, home for some 200 years to the Howards, Earls of Wicklow. At this time the last of the family to live there, William Howard, 8th Earl Wicklow, was in residence. In 1932 he had converted to Catholicism, much to the disgust of his father (seemingly, he was appalled at the idea of Shelton Abbey's heir attending the same church as the servants). Father Browne had visited the house in November 1946, but the following April he sought permission to go there again, as Lord Wicklow had recently told him 'that owing to his circumstance, he proposes utilising Shelton Abbey as a kind of hotel or "Country Club"'. He therefore wanted Father Browne to return to the house and take further photographs 'before the necessary alterations are made'. The building was then still filled with treasures accumulated by generations of Howards, many of them captured *in situ* by Father Browne as he and his camera went from room to room. His visit was timely – the hotel venture was not a success and after just three years Lord Wicklow was obliged to sell Shelton Abbey's contents in a spectacular auction that lasted for thirteen days. The great majority of

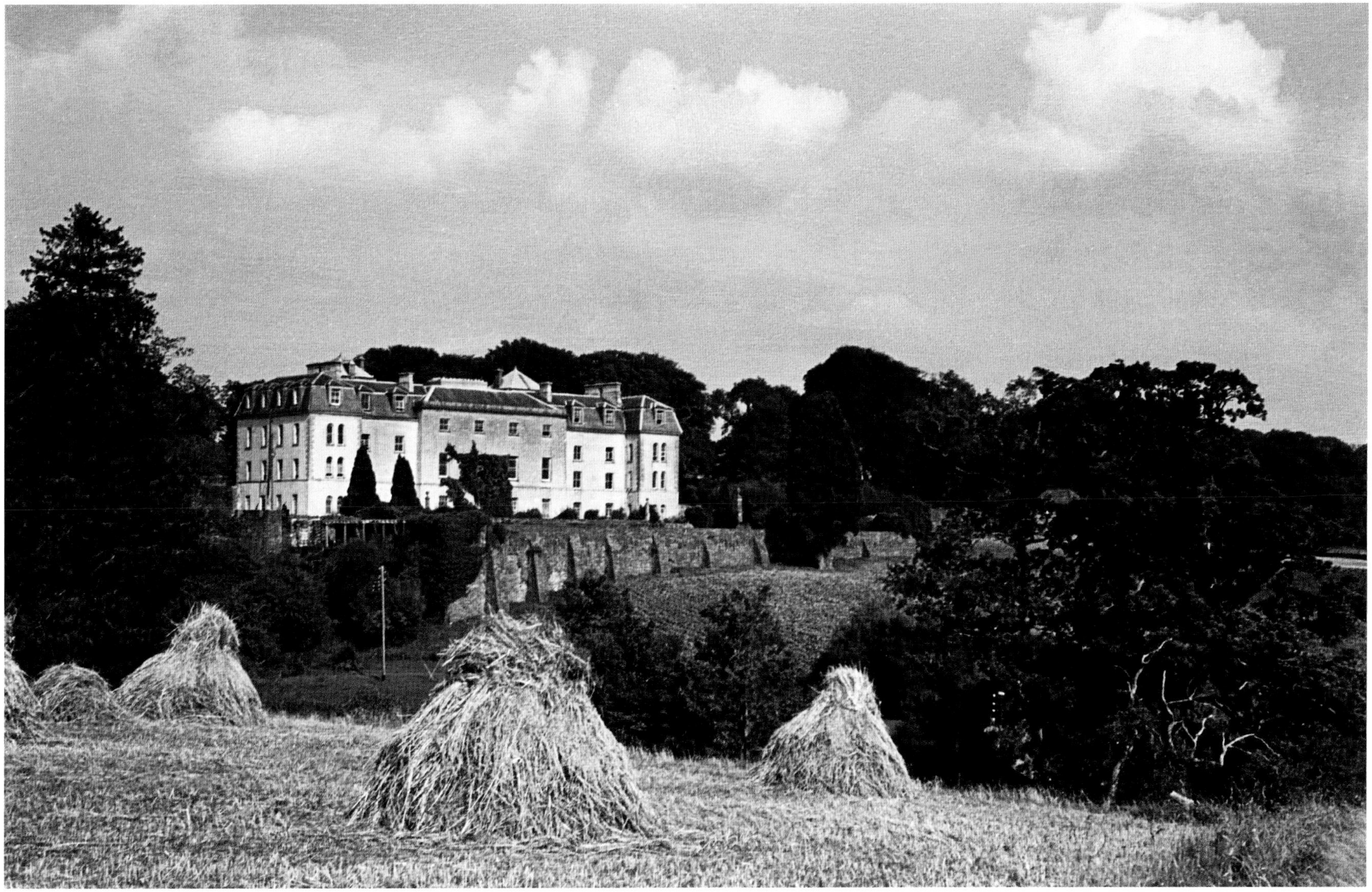

Heywood, County Laois, photographed 8th September 1943, destroyed by fire 1950

lots went to overseas buyers and left Ireland, making Father Browne's photographs priceless as a guide to how the house once looked. Today, Shelton Abbey is an open prison.

Other houses photographed during this period have either since been demolished, such as Rockingham and Frenchpark, both in County Roscommon, or left in ruins, like Killeen Castle in County Meath. Among those included here, two – Adare Manor, County Limerick, and Dromoland Castle, County Clare – are now hotels. Many more, the likes of Knocklofty, County Tipperary, and Glananea, County Westmeath, have changed hands on more than one occasion and have long lost their original contents; as recently as September 2021 the contents of Howth Castle, County Dublin – shown in photographs taken by Father Browne in July 1947 – were dispersed at auction. Happily, the story of what has happened since that time is not all bad. Some of the houses Father Browne visited, not least Castletown, County Kildare, and Malahide Castle, County Dublin, are now in public ownership and open to visitors, while Ormond Castle, County Tipperary, has, since passing into the care of the Office of Public Works, benefitted from an extensive programme of restoration. And a few of the houses shown over the coming pages remain in the same hands and have experienced relatively little change, among them Curraghmore and Lismore Castle, both in County Waterford, and Dunsany Castle in County Meath.

During his lifetime, and most particularly in the 1940s and '50s, Father Browne photographed more than fifty Irish country houses. However, as this selection indicates, they do not cover all of Ireland. Had he been a free agent, he might have taken pictures of a great many other places, but he could only go where he was permitted to go by his superiors; many visits to these historic properties were tagged on to other trips undertaken in the course of his work as a Catholic priest. In consequence, there are omissions. An obvious absence is Northern Ireland which, in the decades after independence, Father Browne does not appear to have visited. Most of the houses he photographed were in the east, the Midlands and the south. Other than the two Roscommon properties already mentioned, the west is unrepresented, and, aside from two houses in Louth and one in Monaghan, he took no pictures of houses north of Dublin.

These gaps are regrettable but, given the photographer's circumstances, understandable. We must be grateful that Father Browne managed to visit so many old houses and record them for posterity before the majority underwent irrevocable change. Not all of them feature here. Limitations of space and the desire to give adequate room to the houses included in this book means many more had to be left out. In a small number of cases, the pictures are not of the best quality or of insufficient number to merit their presence. In others, the houses have already been well documented, and images of them are easily available to anyone interested. Pictures of a few more are included in this introduction, such as Mespil House in Dublin, home for many years to the pioneering artist Sarah Purser, which Father Browne photographed just a couple of months after her death in August 1943. Within a decade, the mid-eighteenth-century building had been demolished, although thankfully three of its remarkable ceilings, attributed to the stuccodore Barthélemy Cramillion, were salvaged; two of them are now in Dublin Castle, and one in Áras an Uachtaráin. Then there was Lamberton in County Laois, a large two-storey Georgian house that Father Browne visited in January 1944, just a few months before it was stripped of everything worth salvaging and then demolished. Heywood, also in Laois, had been acquired by the Salesian order in 1941 and Father Browne photographed it on two occasions, in July 1943 and September 1945. Again, these images are important because in January 1950 the house was gutted by fire and later levelled.

After the pictures of Shelton Abbey appeared in the *Irish Tatler & Sketch* in 1947, further examples of Father Browne's country house photographs continued to appear in the magazine for a number of years, as they did in other publications, including *Ireland of the Welcomes* in 1953–54, and *The Irish Digest*. By then he had stopped travelling so much – he was, after all, in his mid-seventies – and would lead a more retired life until his death in 1960. Like the rest of his output, for a long time his photographs of Irish country houses were forgotten, and even when other pictures had been rediscovered and published, this particular group has not been given much attention. The present volume therefore serves two purposes: it allows us to see how these buildings looked in the middle of the last century and it gives us an opportunity to celebrate once more the outstanding talents of Father Francis Browne, photographer.

ADARE MANOR

COUNTY LIMERICK

11TH AUGUST 1949

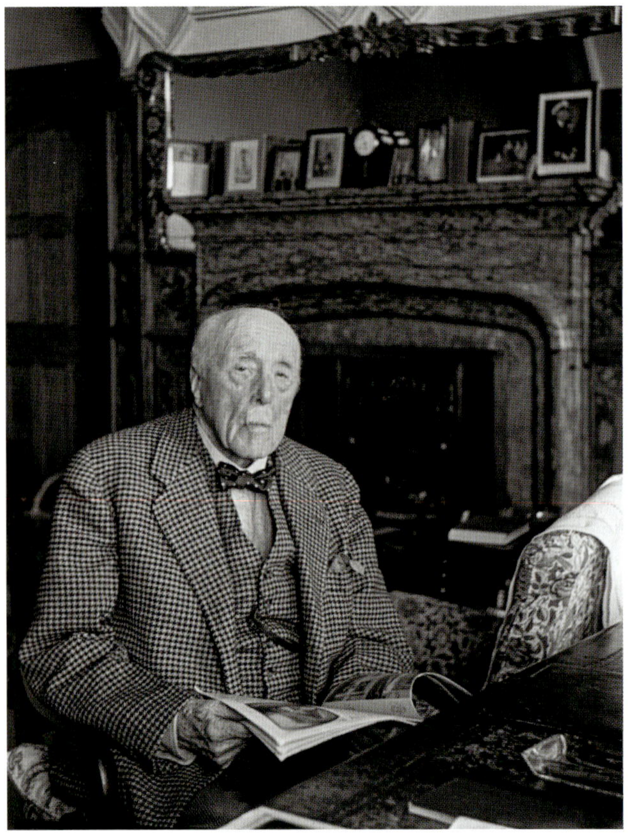

Above: The 92-year old 5th Earl of Dunraven who had inherited Adare Manor from a cousin in 1926

Opposite: The Manor's Great Hall seen from the south-west corner

Now a hotel, Adare Manor in its present form dates from the second quarter of the nineteenth century when it was built for the second and third earls of Dunraven. Descended from the O'Quins of Inchiquin, County Clare, their forebear Donagh Quin (died 1671) is thought to have been the first member of the family to have settled in Adare on lands formerly owned by the FitzGeralds. His son Thady Quin, a successful lawyer, made a series of financially advantageous marriages and was able to acquire a great deal of land in the area, thereby creating the estate enjoyed by future generations. Thady's heir, Valentine Quin, likewise married a wealthy heiress, Mary Widenham, and around 1725 the couple commissioned a new residence, Adare House. A relatively plain, south-facing, two-storey building of seven bays with a three-bay pedimented breakfront, Adare House had an additional storey added by the next generation, Windham Quin and his wife Frances Dawson.

Their son, another Valentine, was created Baron Adare, then Viscount Mount-Earl and, finally, in 1822 was made 1st Earl of Dunraven. However, in the early nineteenth century he had handed over responsibility for the family estate to his son Windham who, in 1810, married wealthy heiress Caroline Wyndham; in 1815, following his father-in-law's death, Windham Quin changed his surname by royal licence to Wyndham-Quin.

Over the following decade, the Wyndham-Quins – by now 2nd Earl and countess of Dunraven – embarked on the transformation of their Georgian house in Adare. They turned for advice to Limerick-based architect James Pain; in 1826 he had designed a mausoleum for the family beside the medieval Augustinian priory (today St Nicholas' Church of Ireland parish church). Pain and his brother George now came up with a number of options for a new house, including a classical pedimented mansion, but their clients preferred the alternative: a romantic Tudor-Revival manor. The style was then very much in vogue, and it suited the Dunravens' desire to emphasise their ancient lineage.

The Pain brothers' most significant contribution to the new house was the Gallery, intended to reflect their clients' love of medieval cathedrals. At the time of its construction the Gallery, more than 132 feet long, 21 feet wide and over 21 feet high, was the largest domestic space in the country. In the late 1830s, Lord Dunraven sought advice from English architect L.N. Cottingham, who had pioneered the study of the Gothic style. He assisted with the design of the new manor's interiors although he never came to Ireland. Augustus Pugin was also employed and the 3rd Earl later turned to Philip Charles Hardwick for completion of the south range and tower.

Yet, strangely, when the widowed Lady Dunraven came to write an account of the house, she claimed 'the greater portion of the building, and that the boldest in conception and most picturesque in effect, was designed by an amateur, not a single drawing having been

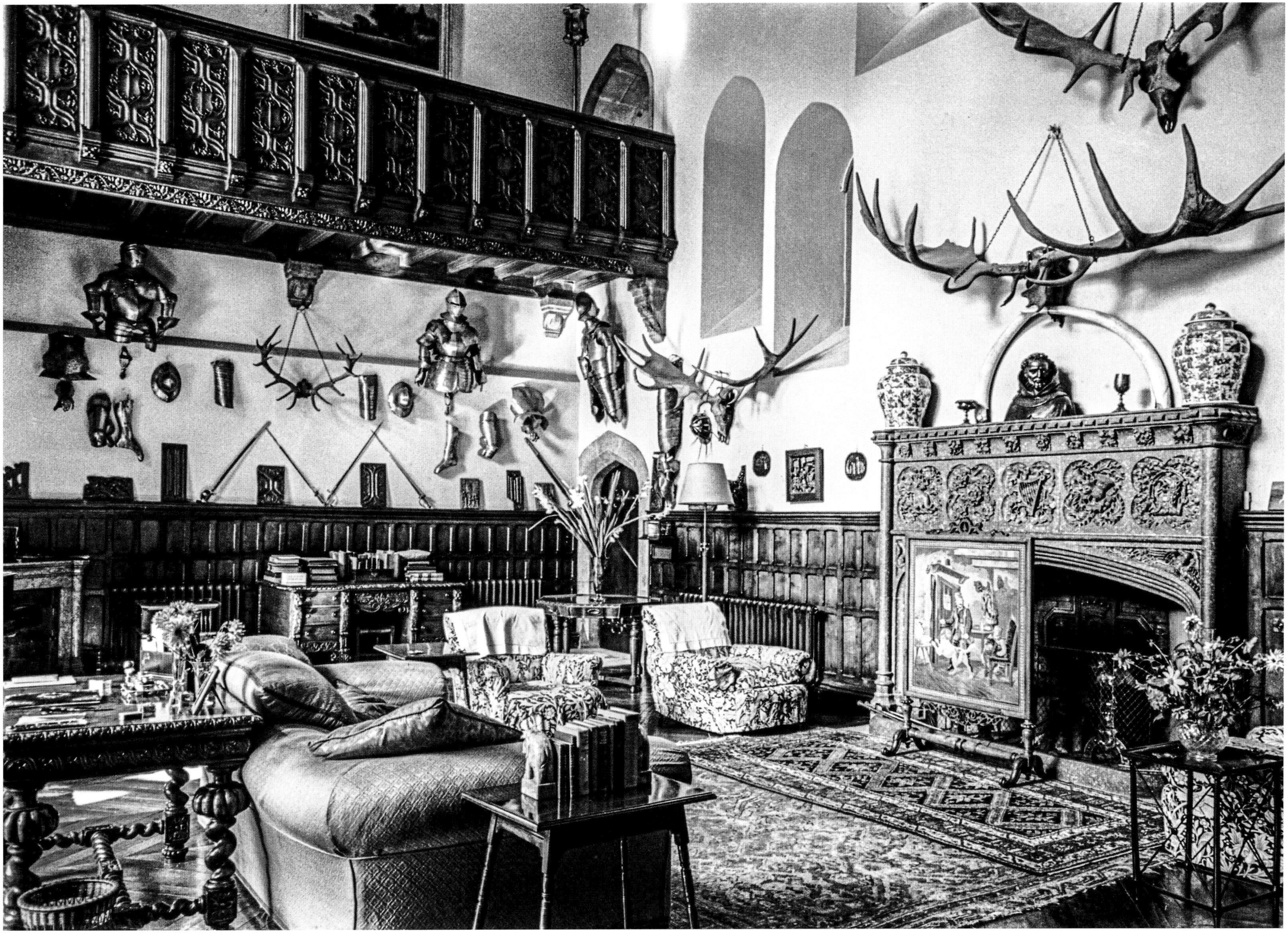

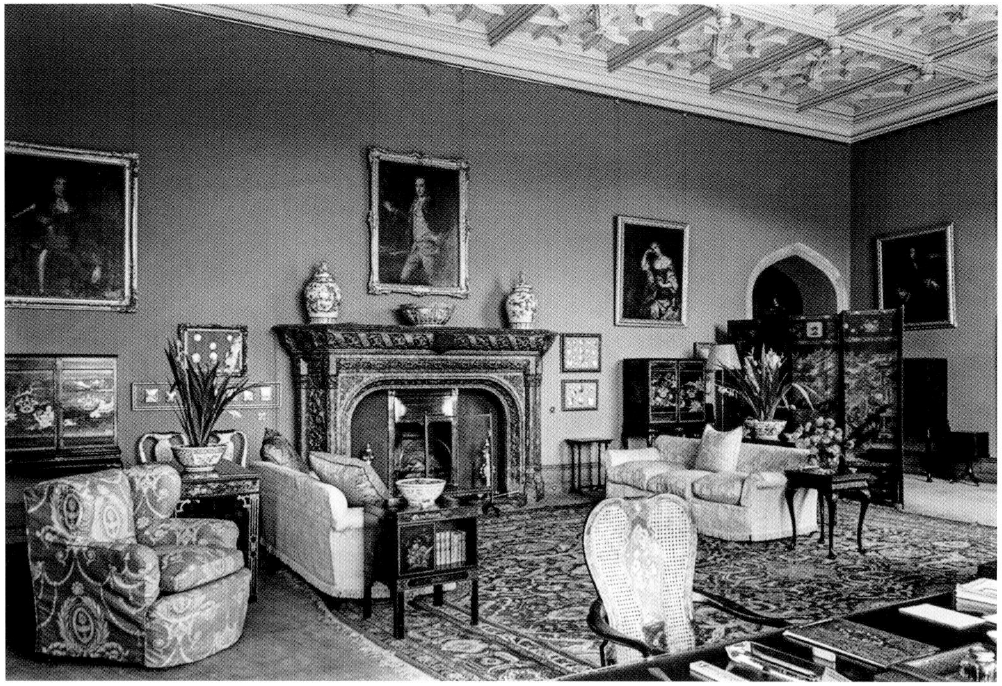

furnished by an architect'. The only person she credited with being involved was a local stonemason, James Conolly, whose contribution is commemorated on the east front of the manor.

Browne's photographs, taken in 1949, unusually include a couple of images of its owner, Windham Wyndham-Quin, 5th Earl of Dunraven – then aged ninety-two – who had inherited the property from his cousin, the fourth earl, twenty-three years earlier. As shown here, the interiors still look much as they did a century before, when first arranged by his grandparents and filled with the pictures and furniture they had either inherited or acquired. Many of these items were dispersed in an auction held on site in June 1982, after the 7th Earl and his wife, no longer able to maintain the property, had sold the house and demesne.

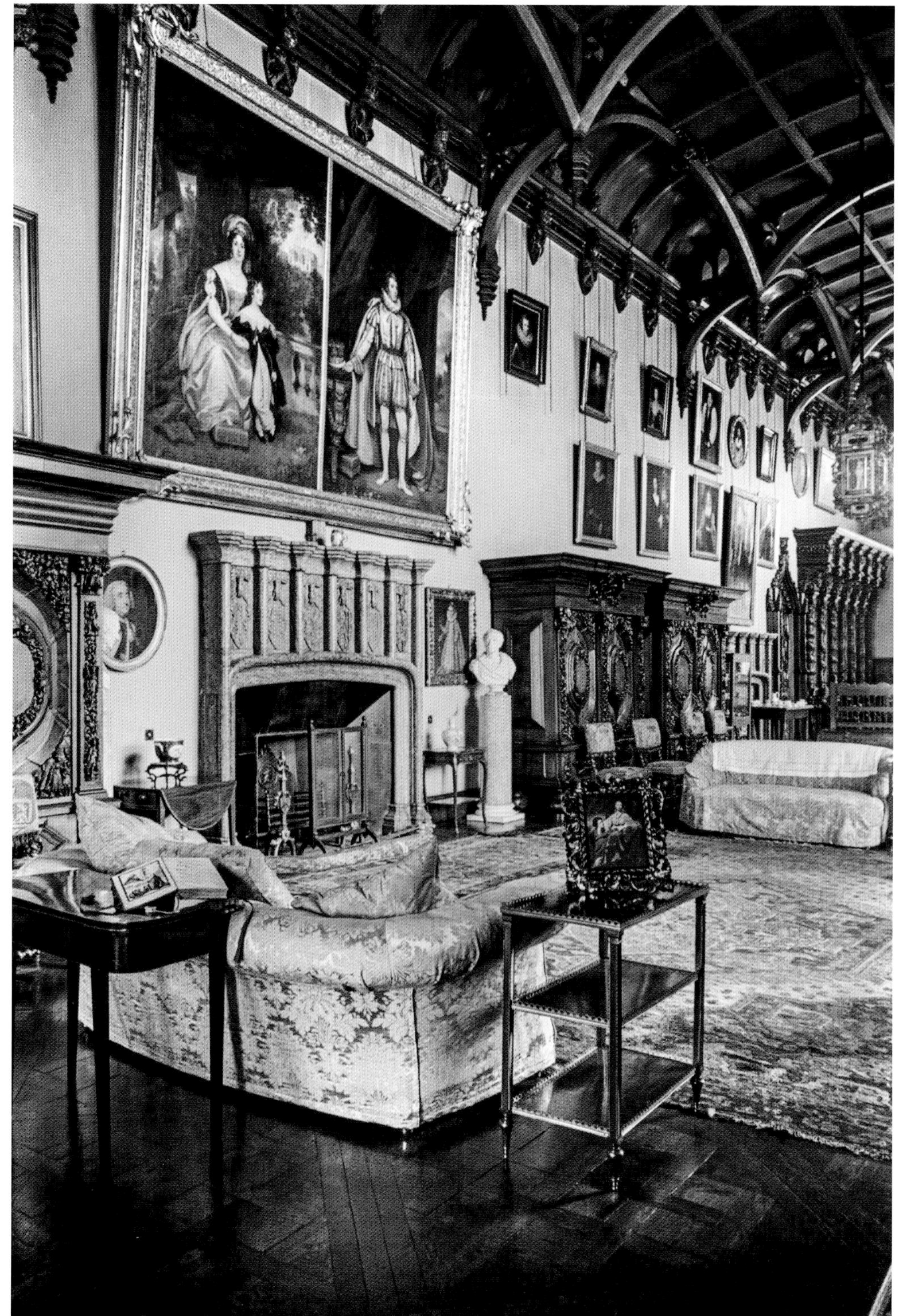

Above: The Drawing Room, its walls lined with family portraits.
Right: The Long Gallery with portraits by Thomas Philipps of the 2nd Earl and his wife above the chimneypiece

Opposite: The Dining Room, its table set for luncheon

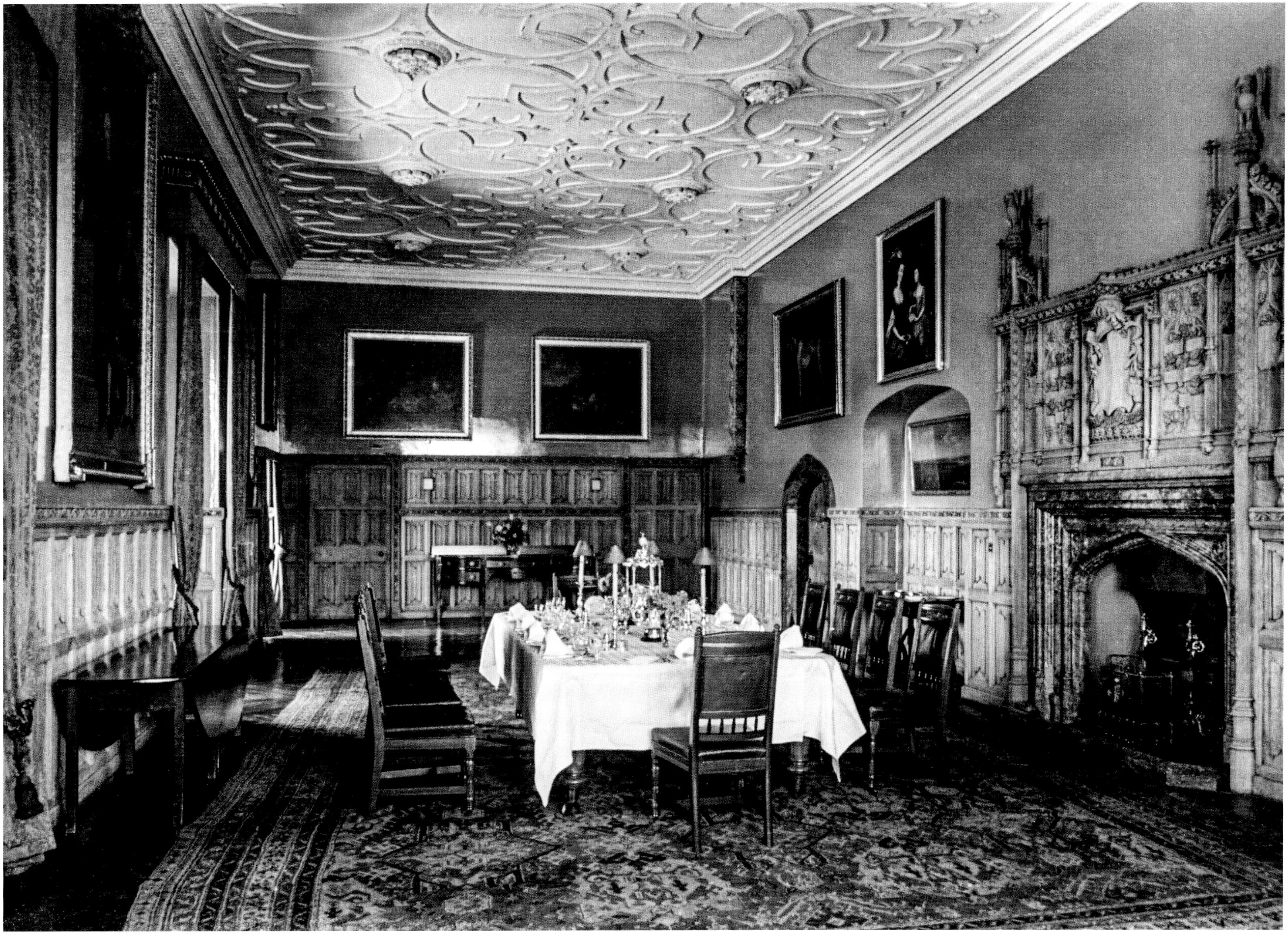

Corbalton
County Meath

27th August 1950

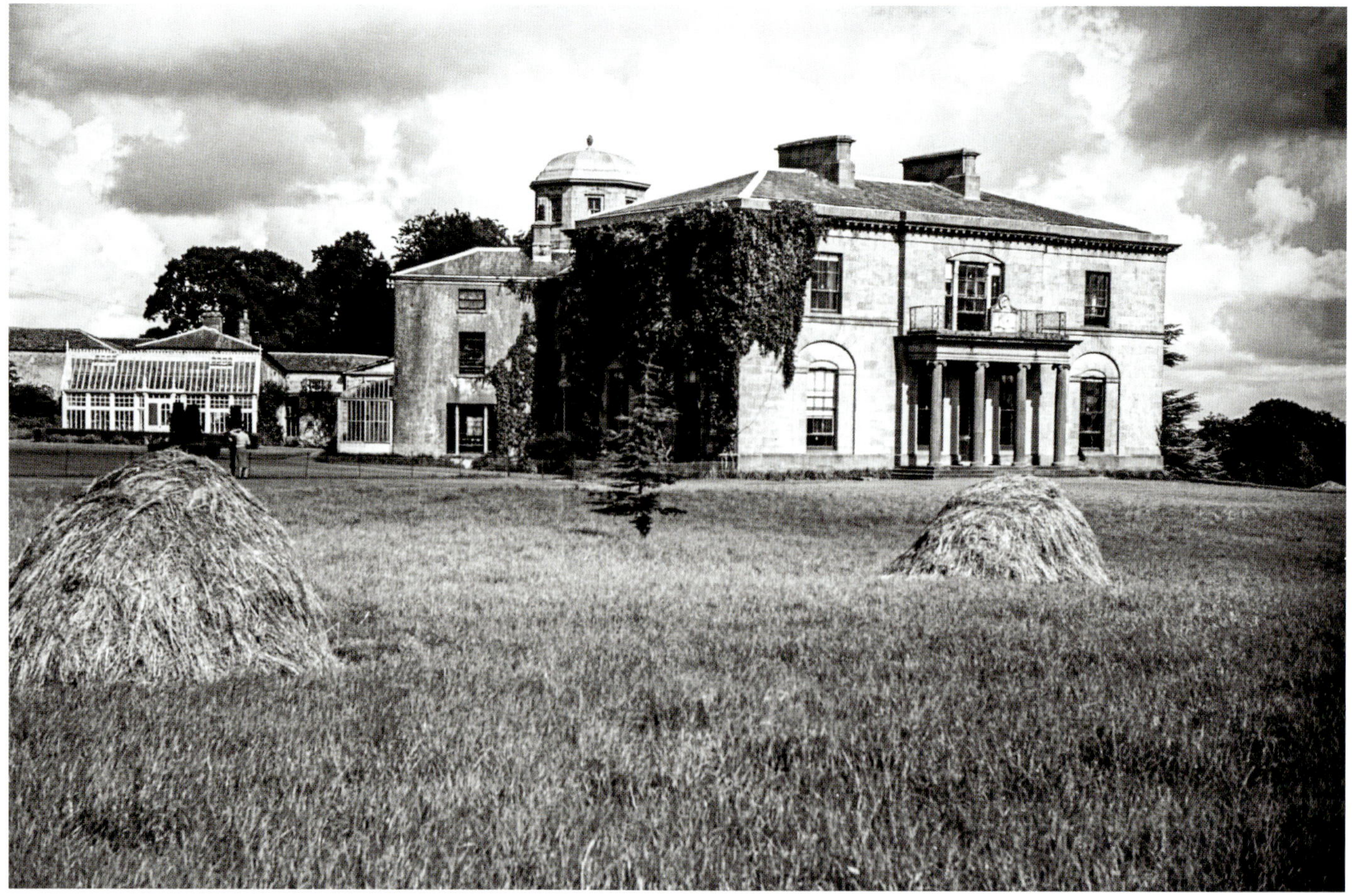

Nestling amidst the verdant landscape of County Meath, Corbalton dates from 1801, when it was designed by Francis Johnston. The foremost architect of the period, Johnston was responsible for some of Ireland's most significant buildings, such as Dublin's GPO and the Chapel Royal in Dublin Castle, as well as many other country houses. His client on this occasion was Elias Corbally, a wealthy miller who bought the estate on which an older three-storey house, Cookstown, already stood. To commemorate his family, Corbally decided to rename the house Corbalton.

A flawless example of fashionable neo-classical taste, Johnston's Corbalton was joined at an acute angle to the old Cookstown. Faced in crisp limestone, the villa's two-storey facade is defined by a freestanding Ionic portico. The windows on either side are set in shallow recesses with semi-elliptical fluted panels above them. Inside, the building follows a tripartite plan, with a central entrance hall flanked by the main reception rooms, accessed through meticulously finished mahogany doors. To the rear of the hall is the cantilevered staircase in pale Portland stone, the whole space amply lit by a generous bow window on the return and leading up to a series of bedrooms. The drawing room and dining room have exactly the same proportions, except that the former has a large bow window offering views across the demesne. All the windows on this floor are set in shallow recesses holding shutters, at the top of which can be seen a design detail typical of Johnston's work: a fan-like, fluted semi-circular motif.

Elias Corbally was a Roman Catholic, a keen campaigner for the repeal of the Penal Laws and full civil rights for members of his faith. As a result, the Corballys became associated through marriage with other notable Catholic families elsewhere in County Meath. In 1817, Elias's only daughter, Louisa Emilia Corbally, married Arthur Plunket, 10th Earl of Fingall. The Fingalls lived not far away at Killeen Castle, which had only recently been enlarged and altered by Francis Johnston. They had always been Catholic, as were the Prestons, Viscounts Gormanston. In 1842 Elias's son and heir Matthew married the Hon. Matilda Preston, daughter of the 12th Viscount. In 1865 their only child, and Elias's granddaughter, Mary Margaret Corbally, would marry

Above: A view of Corbalton showing Francis Johnston's house joined at an acute angle to the older Cookstown behind

Opposite: A sparsely furnished sitting room: the double doors behind led to the original house on this site

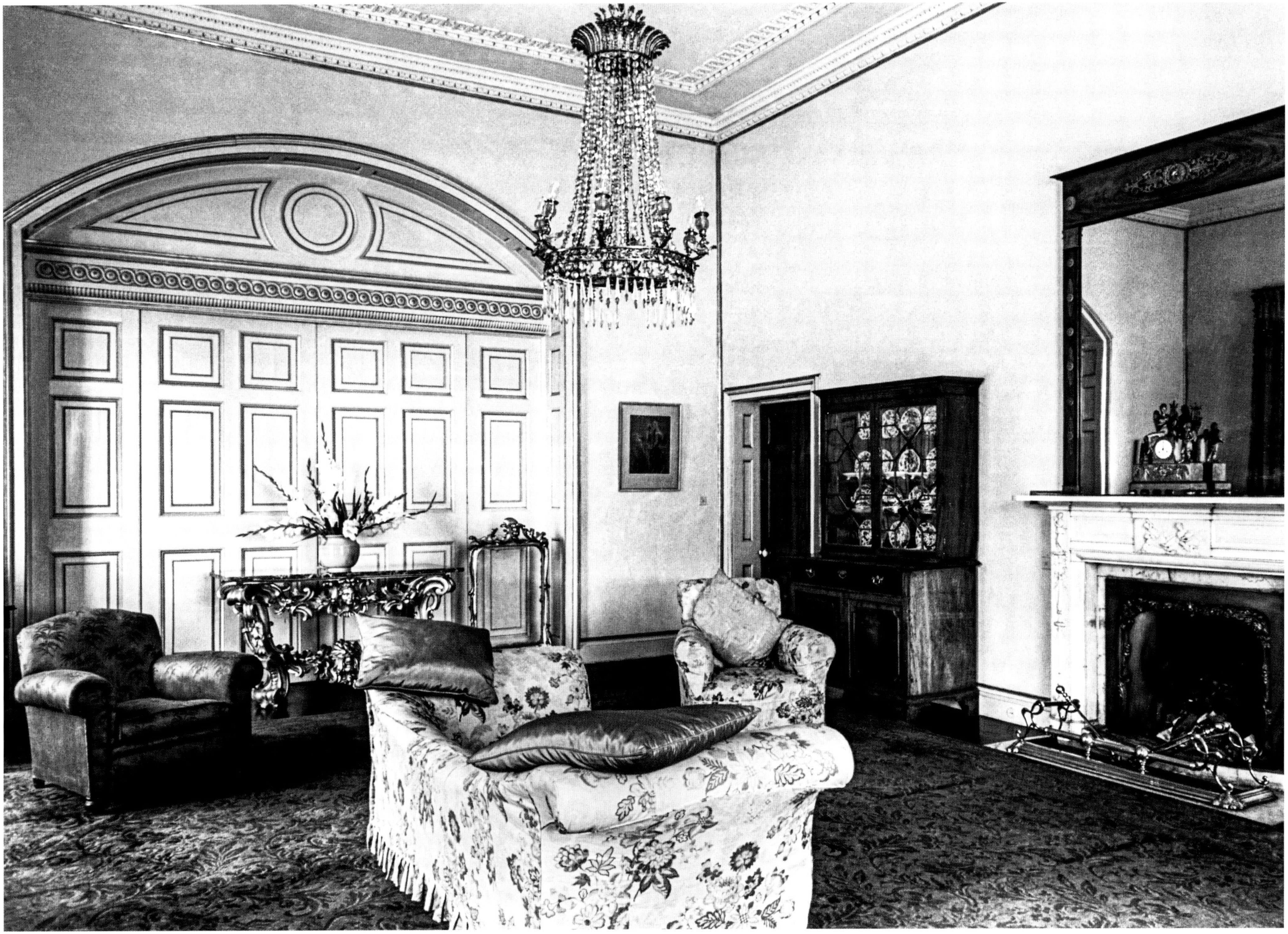

Alfred Stourton, 24th Baron Segrave, whose family title went all the way back to 1283; like the other families, his ancestors had always remained Catholic.

Their son, the Hon. Edward Plantagenet Joseph Corbally Stourton, was the last of the family to live at Corbalton Hall. A year after Browne took these photographs, the estate was sold and the images are accordingly a valuable record of how the house looked prior to the departure of the original owners. The interiors appear to have been in poor condition and, like so many other similar properties at that time, thinly furnished. In 1970 the original Cookstown House was demolished, leaving an empty space between Johnston's villa and the stable block, which he had also designed. At the start of the present century, an extension designed by conservation architect David Sheehan was added to the rear of the house, on the footprint of the demolished Cookstown, thereby restoring coherence to the site. In recent years Corbalton Hall has been extensively restored and refurbished by its current owner.

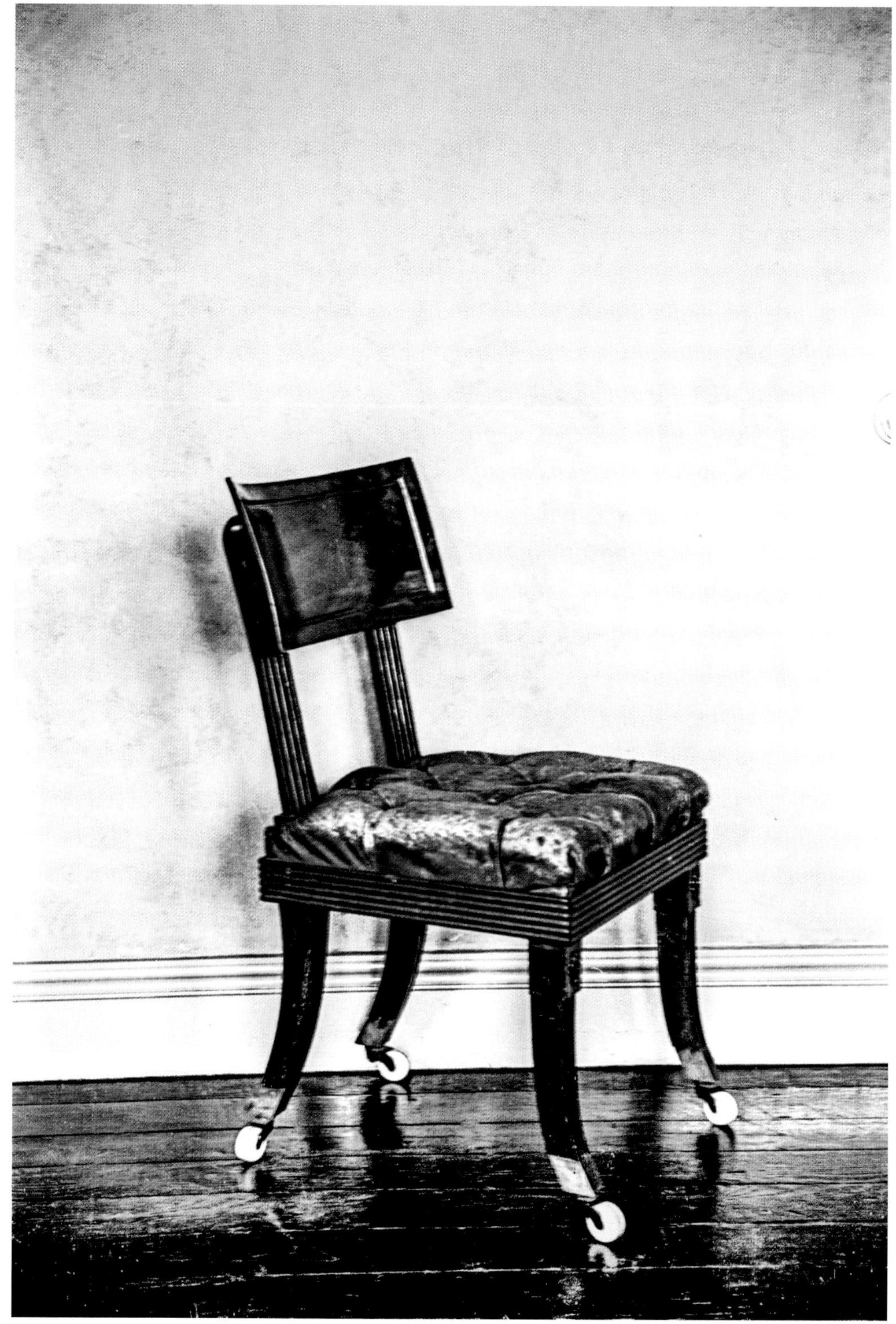

Right: A leather-upholstered chair in the Dining Room

Opposite: A view up the main staircase to the ceiling, the walls showing evidence of the house's poor condition at the time

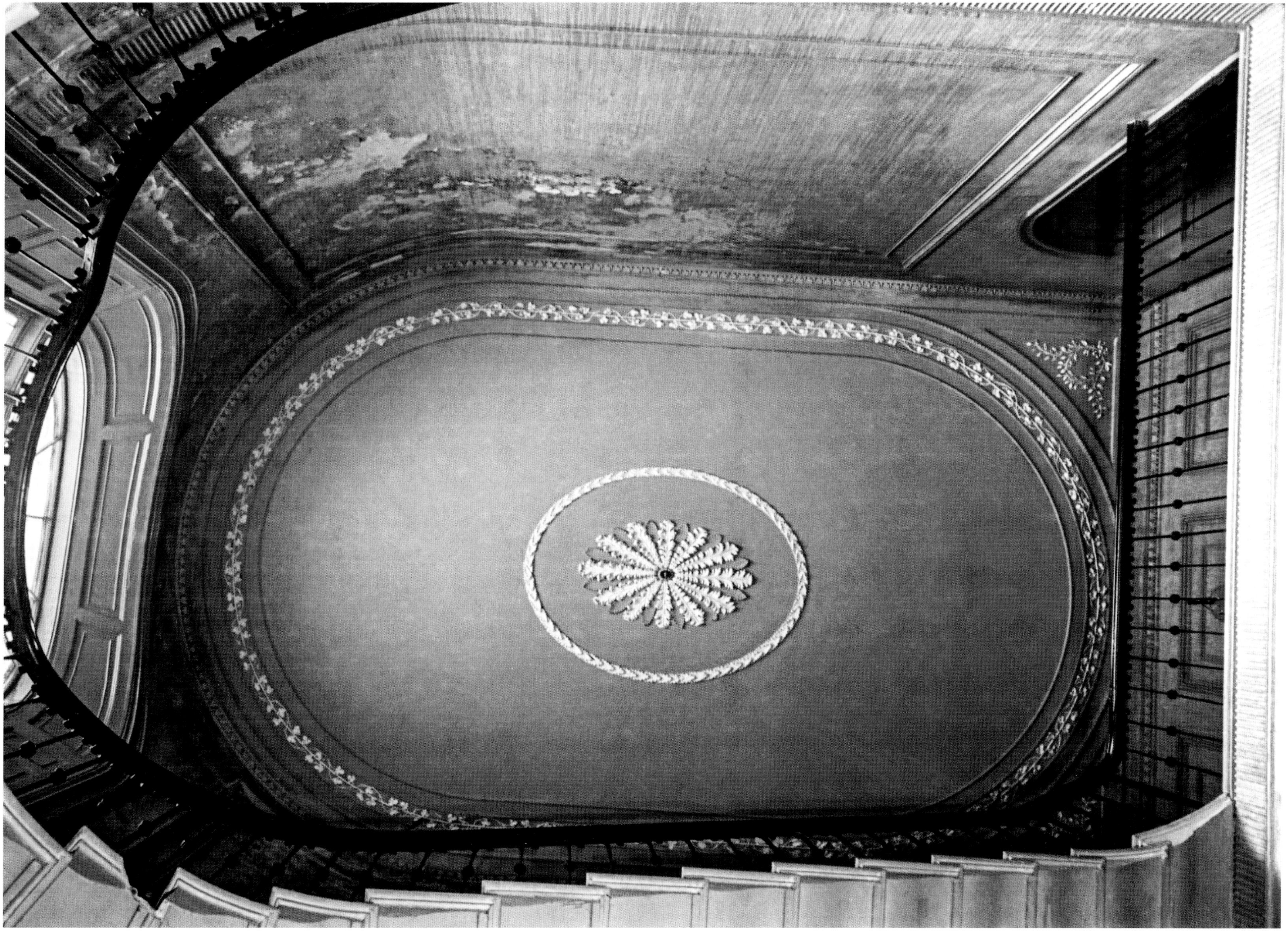

Castletown
County Kildare

18th July 1947

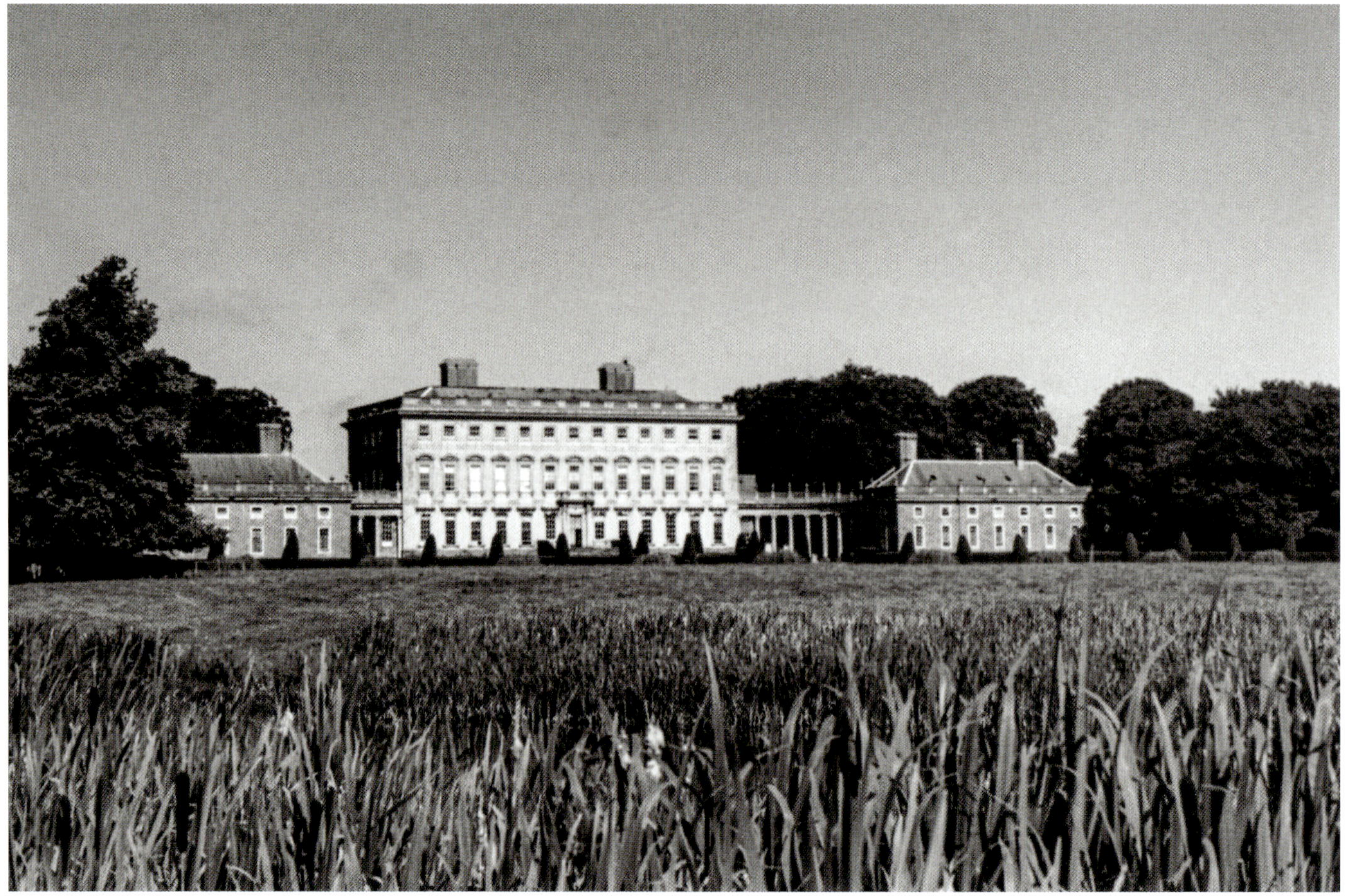

The largest and finest Palladian house in Ireland, Castletown was built for William Conolly, Speaker of the Irish House of Commons and the richest man in the country. He had purchased the land on which the building stands in 1709, but work started here only in 1722, using designs supplied by Italian architect Alessandro Galilei, who had visited Ireland some years earlier. Since Galilei did not stay in the country, it is thought that the execution of his designs was entrusted to Sir Edward Lovett Pearce, who was responsible for the new Houses of Parliament (now the Bank of Ireland) in central Dublin.

Work was still ongoing when Conolly died in 1729, but his widow Katherine continued to live in the house until her death twenty-three years later. The interiors of Castletown remained incomplete during this period; the main staircase, for example, had yet to be built. When Mary Delany visited in 1732, she described the house as 'a large heavy building, a vast deal of room in it, but not laid out with a good taste, the furniture good, but not disposed to the best advantage'.

Following Katherine Conolly's death in 1752, Castletown was inherited by her late husband's nephew, another William Conolly, and when he died just two years later, the house and estate passed to his only son, Thomas Conolly. Following the latter's marriage in 1758 to Lady Louisa Richmond, a daughter of the 2nd Duke of Richmond, the couple moved into Castletown and embarked on finishing the interiors. The staircase hall was now completed, its walls and ceiling covered with plasterwork by master stuccodore Filippo Lafranchini, and the first floor Long Gallery created, the walls here covered in Pompeian-style painting by Charles Reuben Riley. In her re-ordering of the ground floor, Lady Louisa was also responsible for a Print Room, completed in 1769 and today a rare surviving example of this genre.

Thomas Conolly died at Castletown in 1803 and his widow remained there until her death eighteen years later. The couple had no children, and the house and estate next passed to a grandson of Thomas's sister, Edward Pakenham, who assumed the name and arms of Conolly. When he died in 1848, his son Thomas inherited Castletown. Only a few alterations to the place were made in the nineteenth century, such as the installation of gas lighting and the creation of additional

Above: A view across the parkland towards Castletown's Palladian façade

Opposite: The double-height Entrance Hall filled with furniture and pictures, many of which would be dispersed when the house's contents were sold at auction in April 1966

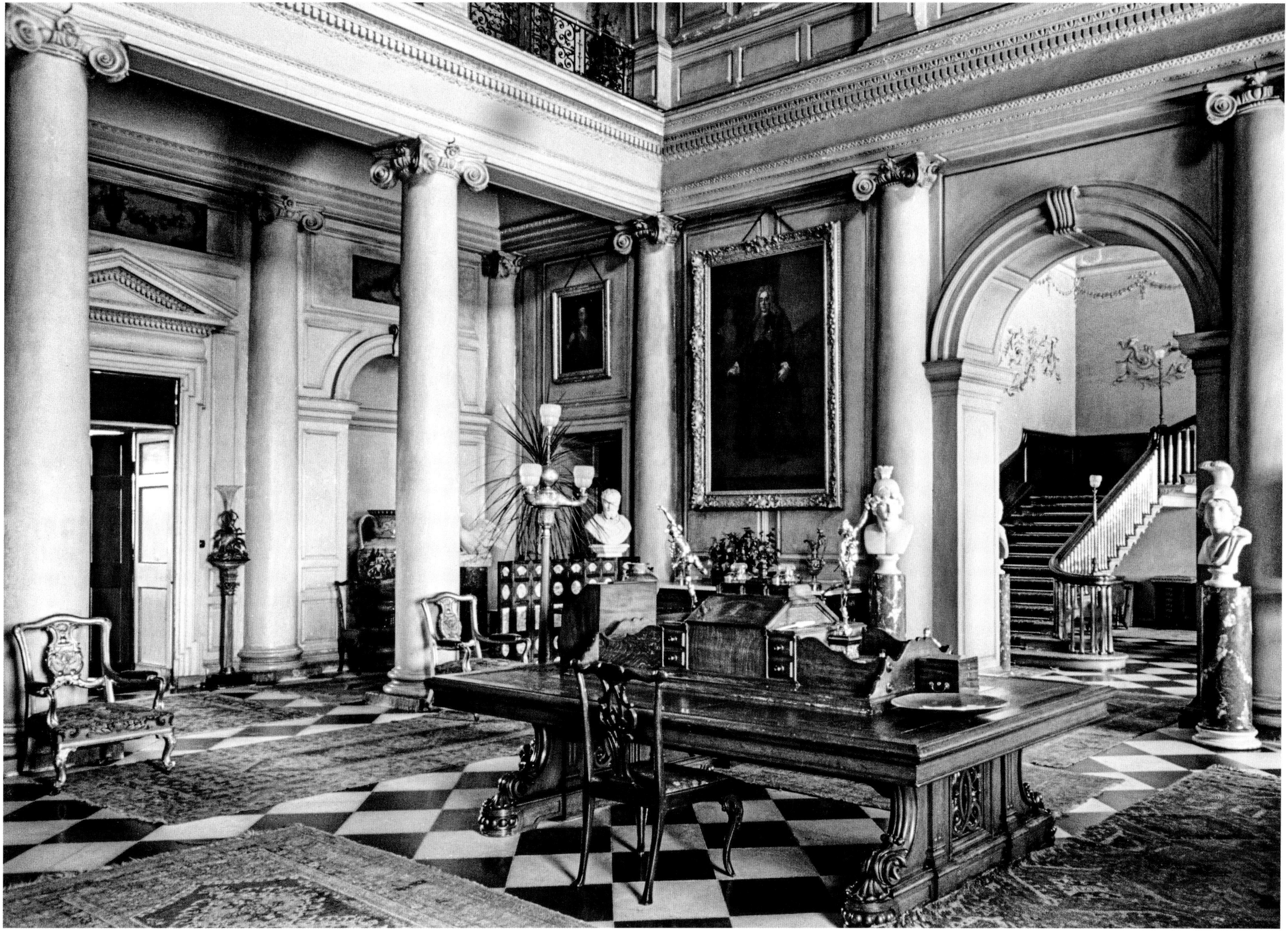

accommodation in one of the wings. At the beginning of the last century, some parts of the building came to benefit from central heating, but little else had changed by 1956 when Major Edward Conolly died and Castletown was inherited by his nephew, the 6th Baron Carew. In 1965 he sold the house and surrounding 500 acres, and a year later many of the contents were dispersed at auction.

Left neglected, Castletown was vandalised, with lead stripped from the roof and windows broken. Fortunately, in 1967, the Hon. Desmond Guinness who, nine years earlier had established the Irish Georgian Society with his wife Mariga, purchased the house and 120 acres of land. Soon afterwards he opened it to the public. Castletown's restoration was undertaken by the Irish Georgian Society, which also undertook to acquire furniture and paintings for the building. While some of the original furnishings had already been bought by Desmond Guinness, other pieces came to the property thanks to the support of private benefactors. The Castletown Foundation was established in 1979 to take over ownership and management of the house, but this responsibility eventually proved too onerous. In 1994 the Office of Public Works accepted Castletown on behalf of the state and has run the property ever since. Father Browne's valuable photographs were taken when the house was occupied by Major Conolly and was still filled with its original contents.

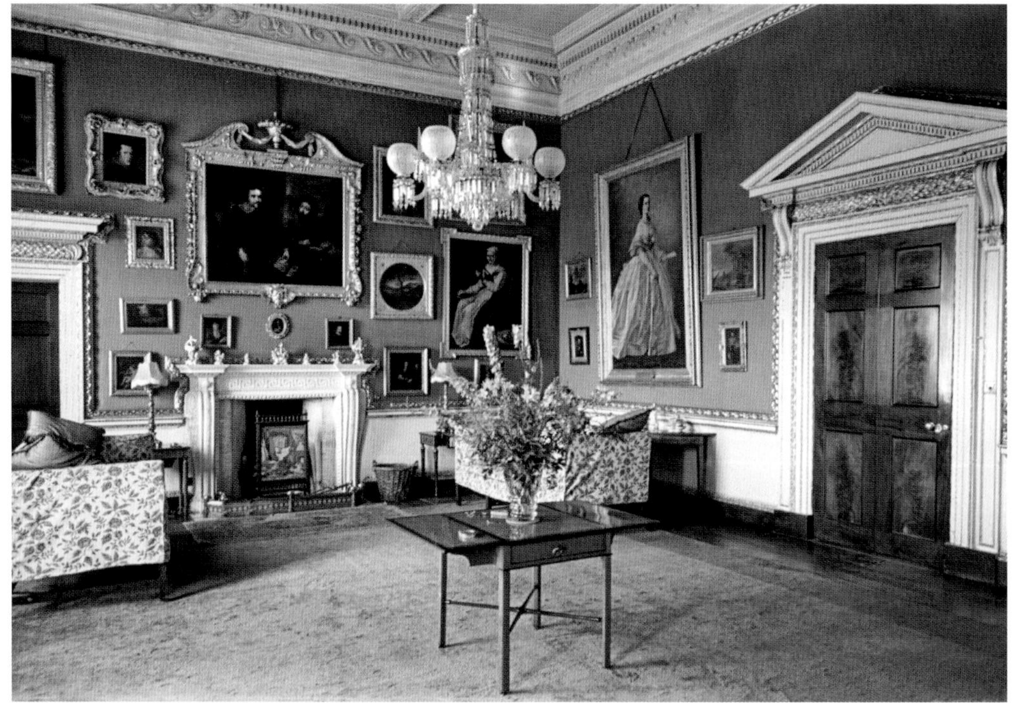

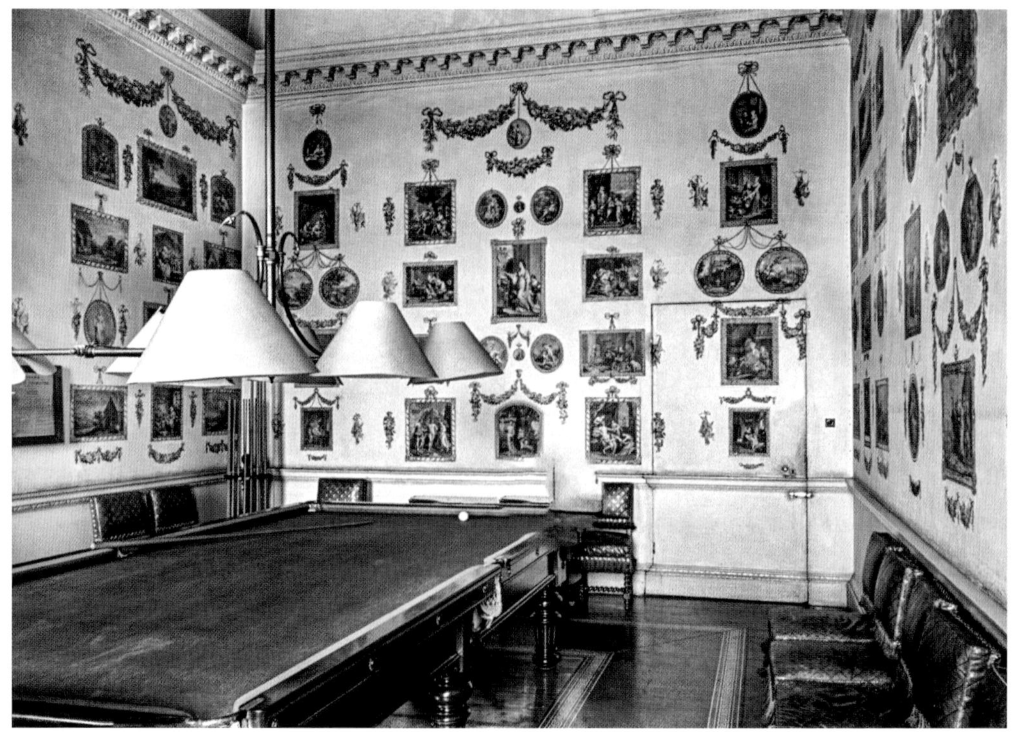

Top: The Green Drawing Room, one of an enfilade with views looking across the demesne
Bottom: Lady Louisa Conolly's Print Room, created in 1769, used as a billiard room in the last century

Opposite Page: The Dining Room; here, as elsewhere, much of what was photographed would be sold within a couple of decades

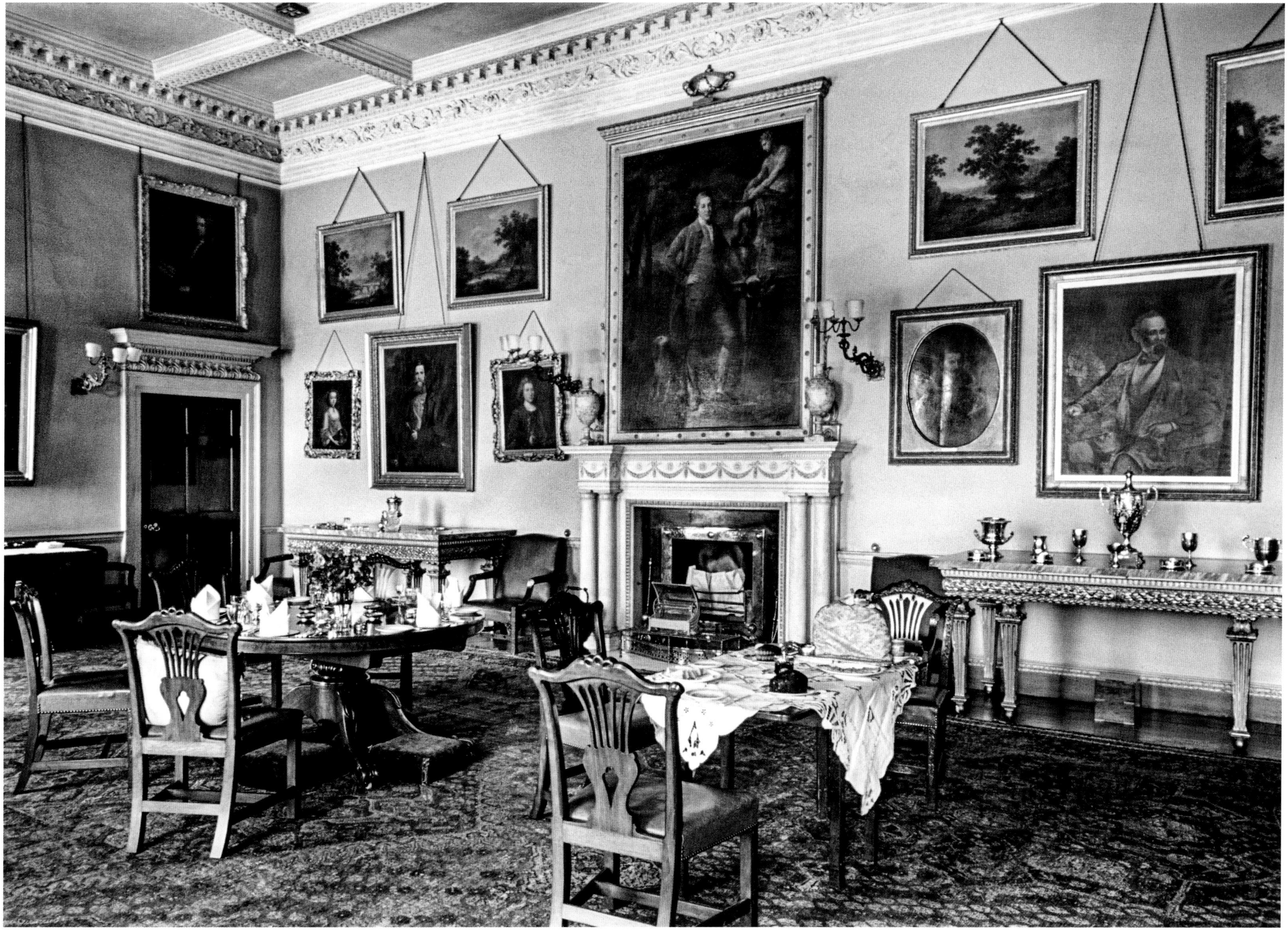

Mount Congreve

County Waterford

17th October 1949

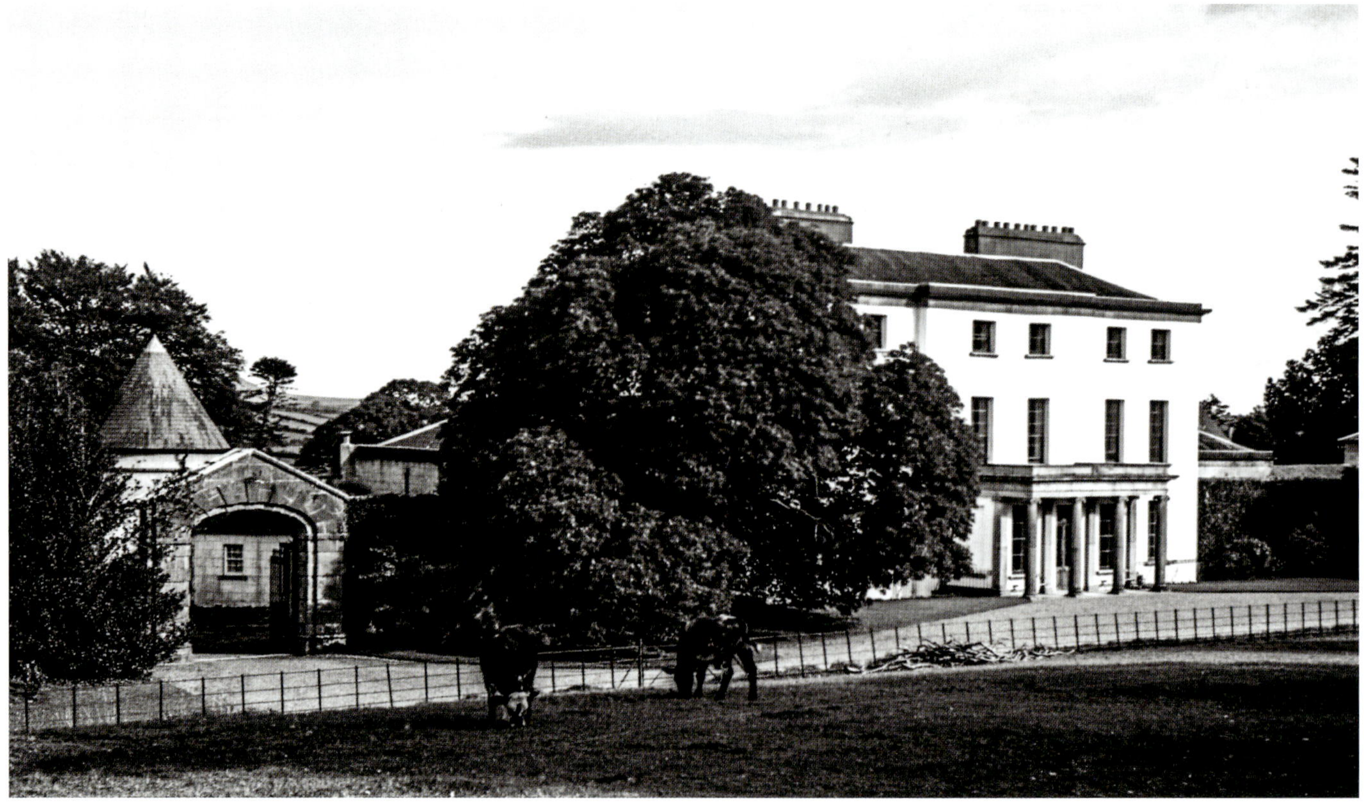

In July 1957, the *Irish Times* announced that the gardens of Mount Congreve, County Waterford, 'are to be open to the public for the first time' on three afternoons each week over the following two months. The unnamed journalist declared that few finer gardens of their kind were to be found on either side of the Irish Sea, those at Mount Congreve including a large eighteenth-century conservatory and a walled garden where the quarter-mile of herbaceous borders held some 15,000 plants in hundreds of varieties 'timed to flower in the coming weeks'.

Originally from Staffordshire, and collaterally related to the Restoration playwright William Congreve, members of the Congreve family first arrived in Ireland in the seventeenth century, one of them, the Rev. John Congreve, settling in County Waterford. His grandson, another John, was responsible for building Mount Congreve c.1760. Its design is sometimes attributed to local architect John Roberts. As first built, the house was of three storeys and seven bays, with slightly projecting two-storey wings on either side, beyond which lay the service yards. Successive generations of the family lived there, alternating the first names John and Ambrose until the last of these, Ambrose Christian Congreve, died in 2011 at the age of 104, leaving no heir.

Above: The house's façade before changes were made to the building by the late Ambrose Congreve in the 1960s

Opposite Page: The Entrance Hall with its screens of fluted Corinthian columns, beyond which snakes the cantilevered staircase

Thanks to his considerable wealth, Ambrose Congreve was responsible for transforming both the house and surrounding gardens. As a young man he was inspired by Lionel de Rothschild's gardens at Exbury in Hampshire, and from the early 1930s onwards he set about emulating this example, not least by planting the same species in large groups. Thanks to its size – it runs to some 70 acres – Mount Congreve's garden holds over 3,000 different trees and shrubs, more than 2,000 Rhododendrons, 600 Camellias, 300 Acer cultivars, 600 conifers, 250 climbers and 1,500 herbaceous plants.

As for the house, photographed by Browne when still occupied by Ambrose Congreve's father, it was considerably enlarged in the years after the latter's death in 1957, not least by the addition of a substantial bow with limestone doorcase at the centre of the front entrance. Extensions were also made to the wings and yards, which were given cupolas and limestone doorcases. Mr Congreve had a plutocrat's taste: he liked everything large and abundant, and almost to the end of his life he was making changes to the building and its contents, both of which might be described as plush. In 1979, recognising that he had no direct heir, he transferred ownership of the house and some 71 surrounding acres to a charitable organisation, the Mount Congreve Trust, on the understanding that all of this property would eventually pass to the Irish state. However, part of the arrangement was that 66 acres of gardens would only become national property twenty-one years after his death, and the house and immediate five acres only in

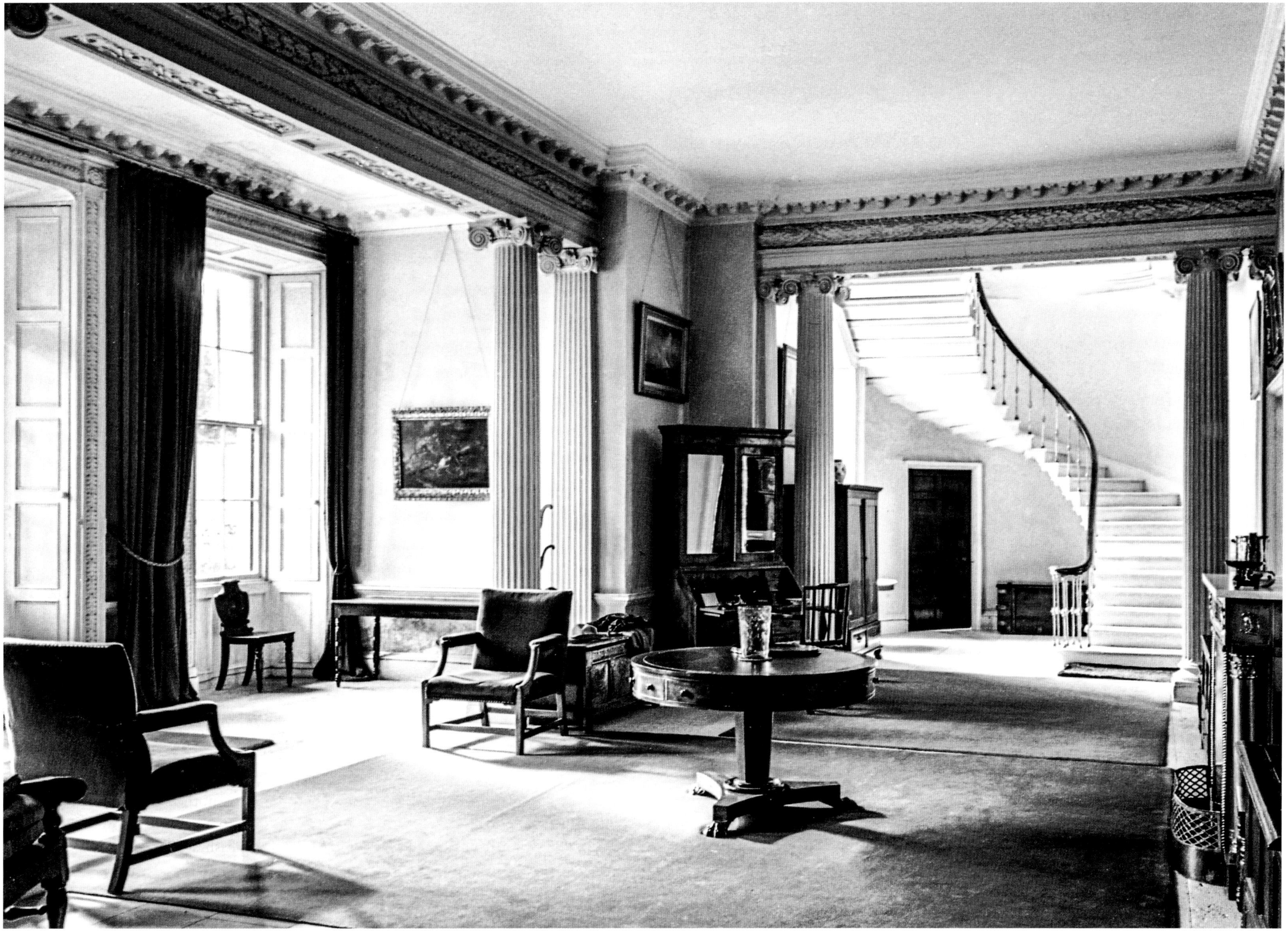

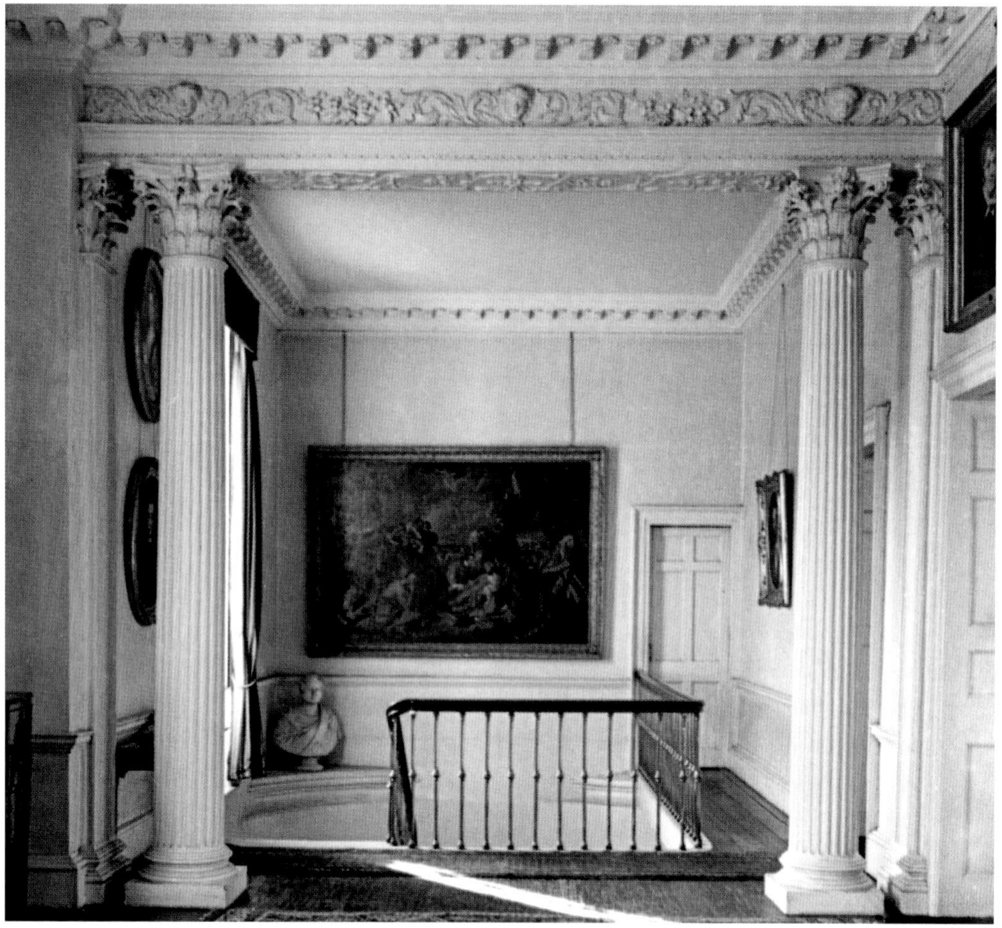

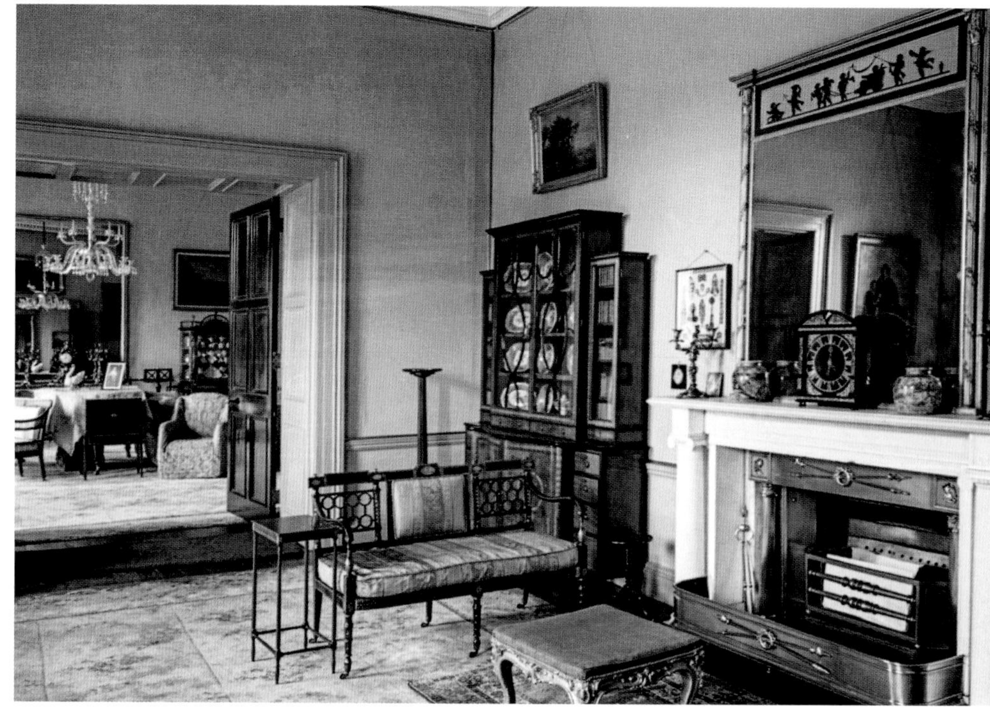

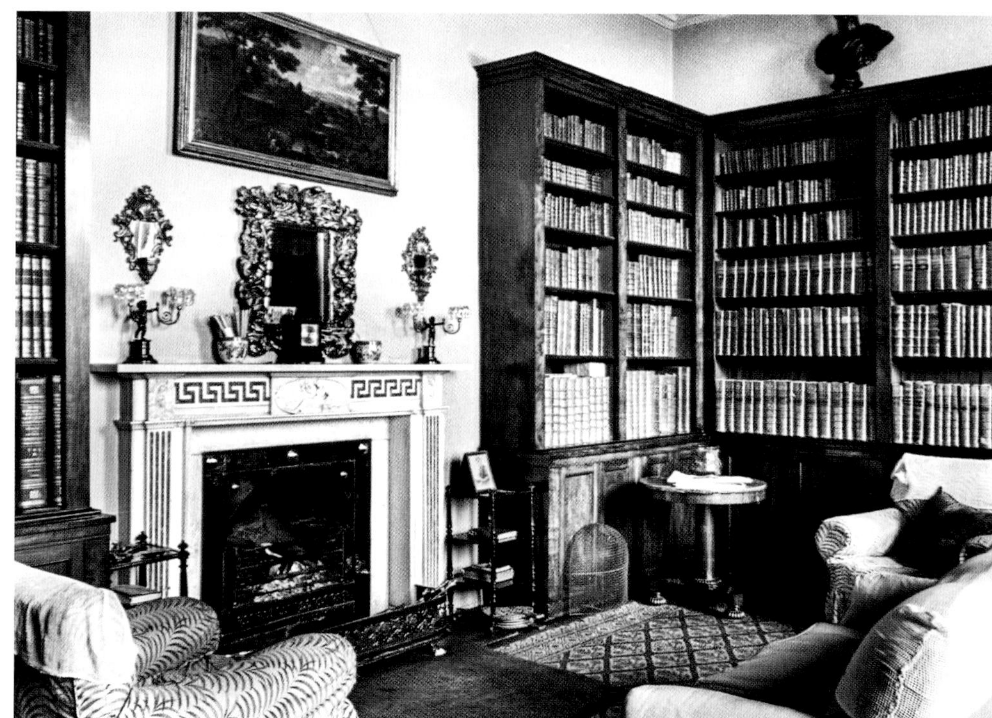

2059. Thus, when he died at the age of 104 in 2011, it appeared that the greater part of the gardens would not be taken under state care until 2032 – and the house and balance of land not for a further twenty-seven years. Inevitably, legal disputes followed, with unfortunate consequences, not least that the contents of the house – including a library dating back to the eighteenth century – were dispersed in a number of auctions, leaving the place empty. Meanwhile, the gardens on which Congreve had lavished so much care and expense also deteriorated. Only in 2019 was agreement reached whereby the trust transferred both the house and gardens to the local authority, which has since opened the gardens and a couple of rooms in the house to the public.

Above: The landing at the top of the main staircase. Right Top and Bottom: The Drawing Room and Library

Opposite Page: The Dining Room, its walls lined with grisaille paintings by Peter de Gree which were later sold from the house and are now in Ballyfin, County Laois

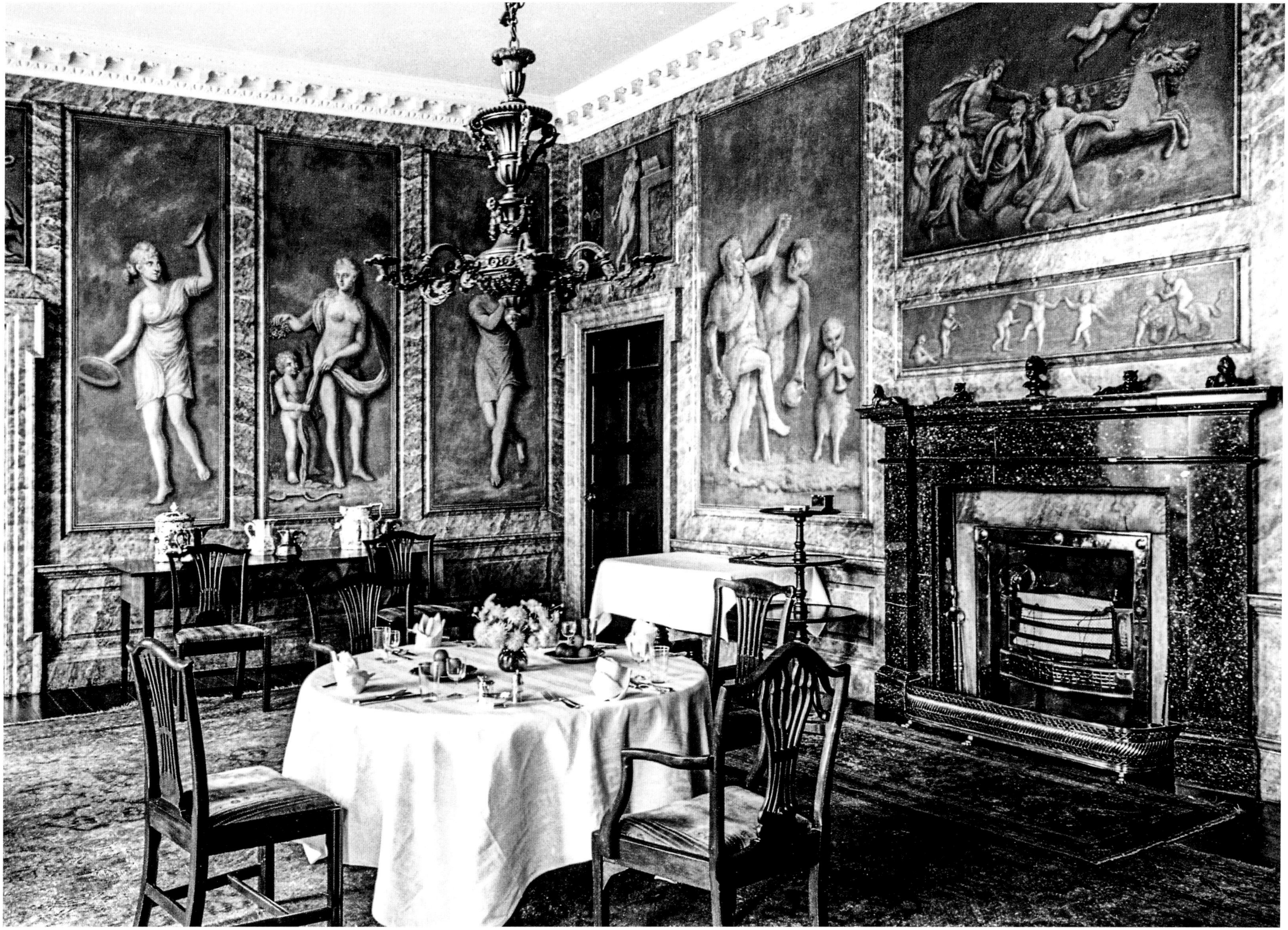

LISMORE CASTLE
COUNTY WATERFORD

7TH AUGUST 1952

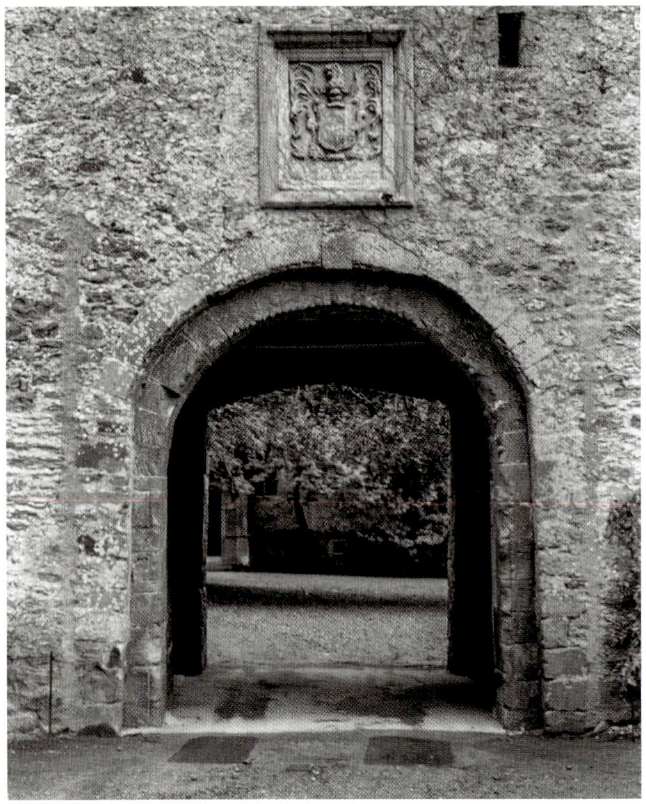

Above: Carrying the Boyle coat of arms, the arch leading to the castle's inner courtyard

Opposite: The Entrance Hall, one of the many rooms given its present appearance in the 19th century

Dramatically sited high above the River Blackwater, Lismore Castle began as a monastery founded in 636 by St Carthage. It remained an important centre of learning and prayer, but in 1185 Prince John, Lord of Ireland (and future King of England), fortified the building, thus turning it into a castle. The former monastery later became a residence for successive bishops of Lismore until the late sixteenth century, when it was granted to Sir Walter Raleigh, along with vast tracts of surrounding land.

Following Raleigh's fall from royal favour and imprisonment in the Tower of London, he was obliged to dispose of his Irish estates, which were bought in 1602 by Richard Boyle, afterwards 1st Earl of Cork, who, having arrived in Ireland with just £27, would end his life one of the richest and most powerful men in the country. Boyle chose to make Lismore Castle his principal seat and undertook extensive work here, creating a substantial residence around a central courtyard entered via a gatehouse tower. The entire site was then surrounded by a further range of high walls and an outer gatehouse tower. Much of what he constructed still survives, as does a series of terraces within the walls, believed to be the oldest continuously cultivated gardens in Ireland.

Boyle's descendants continued to own Lismore Castle, but spent less time there after the building was badly damaged during the Confederate Wars of the 1640s, when it was besieged at least twice and sacked once. By the early eighteenth century, it was little used, the 4th Earl of Cork (better known as the 3rd Earl of Burlington) preferring to live in England. When he died in 1753, the earl's Irish estates were inherited by his daughter, Lady Charlotte Boyle, married to William Cavendish, future 4th Duke of Devonshire: the couple's descendants have owned Lismore Castle ever since.

Nevertheless, the property remained largely unused and unvisited by the family until inherited by the 6th 'bachelor' Duke of Devonshire following his father's death in 1811. Work on transforming the building began almost immediately and continued for the next forty-plus years, giving the castle its present appearance. Initially the architect William Atkinson was employed on tasks such as adding battlements to the range overlooking the Blackwater, but Sir Joseph Paxton, who began his career as the duke's gardener, was later invited to refashion the rest of the site, turning the whole place into a romantic castle, replete with towers and turrets, all of it faced in cut stone shipped over from the Devonshires' Derbyshire estate. A great hall was created out of what was thought to have been the medieval bishops' chapel, its Perpendicular window filled with glass celebrating the many families into which the Cavendishes had married. The room was decorated by John Gregory Crace and includes a large chimneypiece designed by Augustus Welby Pugin and originally shown in London's Great

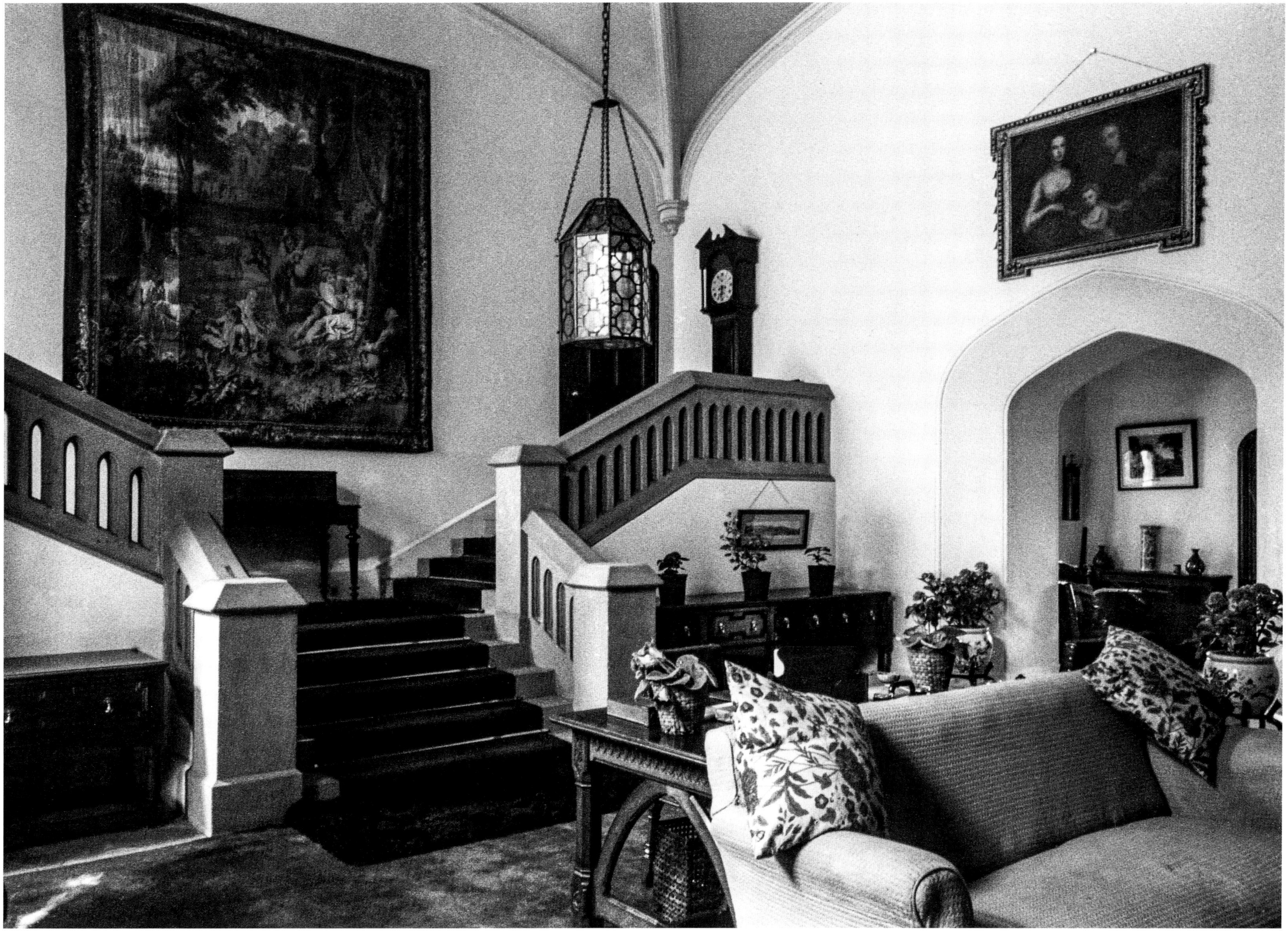

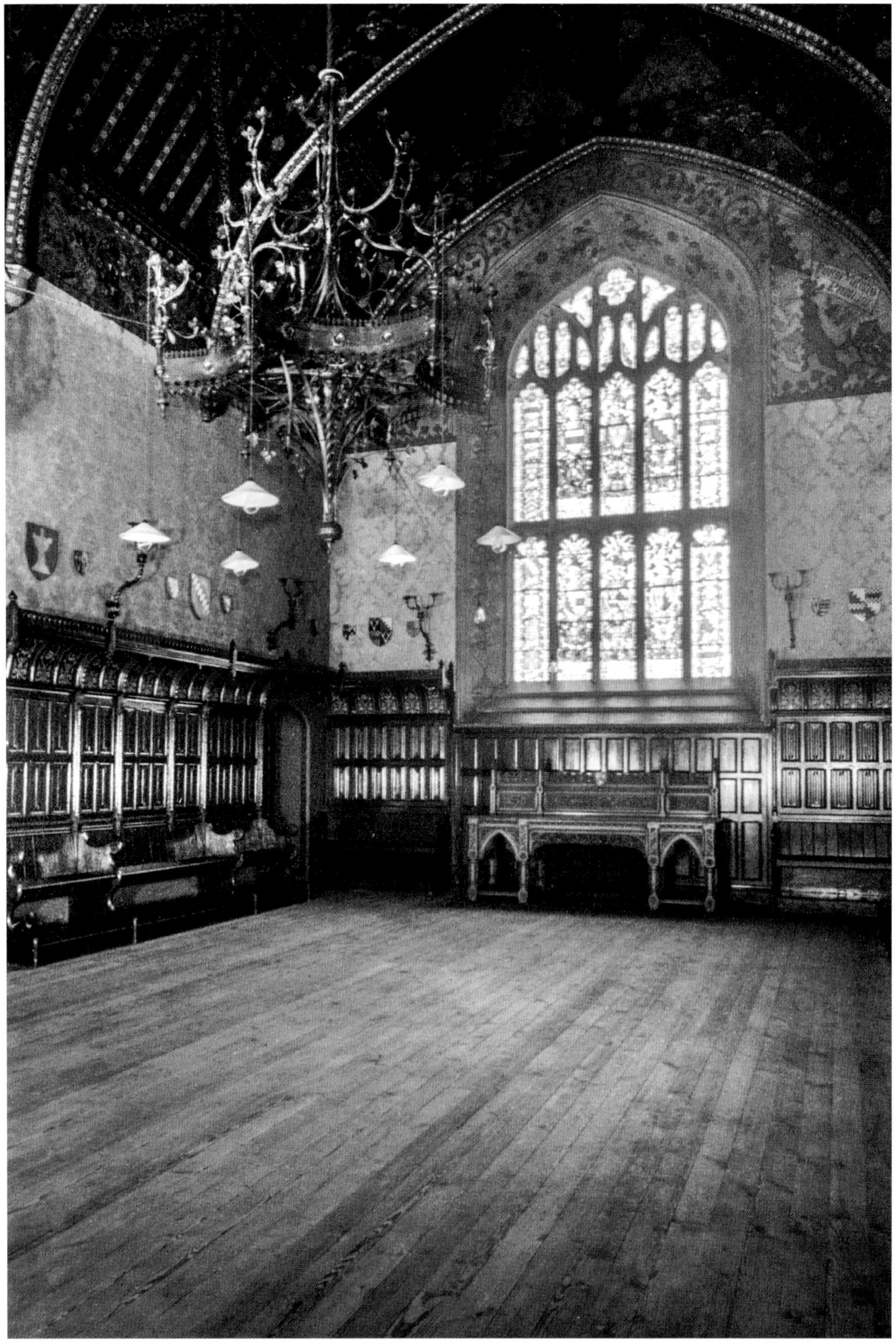

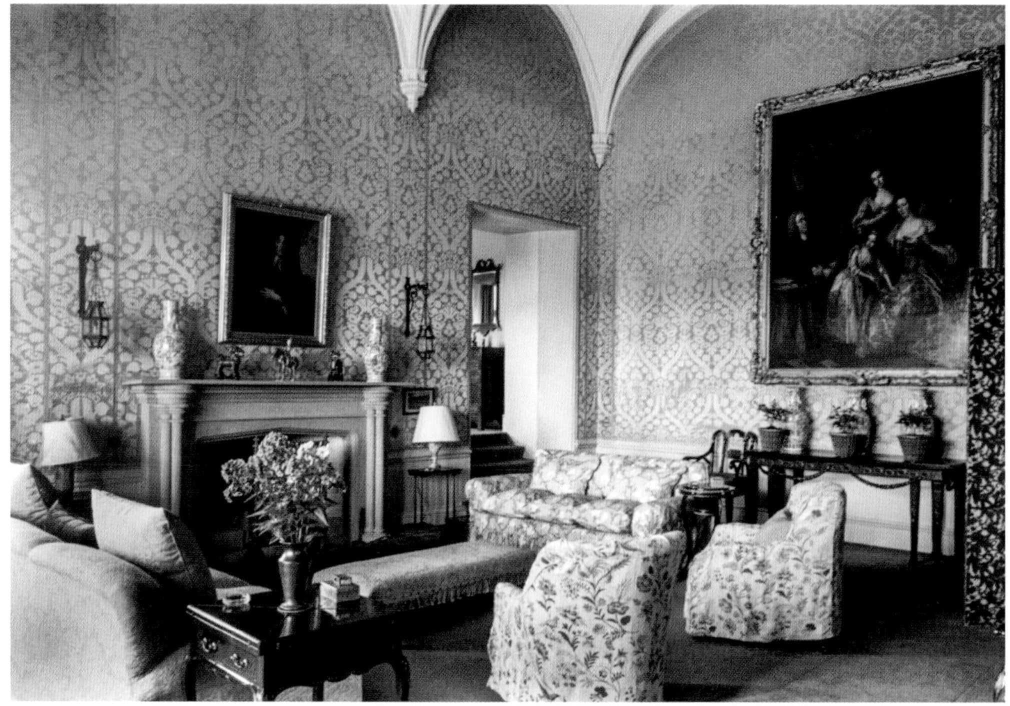

Exhibition of 1851 (where the Crystal Palace had been designed by Paxton).

The other reception rooms seem to have been given similar treatment, but by the time Browne visited in 1952, much of this High Victorian decoration had been covered in white paint and furnished in a sparer style than had previously been the case. The castle was then primarily used by Adele Astaire, sister of Fred Astaire, who in 1932 had married Lord Charles Cavendish, a younger son of the 9th Duke of Devonshire. She continued to spend time there each year even after her husband's death in 1944. She was responsible for installing a swimming pool in the gardens; it has since been turned into a tennis court.

Left: The Great Hall, designed in the early 1850s by Augustus Welby Pugin and decorated by John Gregory Crace
Above and Opposite Page: The Drawing Room and adjacent Sitting Room, both designed for the 6th Duke of Devonshire in the early 19th century by William Atkinson

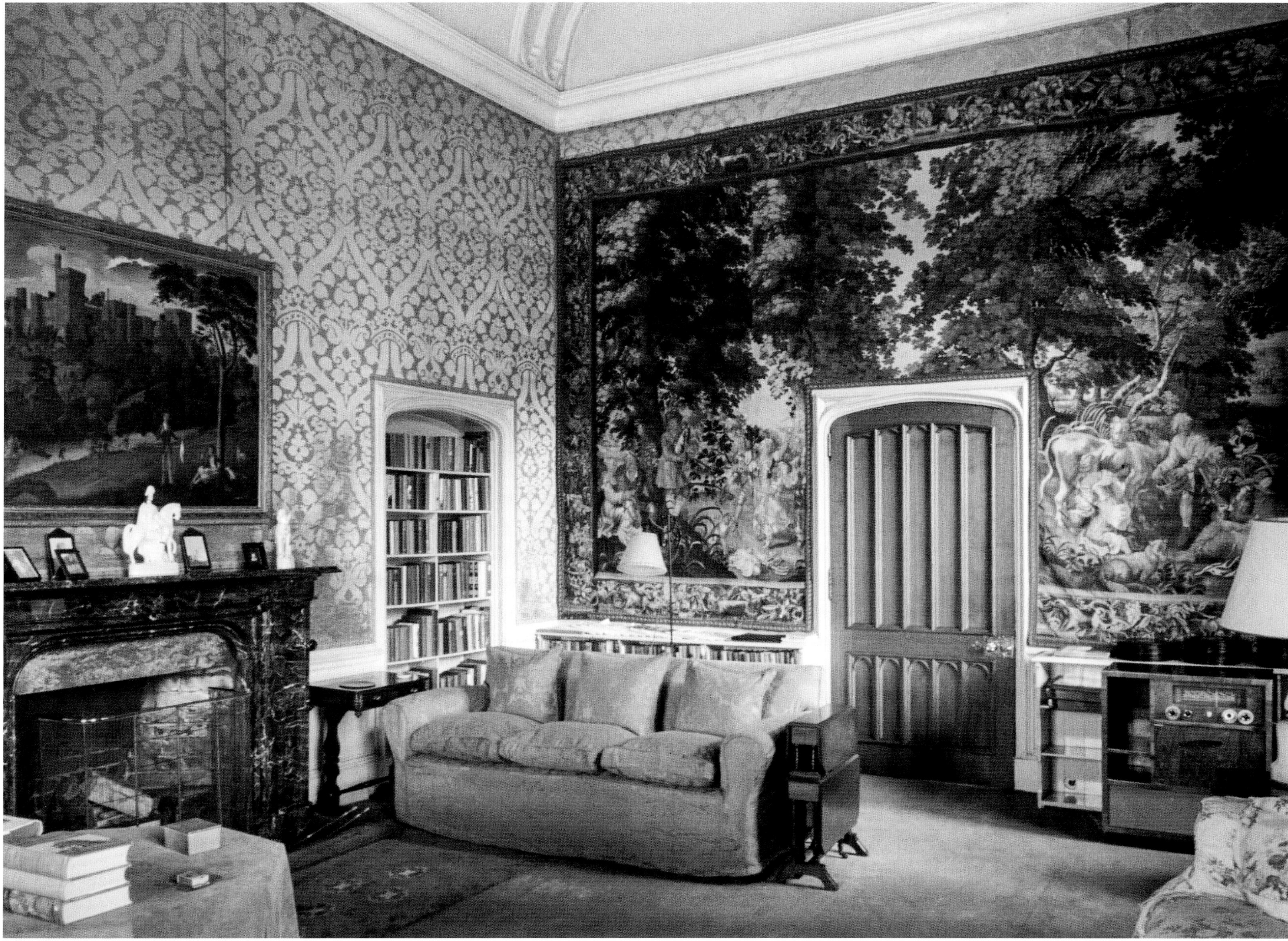

Ormond Castle
County Tipperary
28th February 1944

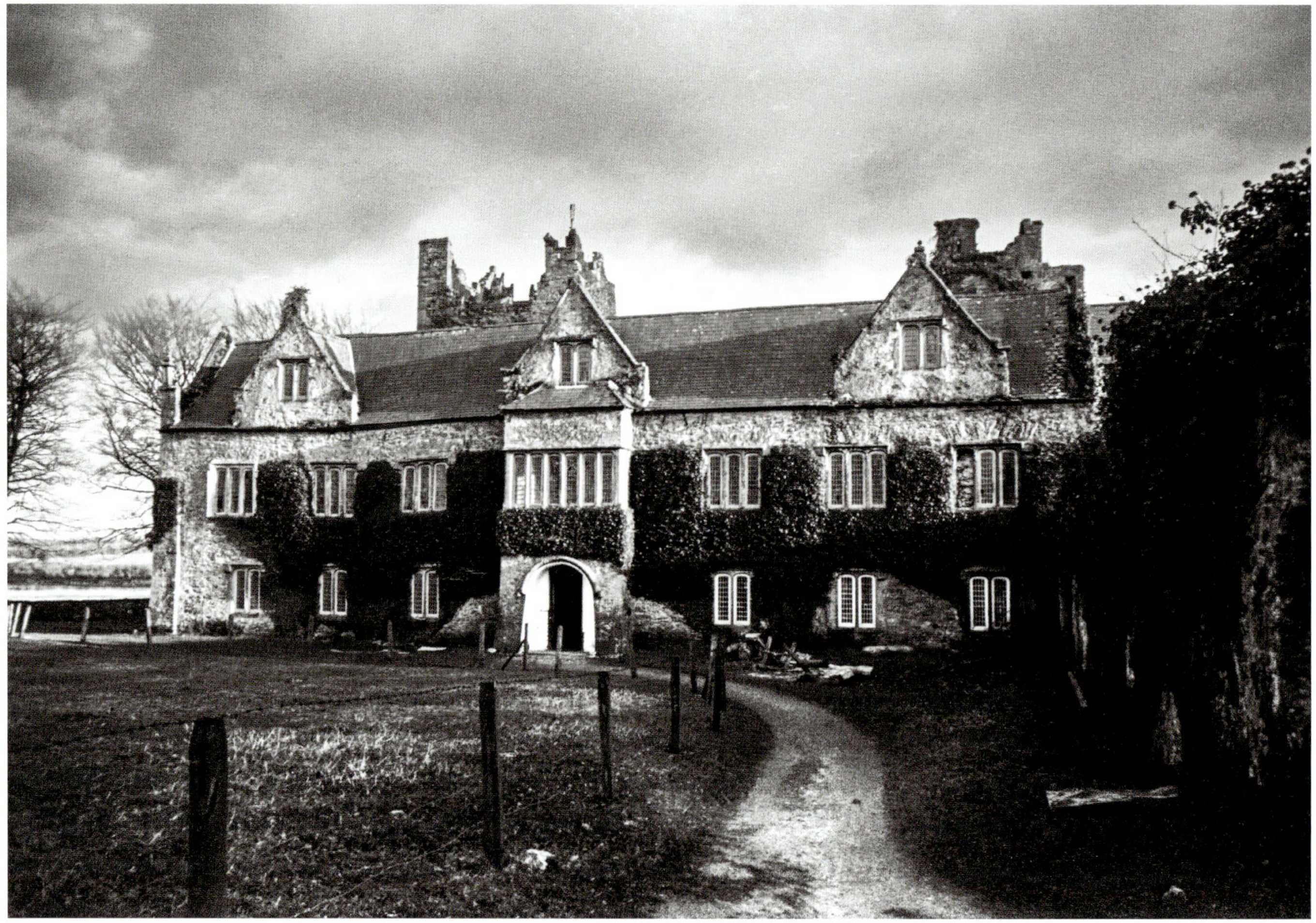

When these photographs were taken, Ormond Castle – the finest surviving example of an Elizabethan manor house in Ireland – was on the verge of being lost for ever. The original castle was constructed on the north side of the River Suir and at the south-east corner of the medieval walled town of Carrick. A D-shaped enclosure with a watergate fronting directly onto the river, this building was enlarged in the fifteenth century, not least by two five-storey towers, before its appearance was radically altered around 1565 with the addition of a large unfortified house in front of the older property. The new work was commissioned by 'Black Tom', Thomas Butler, 10th Earl of Ormond, who had been raised in the English court where he came to know the future Queen Elizabeth I, a distant cousin (the queen's great-grandmother, Lady Margaret Butler, was a daughter of the 7th Earl of Ormond). Appointed Lord Treasurer of Ireland in 1559, the earl returned to his native country and some years later embarked on building a domestic residence that would reflect current architectural taste. Perhaps the most notable feature of his new mansion is that it was unfortified, at a time when thick defensive walls with few window openings were the norm for Irish domestic residences. Demonstrating the earl's confidence in his authority and position of strength, the manor house's facade is replete with large windows, allowing the interior to be lighter and airier than anything previously built in the country.

This is especially the case in what is the building's most important room, the first floor Long Gallery. A common feature in Elizabethan and Jacobean mansions, the gallery is 95 feet long and would have had walls hung with tapestries; an early nineteenth-century account mentions a series recounting the deeds of Samson as still being in the castle. While these have since been lost, the gallery's plasterwork decoration survives. A deep frieze runs much of the room's length and depicts classical figures representing Justice and Equity alternating with busts of Queen Elizabeth and her deceased brother, King Edward VI, as well as their coats of arms. Meanwhile, the geometrically panelled ceiling plasterwork features the Tudor rose and other heraldic devices, along with the queen's initials and personal arms.

Thomas Butler died in 1614 and thereafter his mansion enjoyed mixed fortunes. It suffered assault during the Confederate Wars of the 1640s and their aftermath; in 1661 the Duchess of Ormond described the place as being 'in a ruinous condition'. Her husband,

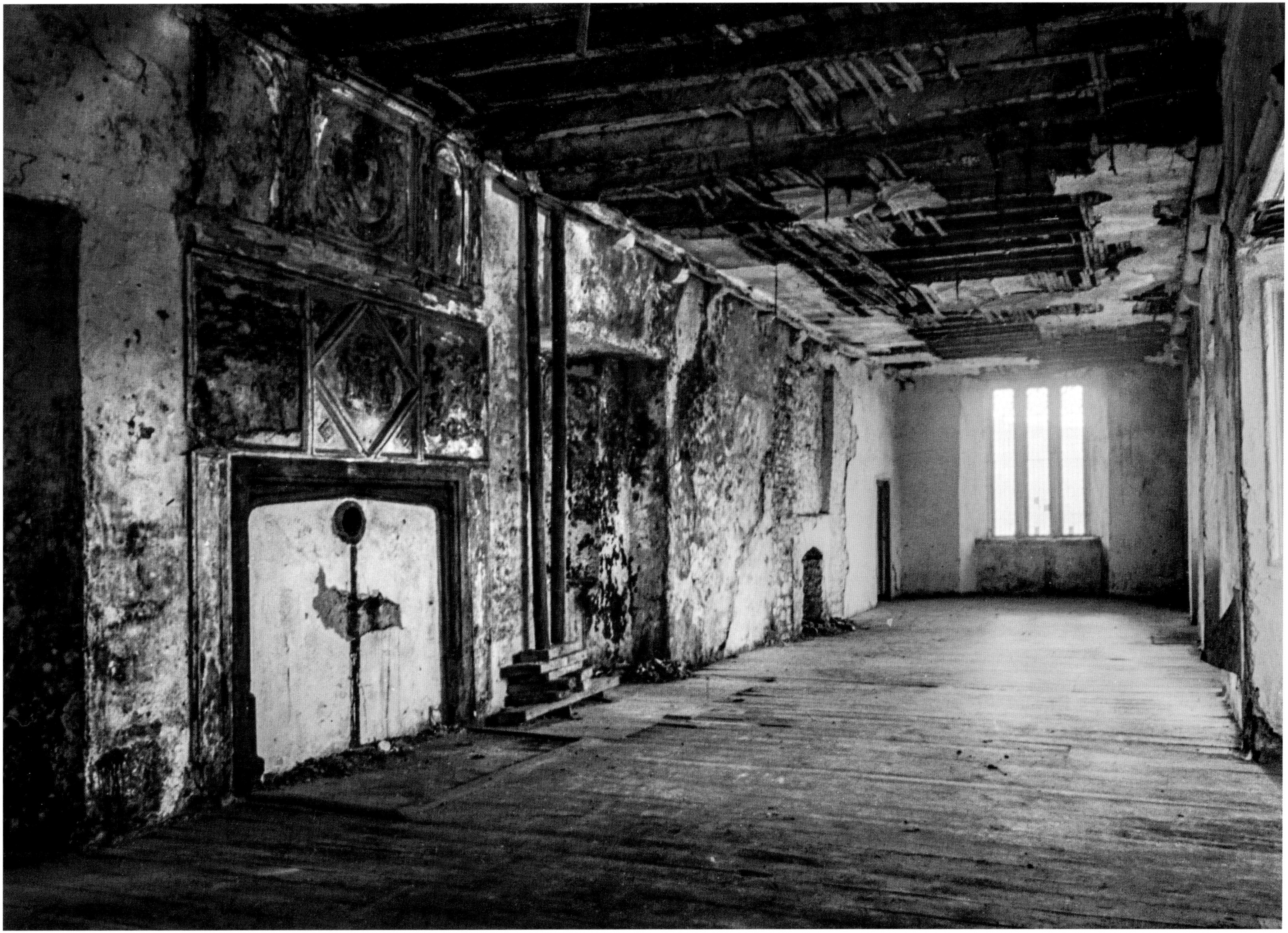

James Butler, 12th Earl and 1st Duke of Ormond, undertook work, but following his death in 1688, the building again fell into neglect. The Butlers preferred to live in Kilkenny Castle and the house in Carrick was let to a series of tenants. In the second decade of the nineteenth century, when the building was taken by a local solicitor, John Wogan, a considerable part of the medieval castle was demolished.

By the time that Browne came to take these pictures, the entire property had fallen into serious dilapidation. Slates had come off the roof, allowing water to enter, and many of the windows were broken. The Long Gallery had been clumsily divided into a series of smaller rooms and here, as elsewhere, much of the sixteenth-century plasterwork had been lost. Dereliction and decay were rampant and it must have seemed as though these photographs would act as the record of a building soon to be lost altogether. Happily, this proved not to be the house's fate. In 1947 the Butler family handed responsibility for the building to the Office of Public Works and the first in a series of restoration programmes was initiated. Ormond Castle is now open to the public.

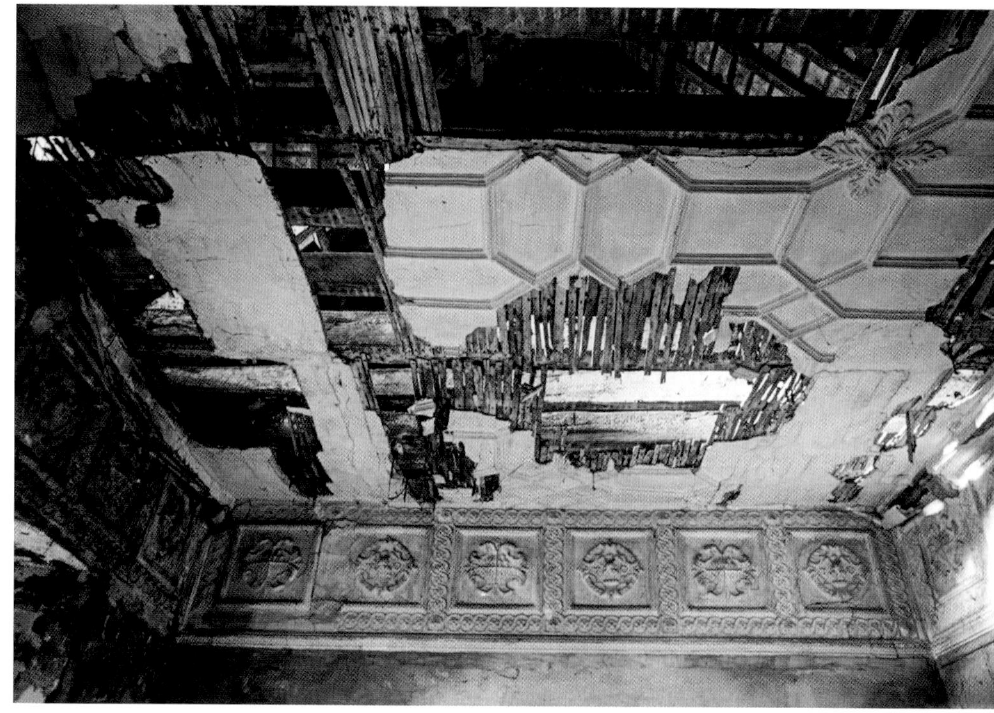

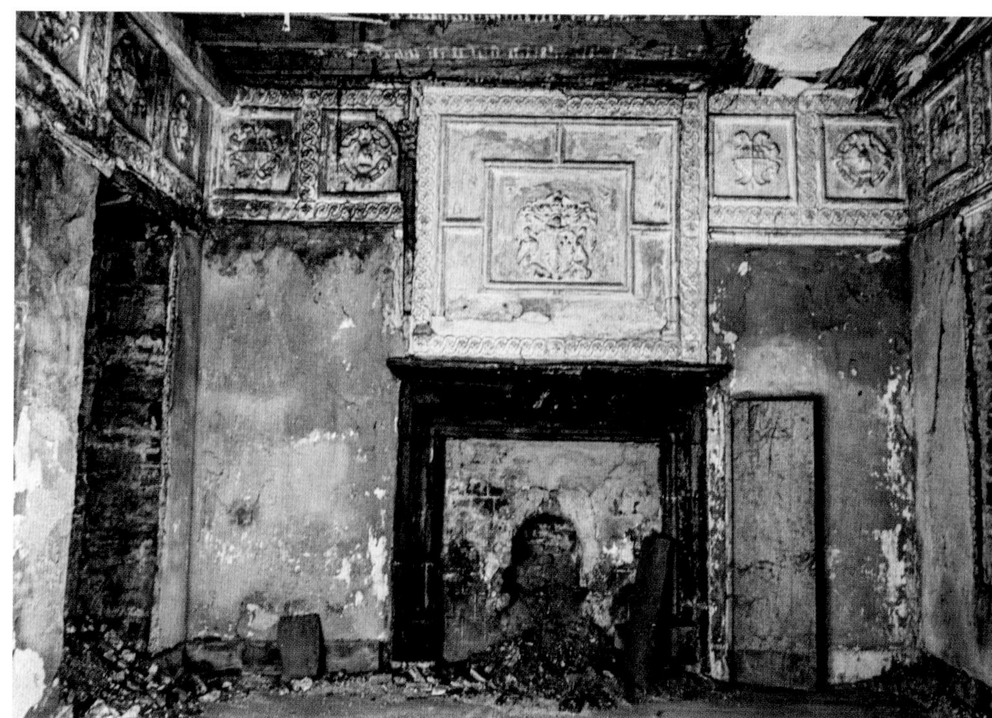

Previous Pages: The façade of the castle and its first-floor Long Gallery, both reflecting the building's very poor condition when photographed in 1944

Right and Opposite Page: Images of two chambers located off the Long Gallery show how close to complete ruin the building had become

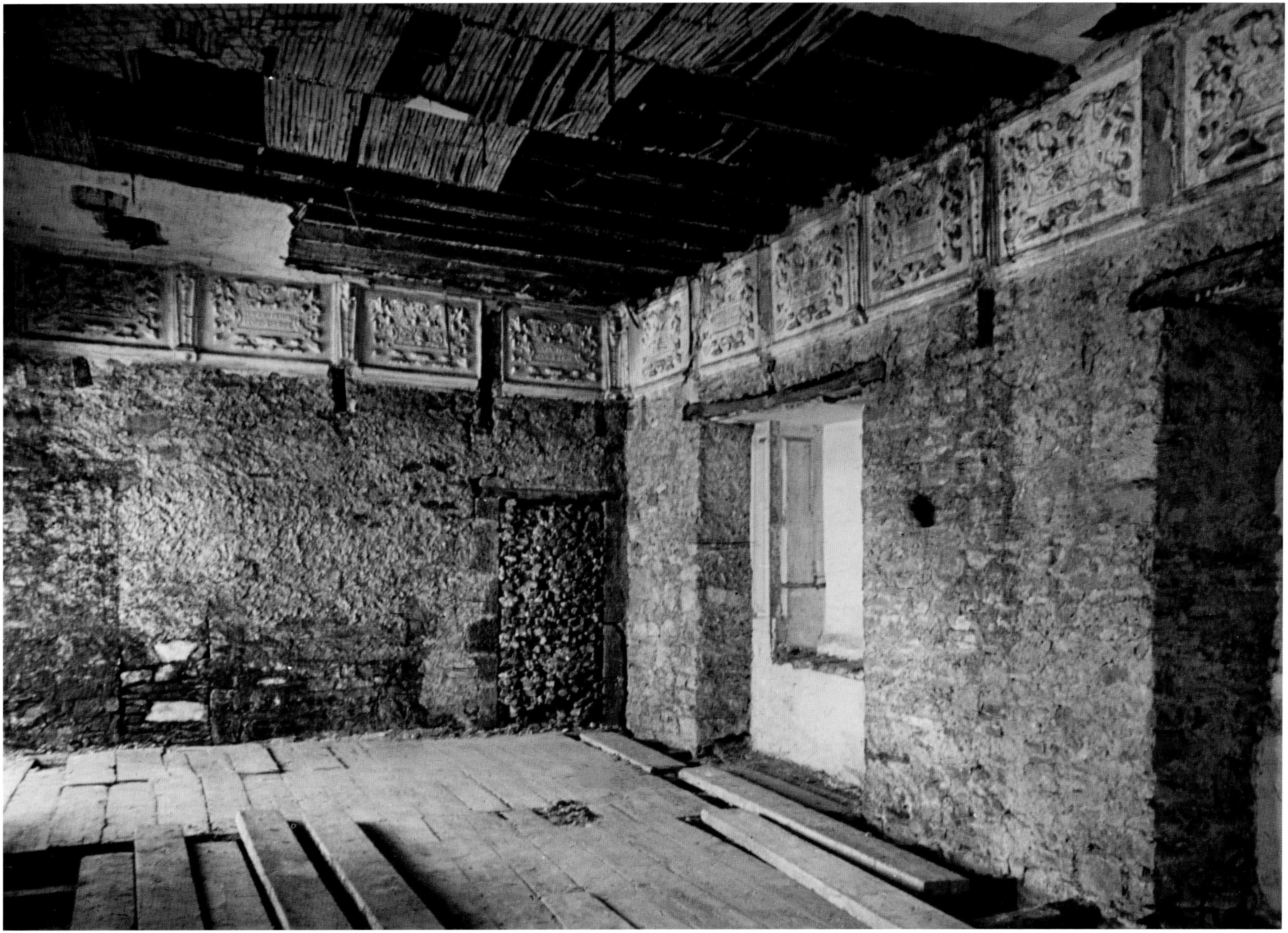

Curraghmore
County Waterford

2nd April 1940

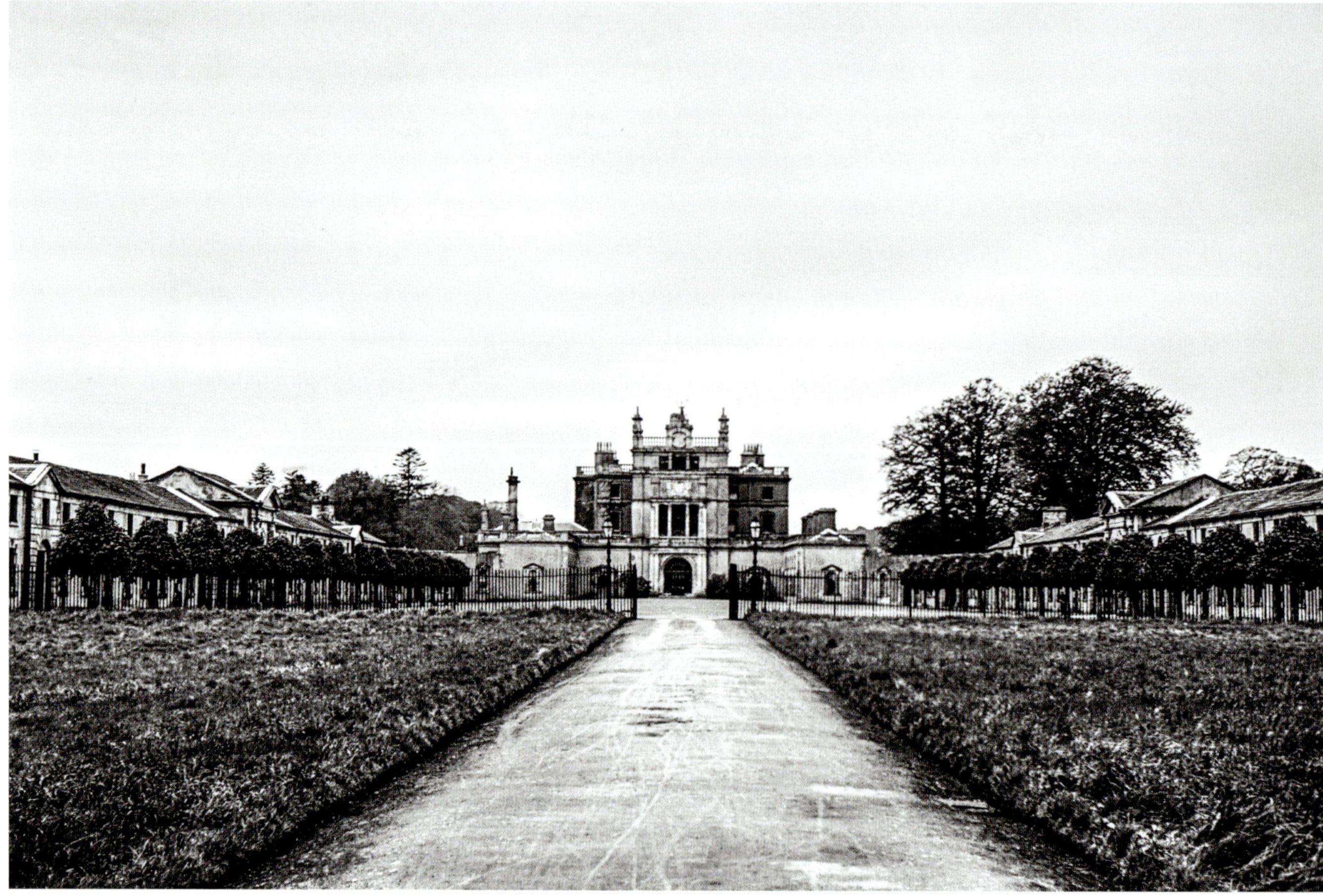

Curraghmore (the name is derived from the Irish *An Currach Mór* – the Great Bog) is a rare example of an Irish country house that looks almost the same today as it did when Browne visited it in 1940. Now occupied by Henry Nicholas de la Poer Beresford, 9th Marquis of Waterford, and his family, the estate has been owned for at least 800 years by descendants of Henry le Poer who settled in the area in the thirteenth century.

Curraghmore evolved with many changes to its character and fabric. But at the building's core is a late-medieval tower house, the walls of which are some 12 feet thick. The 1654 Civil Survey described the estate as containing 'a fayre Castle and a goodly stone house upon the land, there is also an Orchard and Meadow upon the same and stands by the side of a fine wood'. Mention of a 'goodly stone house' suggests that already the original building was being extended.

Substantial changes certainly occurred at the end of the seventeenth century when James, 3rd Earl of Tyrone, embarked on constructing a new residence directly behind the old tower house. In 1746, in his *The Ancient and Present State of the County and City of Waterford*, Charles Smith noted that a pedestal on the doorcase bore the date 1700, indicating this was when work concluded. The new house's entrance hall occupied the site of what is now the Blue Drawing Room, and directly behind rose a staircase that divided in two on the return. Rooms ran around the four sides of the building, which had an open courtyard at its centre. According to Smith the main reception areas were painted by Dutch-born artist William van der Hagen, the staircase hall, for example, having walls covered in columns and festoons, between which were landscape views, and the flat ceiling was made to look like it was a dome raised above more columns.

All this would be swept away towards the end of the eighteenth century, but before then the old tower house was modernised, perhaps with the assistance of architect Richard Castle. Here the ground floor was turned into an entrance hall, its arched ceiling covered in plasterwork, and the room above given an elaborate plaster ceiling, thanks to the artistry of the Swiss-born Lafranchini brothers. Immediately in front of the tower house, long wings incorporating stables and accommodation were built to form an immense courtyard, the only one of its kind in Ireland. This work is thought to have been

Above: Curraghmore's great forecourt, thought to have been designed in the mid-18th century by local architect John Roberts

Opposite: The Blue Drawing Room, designed by James Wyatt, its ceiling decorated by Peter de Gree and, it is thought, Antonio Zucchi

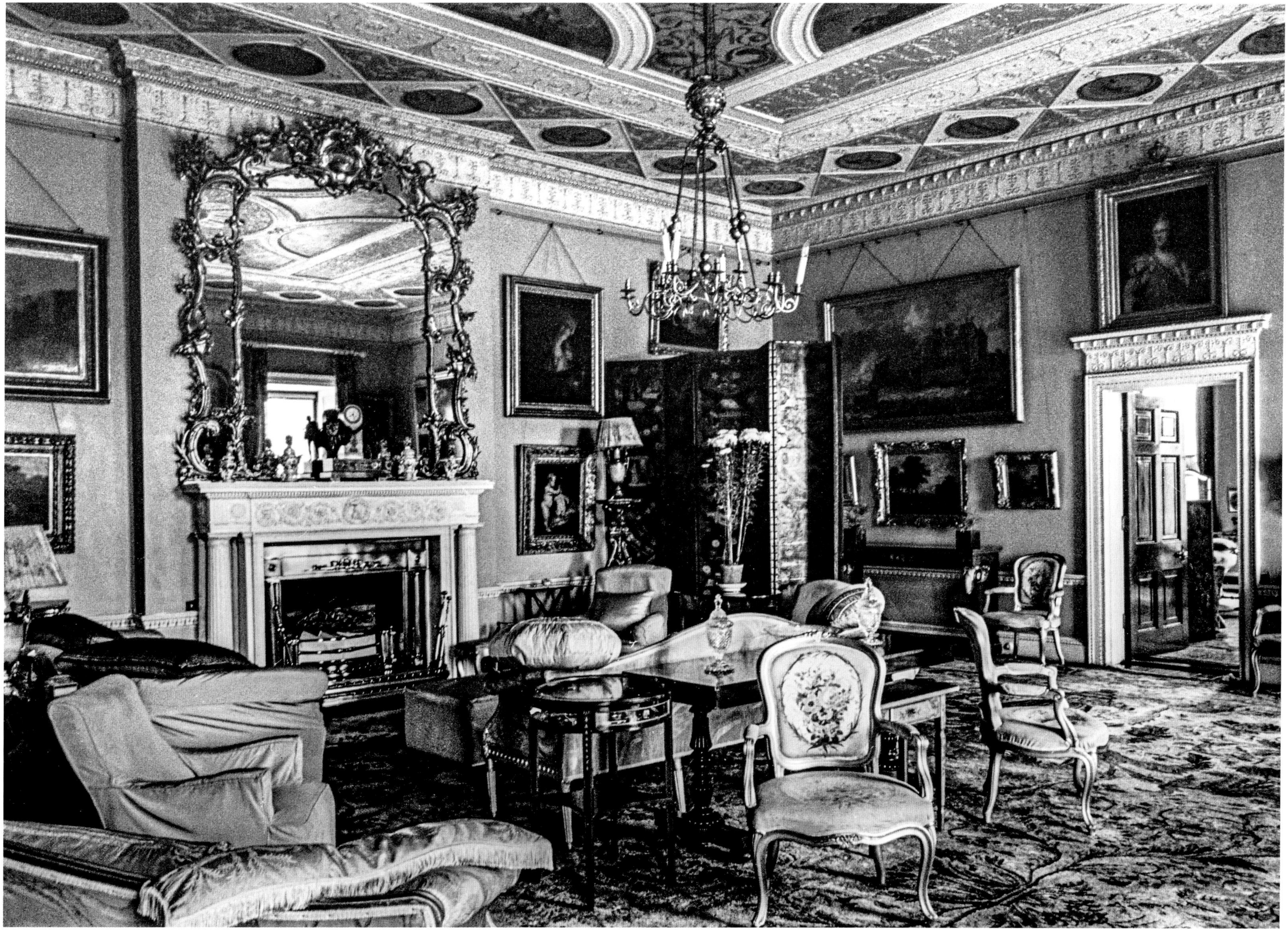

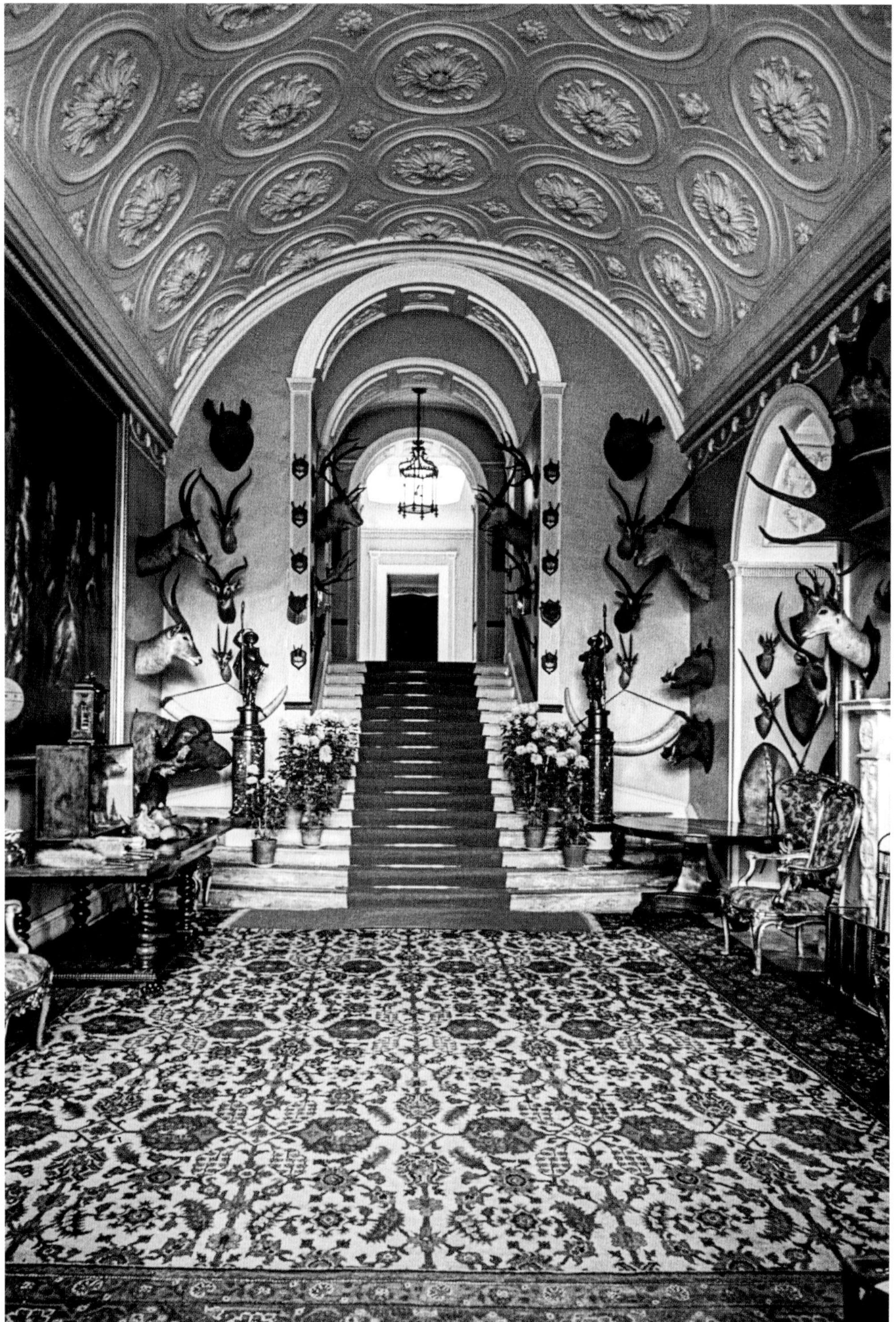

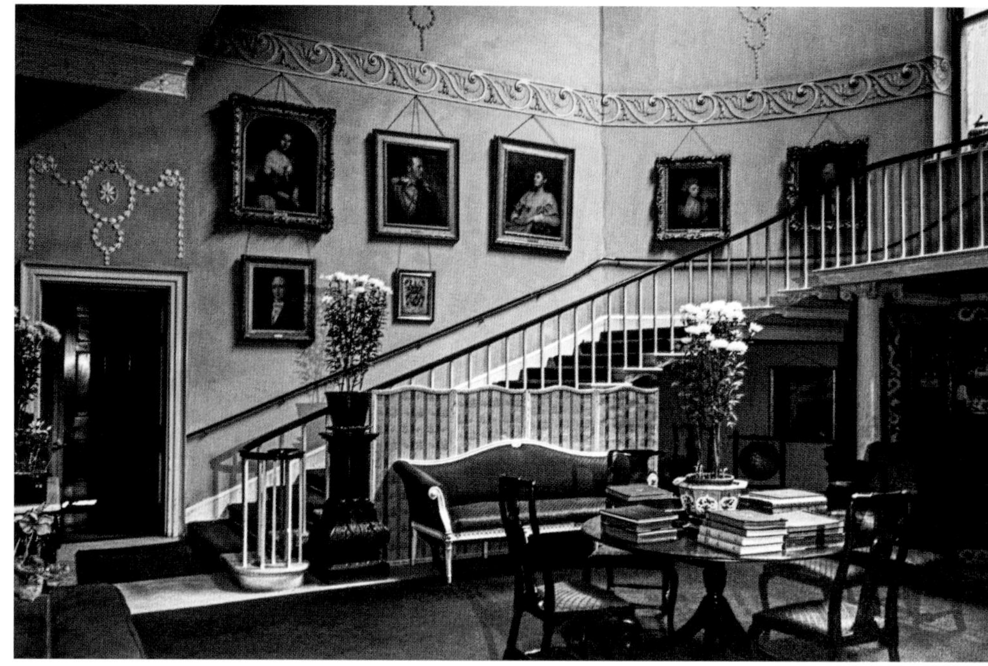

undertaken around 1750–60, and was most likely designed by John Roberts of nearby Waterford city. Then, in the last quarter of the eighteenth century, James Wyatt, the finest neo-classical architect of the period, was asked to redesign Curraghmore's main reception rooms. While it entailed the loss of van der Hagen's painted interiors, the resulting sequence of spaces today offers the pre-eminent example of Wyatt's work within an Irish country house.

Relatively few alterations were made to Curraghmore thereafter, although in the mid-1870s the 6th Marquess of Waterford carried out what were then deemed improvements to the house, putting sheets of plate glass in all the windows and cement render on the exterior. It was also at this time that sculptor Joseph Boehm, who had designed a memorial to the 5th Marquis's first wife, designed the St Hubert stag with a crucifix between its real antlers, which sits atop the facade of the house. Since then, over the course of almost a century and a half, generations of the family have been scrupulous custodians of their legacy, allowing us today to appreciate Curraghmore as an outstanding part of Ireland's architectural heritage.

Left: The Entrance Hall, occupying what would have been the ground floor vaulted chamber in the original tower house here
Above: The Inner Hall, designed by Wyatt, its walls lined with family portraits

Opposite: The Dining Room, likewise designed by Wyatt and decorated once more by Peter de Gree and, it is thought, Antonio Zucchi

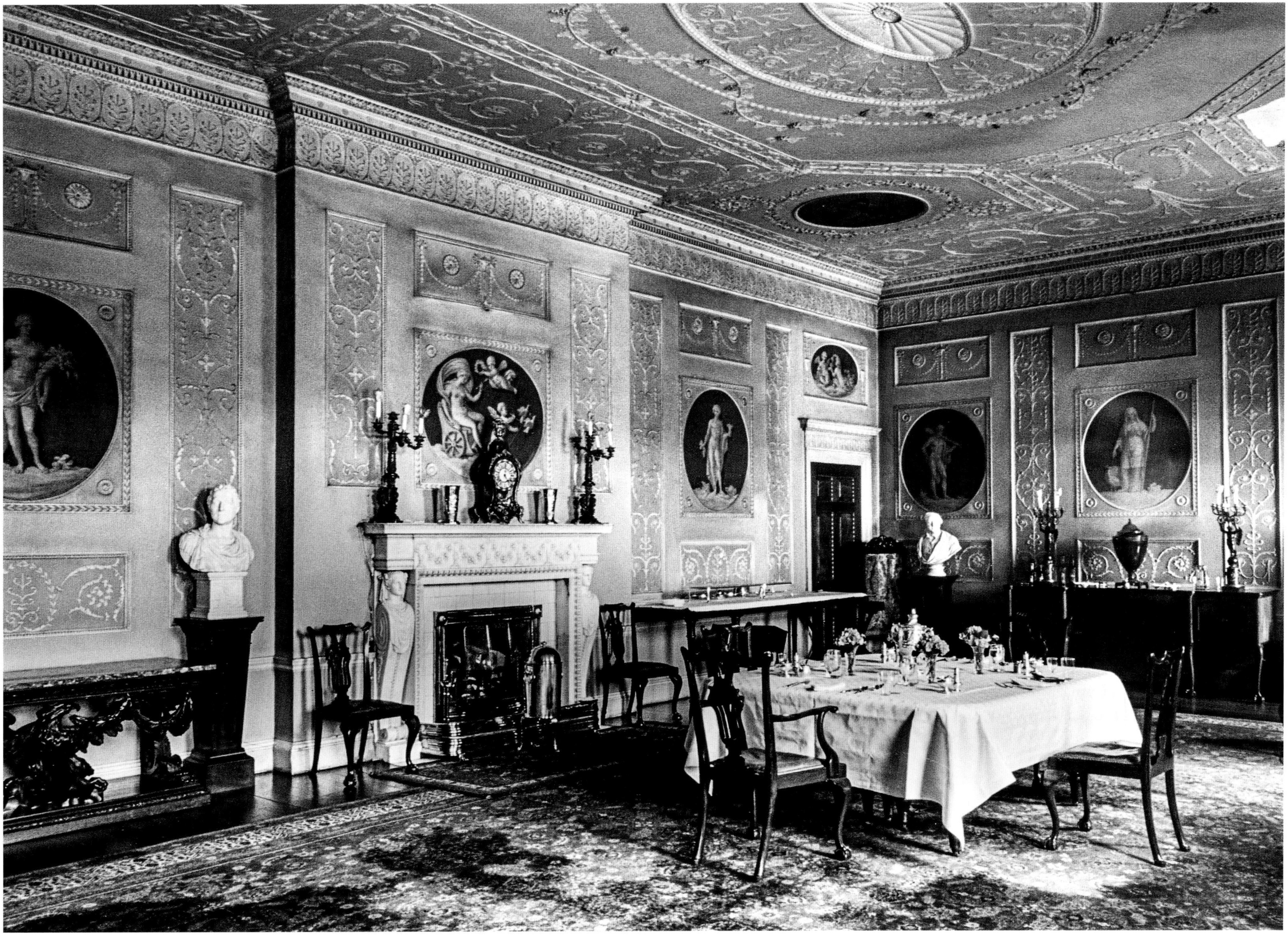

FRENCHPARK
COUNTY ROSCOMMON

28TH APRIL 1948

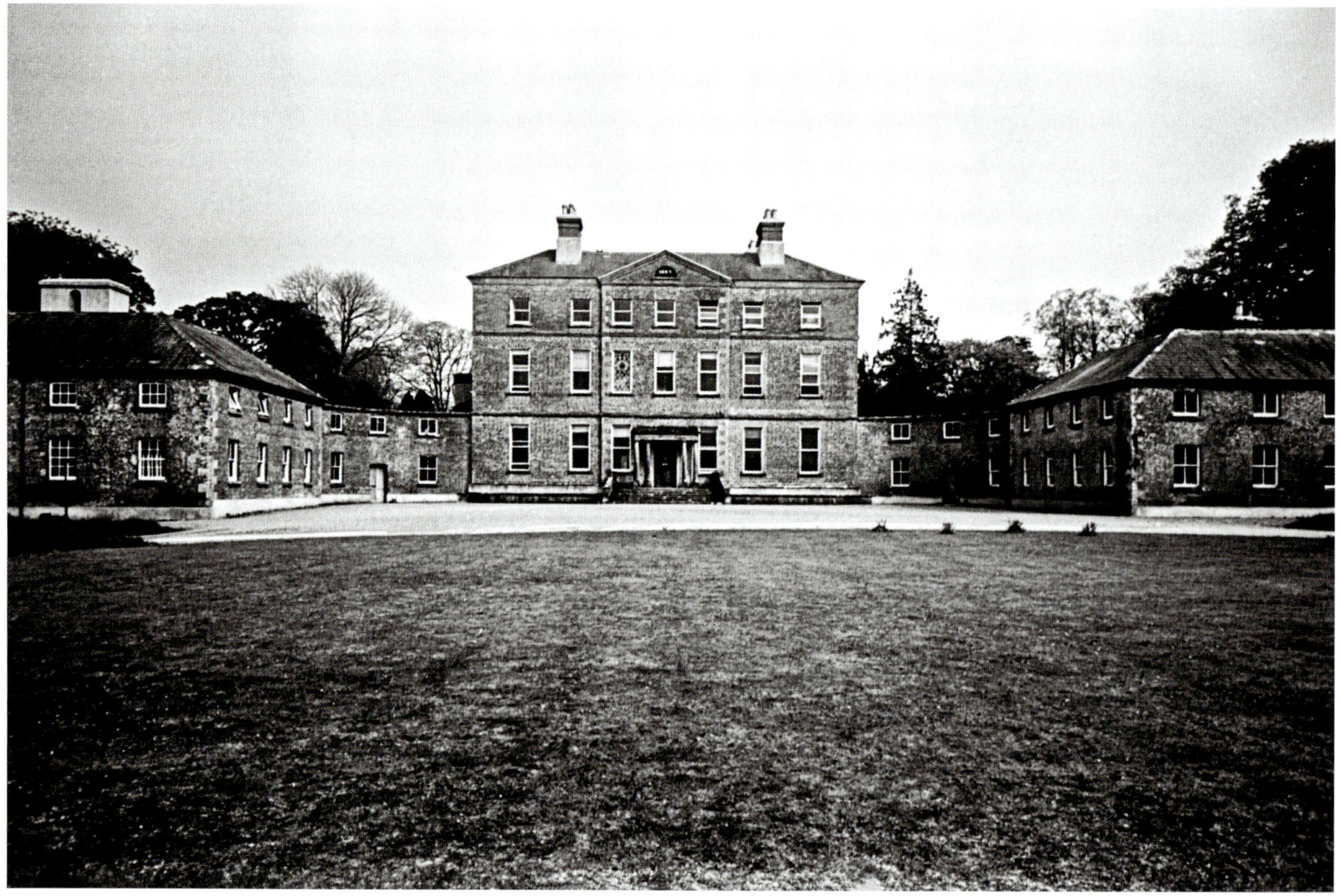

The French family liked to trace their ancestry to Maximillian de Ffrench, descendant of the ninth-century Viking warrior Rollo the Strong, a man so big that no horse strong enough to carry him could ever be found. Rollo and a band of followers were said to have carved out a territory for themselves on the north-west coast of France, which, given that they were Norsemen, came to be known as Normandy. In due course, Rollo was claimed as forebear of both the Frenches and of William the Conqueror, who defeated England's King Harold at the Battle of Hastings in 1066. Given these supposed origins, the surname French has understandably sometimes been thought to refer to France. In fact, it derives from the word *frêne*, meaning ash tree. Hence, when Arthur French of Frenchpark was raised to the peerage in 1839 he took the title Baron de Freyne.

Above: The entrance front of the house, with projecting wings on either side

Opposite: The Drawing Room on the first floor with a Bossi chimneypiece at one end

Long before then, a branch of the family had settled in Galway, where they came to be one of the city's fourteen dominant Tribes. In the sixteenth and early seventeenth century, they began to buy land in the surrounding counties, but this process was disrupted by the upheavals of the Confederate Wars of the 1640s. In the following decade, Patrick French was allotted some 6,000 acres in County Roscommon by the Cromwellian Commissioners, and for the next 300 years this parcel of land formed the basis of the family's estate. Successive generations sat in the Irish House of Commons representing the area. One of them, John French, purchased another estate in 1703, becoming known as an Tiarna Mór (the Great Landowner). He was probably also responsible for commissioning the house called Frenchpark. There may have been a residence on the site already. John French's building dates from c.1729, its design sometimes attributed to Richard Castle, although this is open to question.

The Palladian house consisted of a three-storey over basement, seven-bay block with three-bay pedimented breakfront, the pediment containing a Diocletian window. Two-storey quadrants on either side of this led to five bay wings, the entire building faced in red brick, then an expensive material and possibly imported from the Netherlands. Inside, a panelled hall and carved staircase led to a first-floor gallery. The drawing room was on this level, Browne's photographs showing it to

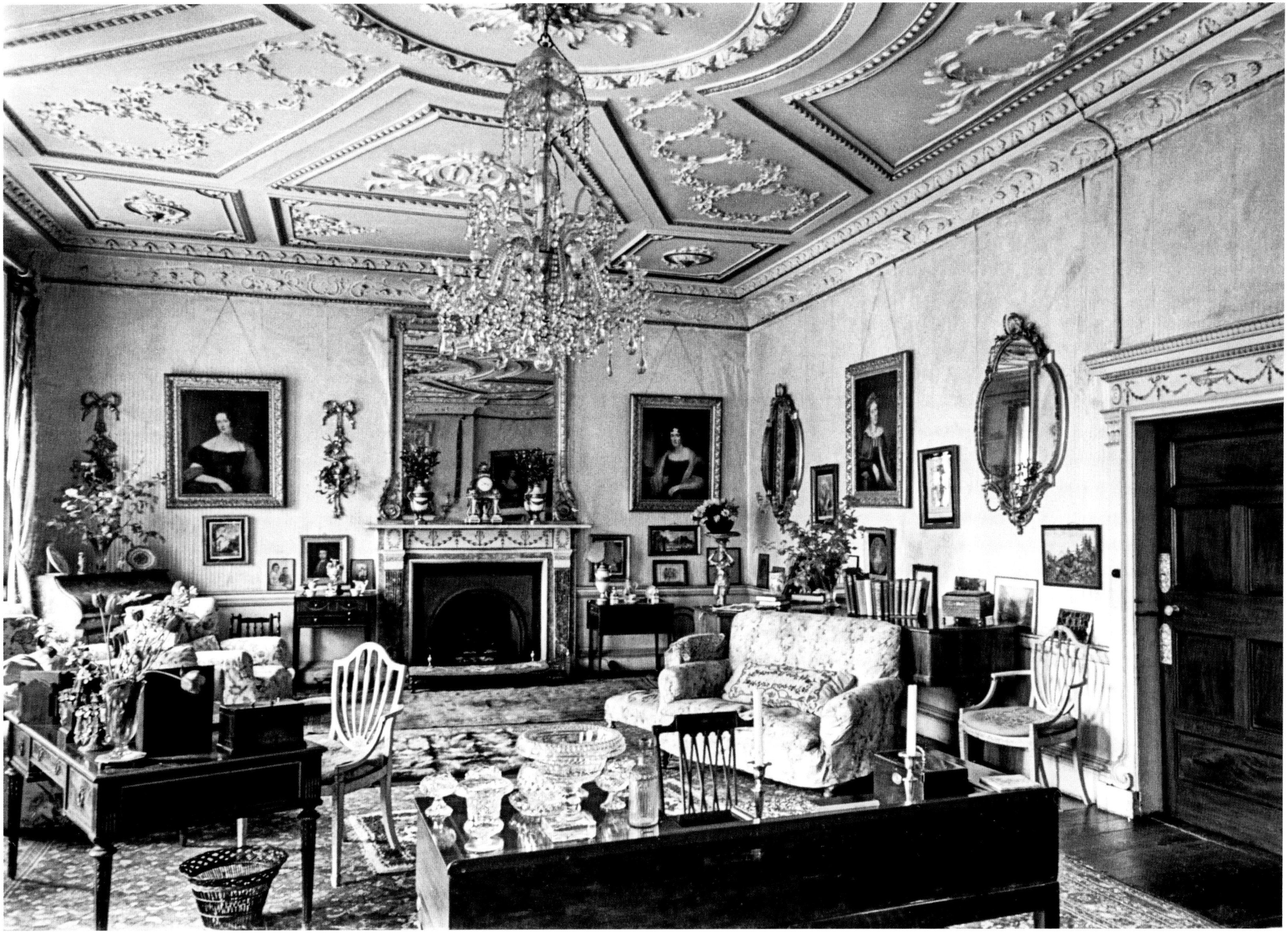

have been a long room with chimneypieces at either end, one inlaid in the style of Bossi, the other with Ionic columns and a carved central panel typical of late eighteenth-century taste. The heavy compartmented baroque-style ceiling here dated from the late nineteenth century, when it was decorated for the fourth Lord de Freyne. The dining room directly below was originally hung with embossed leather, but by the time of Browne's visit, the walls were covered with what appears to have been a Pugin-designed paper.

That visit occurred in 1948, four years before the 7th Baron de Freyne sold the house and remaining 250-acre estate to the Land Commission. The contents of the house, livestock, machinery etc. were auctioned over the course of three days. The house was subsequently unroofed and eventually demolished in the mid-1970s so that nothing remains of it today. An eighteenth-century smokehouse that stood in the former demesne is almost the only surviving evidence that this was once the site of an important estate.

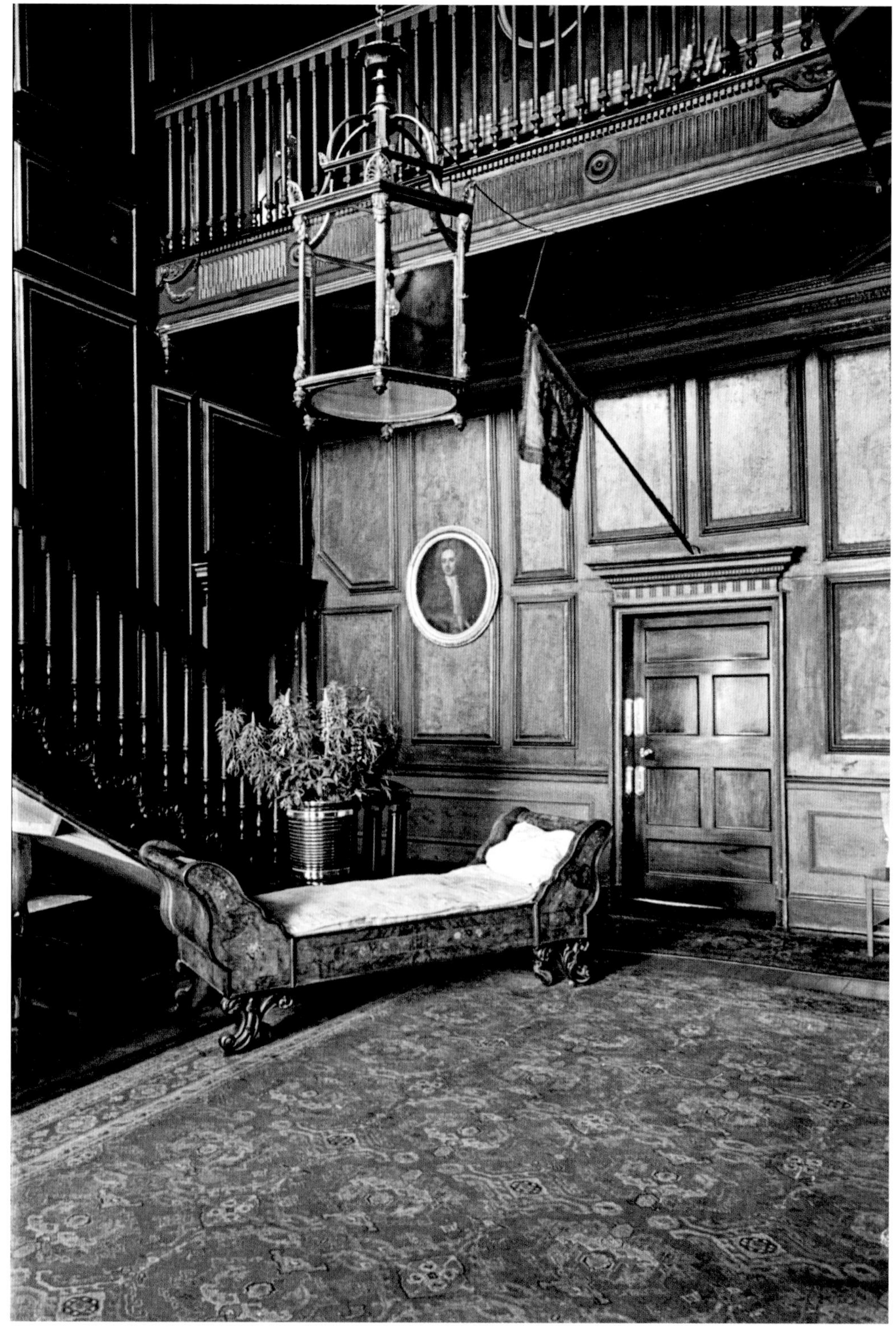

Right: The panelled staircase hall with a gallery around the first floor
Opposite: A panelled boudoir

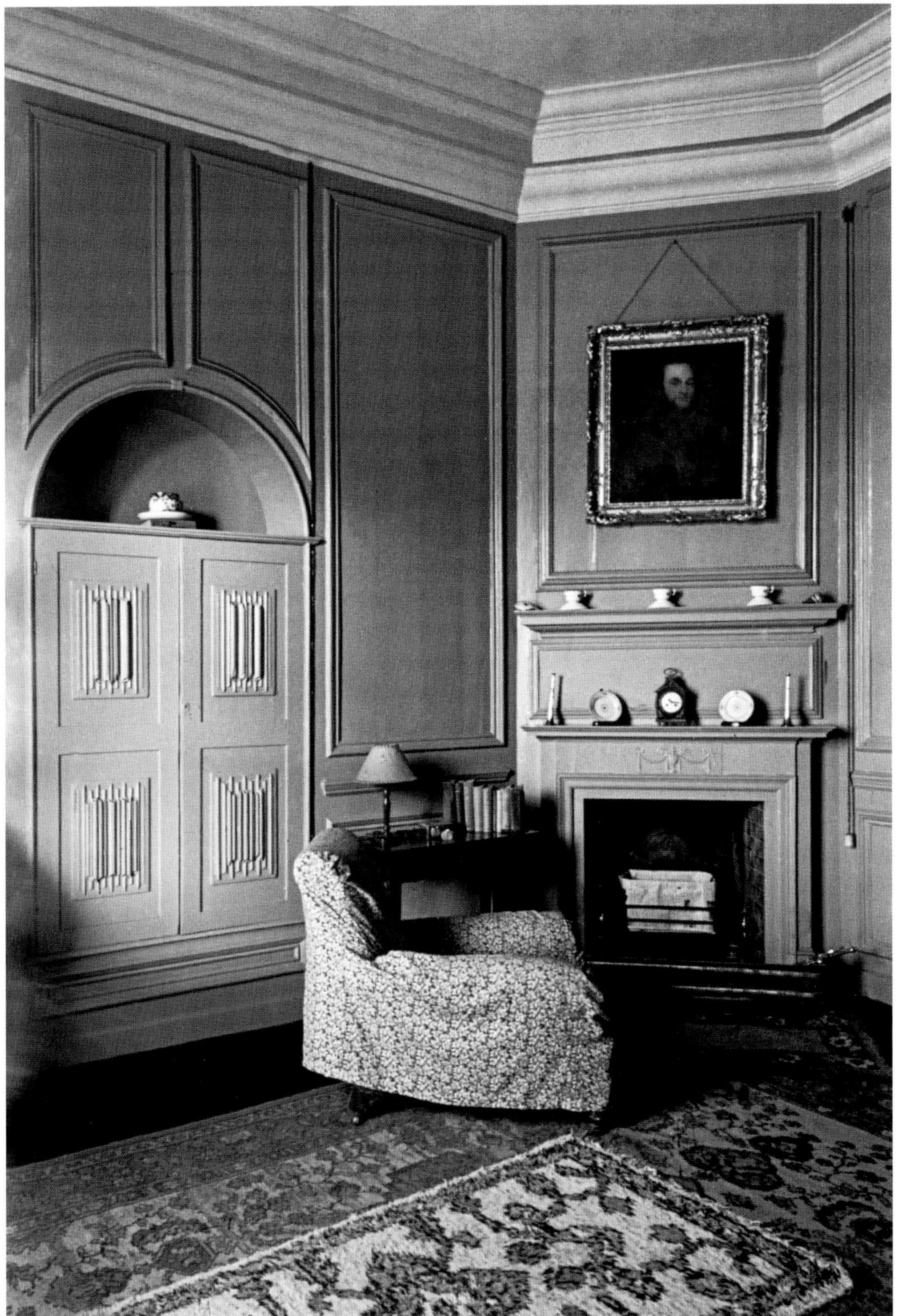

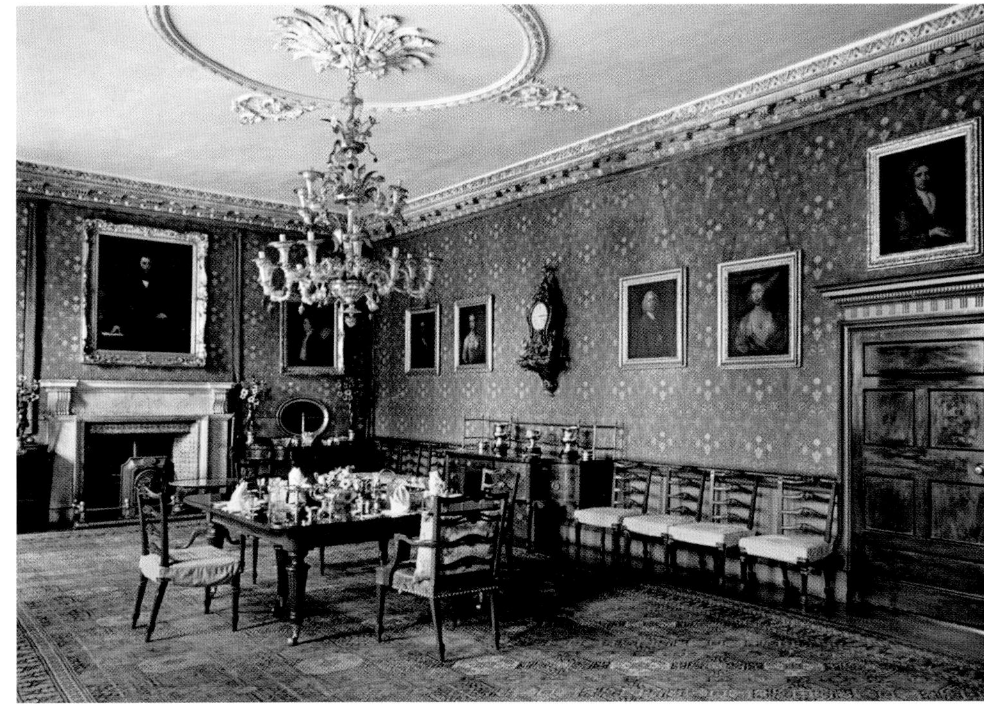

Above: The Dining Room, originally hung with embossed leather but later replaced with wallpaper
Below: One of the bedrooms

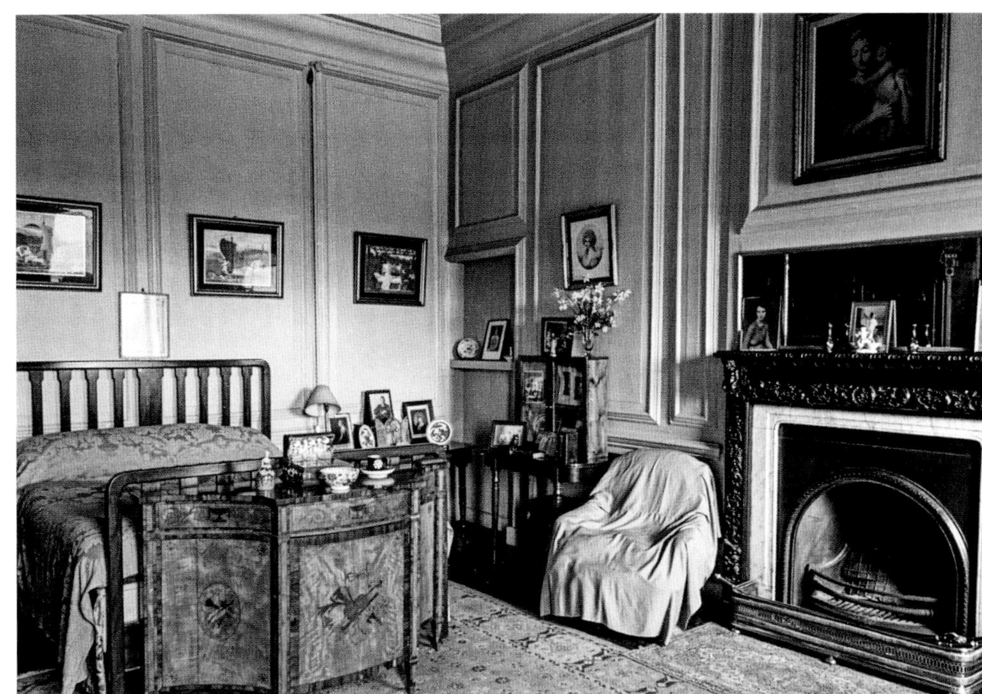

HERBERTSTOWN
COUNTY MEATH

1ST JANUARY 1937

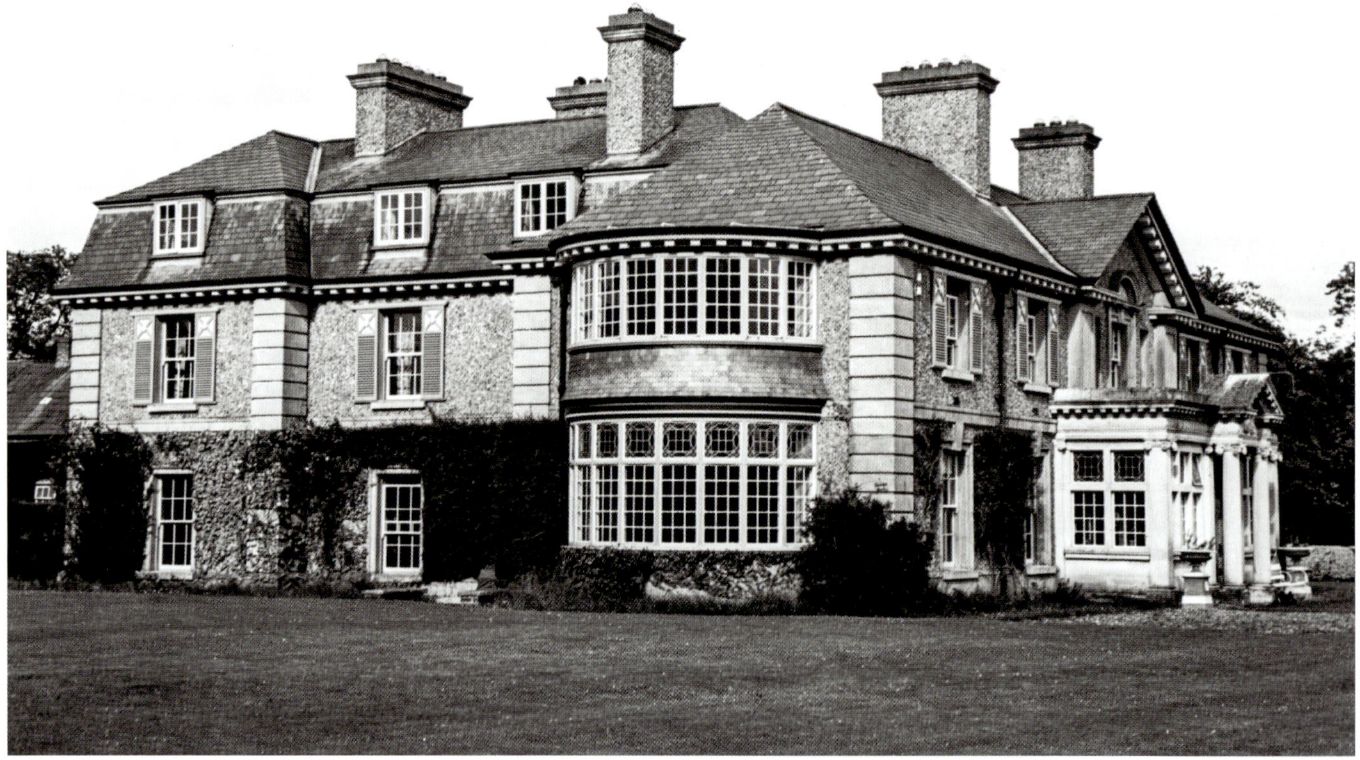

One of the last country houses to be built in Ireland prior to Independence, Herbertstown was designed for a Captain H. Whitworth by the Dublin architectural partnership of McDonnell & Reid. In the centre of the long and deep projecting porch, a pediment supported by engaged Ionic columns carries the date 1916. On either side of this is a series of mullioned and partly leaded windows concluding in Ionic pilasters. Behind the porch, the south-facing, two-storey, five-bay facade is likewise centred on a pedimented gable with a segmental pediment window beneath. On the side elevations, the building features large glazed bows, that to the west being of two storeys, that to the east just one. Behind this are two further bays, with a mansard roof containing dormer windows, the first-floor windows having external shutters. An auction notice for the house in 1954 describe it as having been constructed 'regardless of cost'.

The interior of Herbertstown held a splendid entrance hall, on one side of which rose a carved oak staircase in the seventeenth-century baroque style. The drawing and dining rooms opened off the hall, the former with a modillion cornice and a ceiling on which a large oval holds fan decoration. Both rooms had fine inlaid marble chimneypieces, which may well have come from an earlier property.

Herberstown appears to have been the first country house to have been photographed by Browne, barely two decades after it had been built. His pictures show the interiors somewhat under-furnished, as though between owners at the time. Thereafter it changed hands on a number of occasions and at the time of writing is in the midst of an extensive renovation.

Above: A view of the house from the south-west
Opposite: The Entrance Hall with its carved oak staircase

Overleaf:
Page 52: The Drawing Room, its ceiling dominated by a plasterwork oval with fan decoration
Page 53: Herbertstown's Dining Room

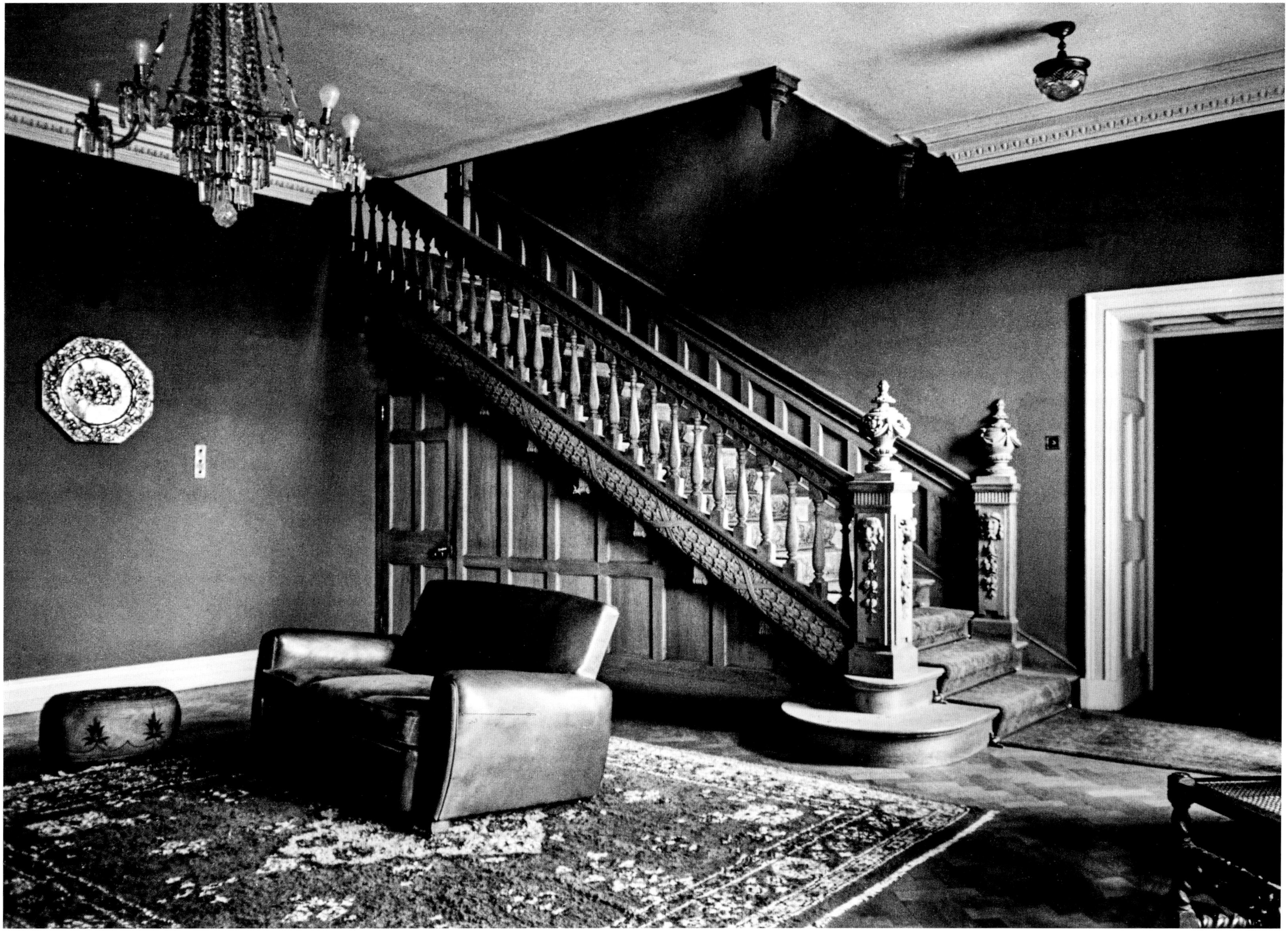

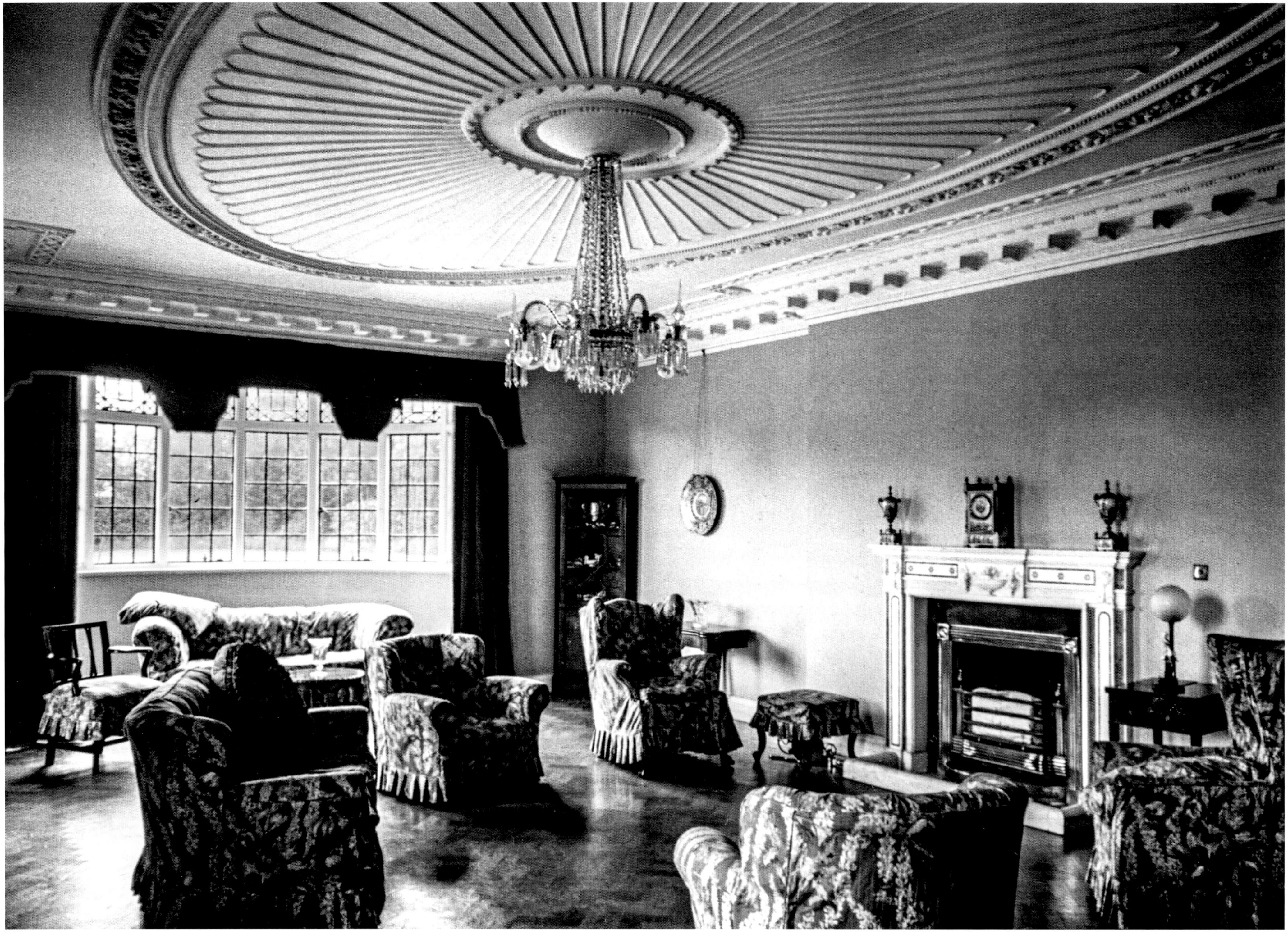

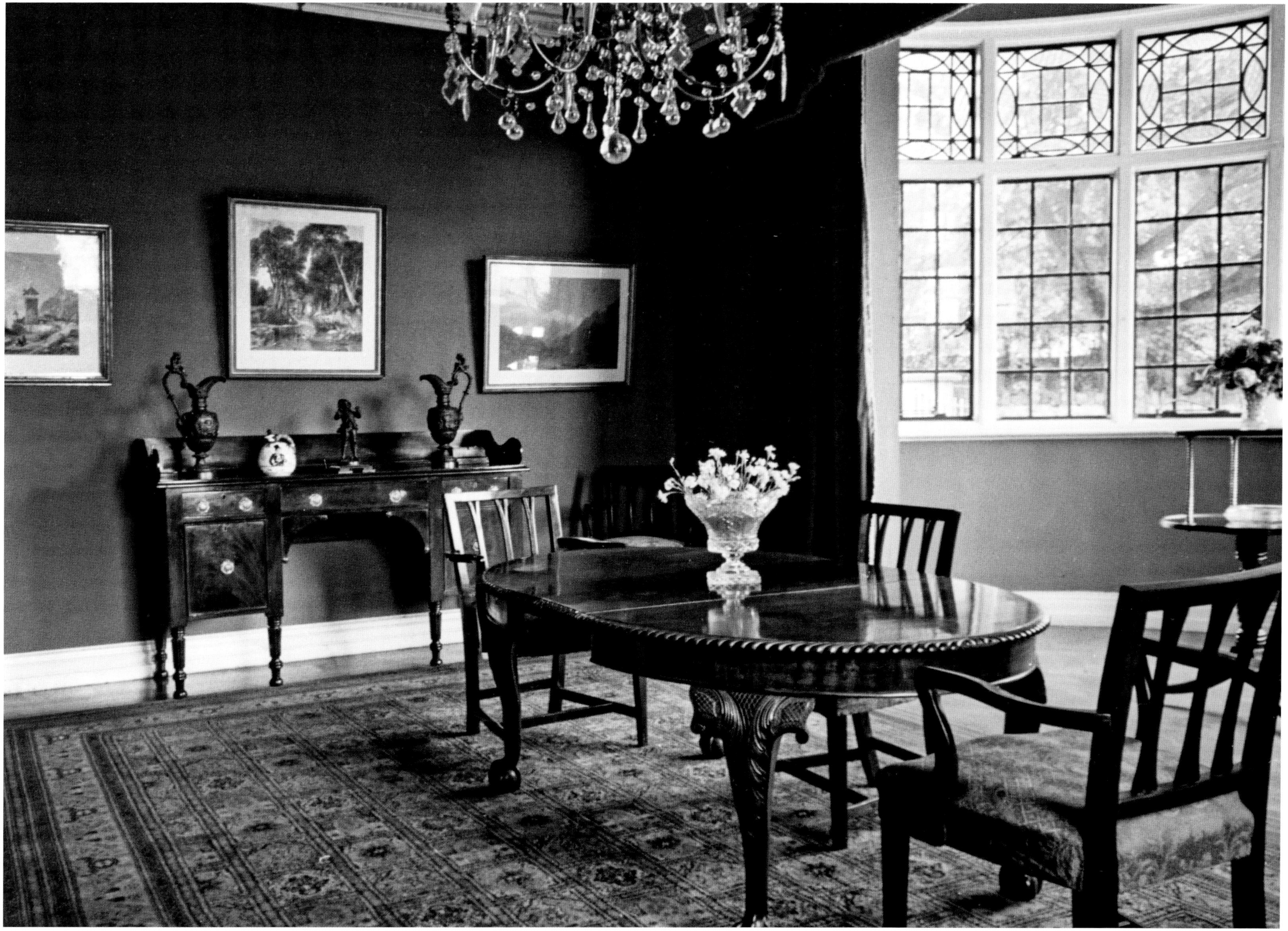

GORMANSTON CASTLE

COUNTY MEATH

15TH AUGUST 1947

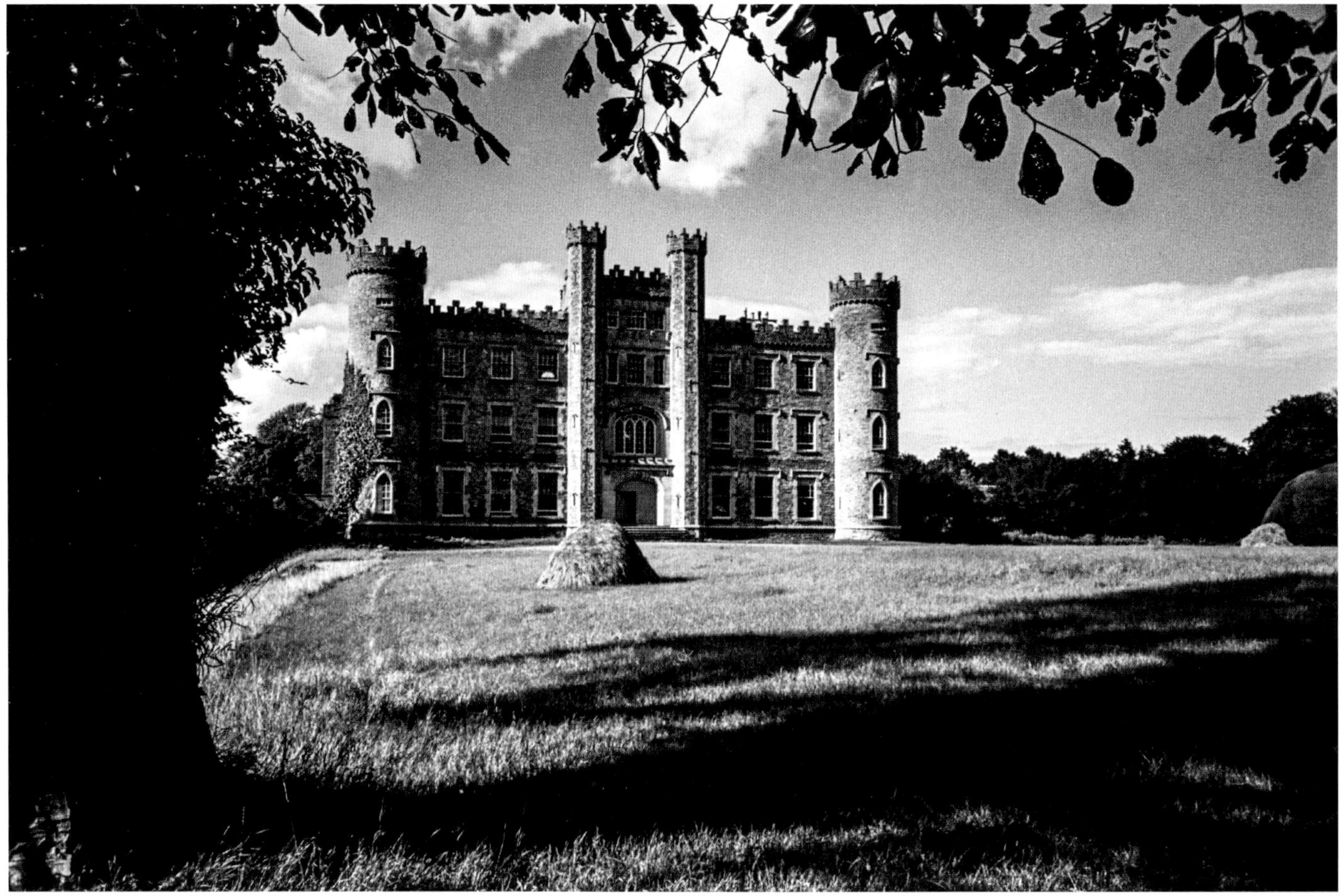

The Preston family originated in the Lancashire town of the same time and first came to Ireland during the early fourteenth century, when two brothers established themselves as merchants in Drogheda. Another sibling, Roger de Preston, was appointed justice in the Court of Common Pleas in 1326 and six years later was made one of the justices of the Court of King's Bench. His heir, Sir Robert de Preston, also a lawyer, served as Chief Justice, briefly as Lord Chancellor and as Chancellor of the Irish Exchequer. In due course, he was created Baron Gormanston, this title deriving from the manor Gormanston, County Meath, that he had purchased in 1363 from Almaric de St Amand, although at that time the Prestons' main residence was at Carbury, County Kildare.

The fourth baron, also called Robert, was appointed Deputy to the Lord Chancellor of Ireland and later made Deputy to Edward IV's son Richard, Duke of York. In 1478 he was created Viscount of Gormanston, and this is now the oldest surviving viscountcy in Ireland. During the sixteenth and seventeenth centuries, the Prestons enjoyed mixed fortunes, falling in and out of favour with the English crown, and on occasion threatened with ruin. The seventh viscount, for example, having remained loyal to the Stuart cause, went into exile with Charles II. His lands were confiscated before being returned to him after the Restoration of 1660. He also supported the cause of James II, fought at the Battle of the Boyne and, following his death in 1691, was declared a traitor, with the family lands forfeited once again.

For the next 100 years, although the title was under attainder, successive heirs continued to call themselves Viscount Gormanston. They also managed to retain the Roman Catholic faith of their forebears and to regain the majority of their land under the terms of the Treaty of Limerick. Only in 1800 did the 12th Viscount succeed in having his ancient titles officially restored. He was also responsible for commissioning the present Gormanston Castle, which replaced an older manor house on the site. Although intended to evoke the Middle Ages, the new castle displays an eighteenth-century fondness for symmetry, its three-storey, eleven-bay facade having matching round corner towers and smaller polygonal turrets on either side of the breakfront entrance, as well as old-fashioned Georgian sash windows. Only the family's ancient private chapel, a carved armorial panel above its door carrying the date 1687, survived this extensive

Above: The façade of the early 19th century castle commissioned by the 12th Viscount

Opposite: The Library, with a series of portraits of members of the Preston family hung around the walls

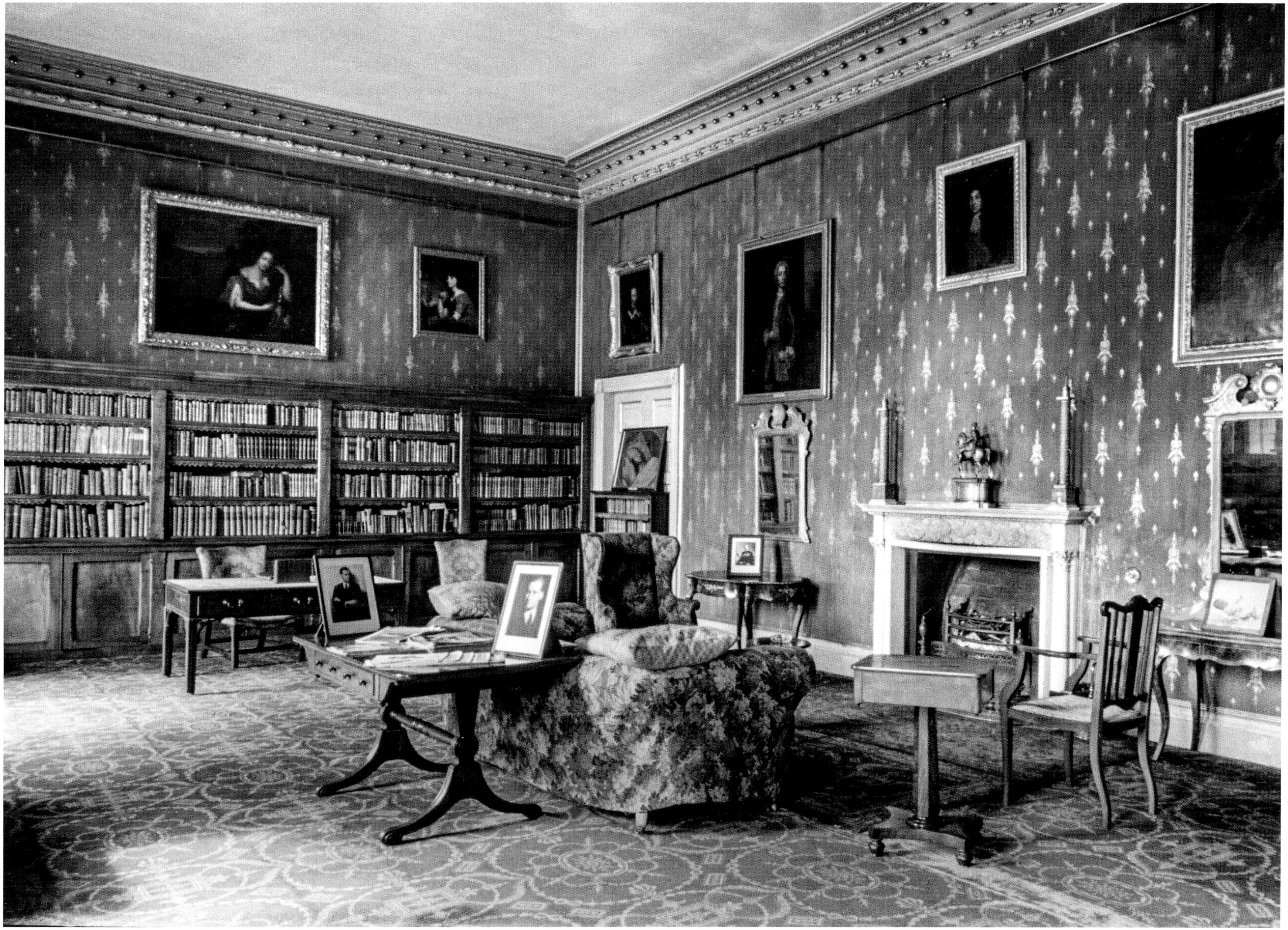

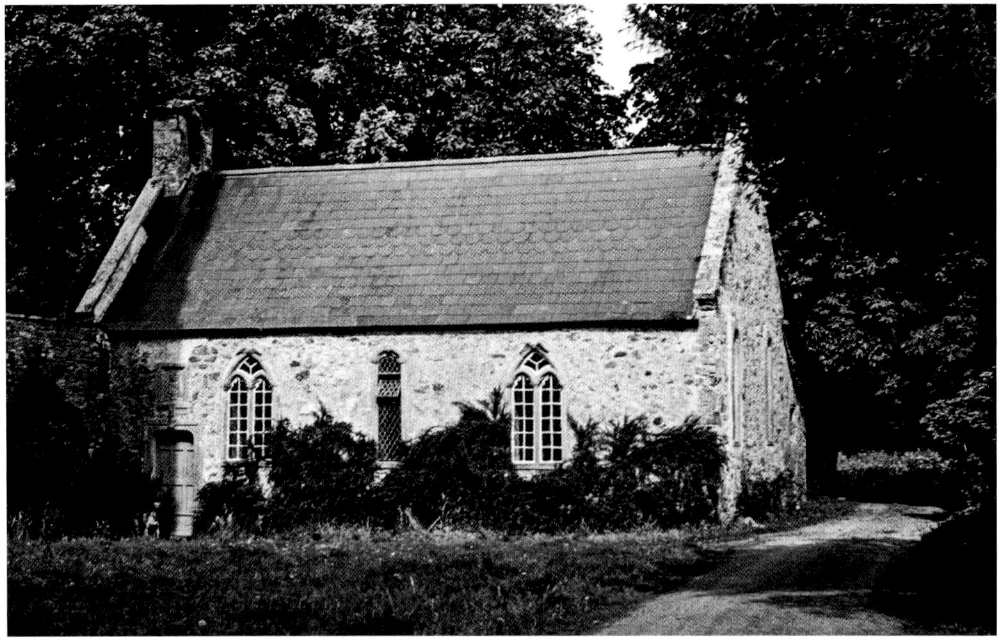

refurbishment. Although the finished castle is very substantial, it is thought that Lord Gormanston discontinued work on the site following the death of his wife in January 1820, when he wrote in his diary, 'This day the light of my life has gone out.' Inside the building, the most notable room was the double-height entrance hall, dominated by a vast oak chimneypiece carved by Georgina Jane Connellan, second wife of the 14th Viscount, and displaying the arms of families intermarried with that of her husband.

The Prestons remained in residence at Gormanston Castle until the middle of the last century. In June 1940, the 16th Viscount, then serving as a second lieutenant in the British army, went missing, presumed killed in action, leaving a baby son as heir. His widow took the decision to sell the property and in 1947, the same year Browne photographed the building, it was bought by the Franciscan order, which opened a boys' boarding school there. Ironically, the Preston family chapel, which had survived the early nineteenth-century rebuilding of the house, was demolished in the mid-1950s and replaced with a vast and ugly block of classrooms and dormitories. Although no longer run by the Franciscans, Gormanston Castle remains a school, with plans to build a replacement nearby announced in 2023.

Above: The family chapel which would be demolished in the mid-1950s
Right: The Entrance Hall, with its oak chimneypiece carved by Georgina Jane Connellan, second wife of the 14th viscount

Opposite: The Dining Room containing a number of paintings by Lady Butler whose daughter had married the 15th Viscount

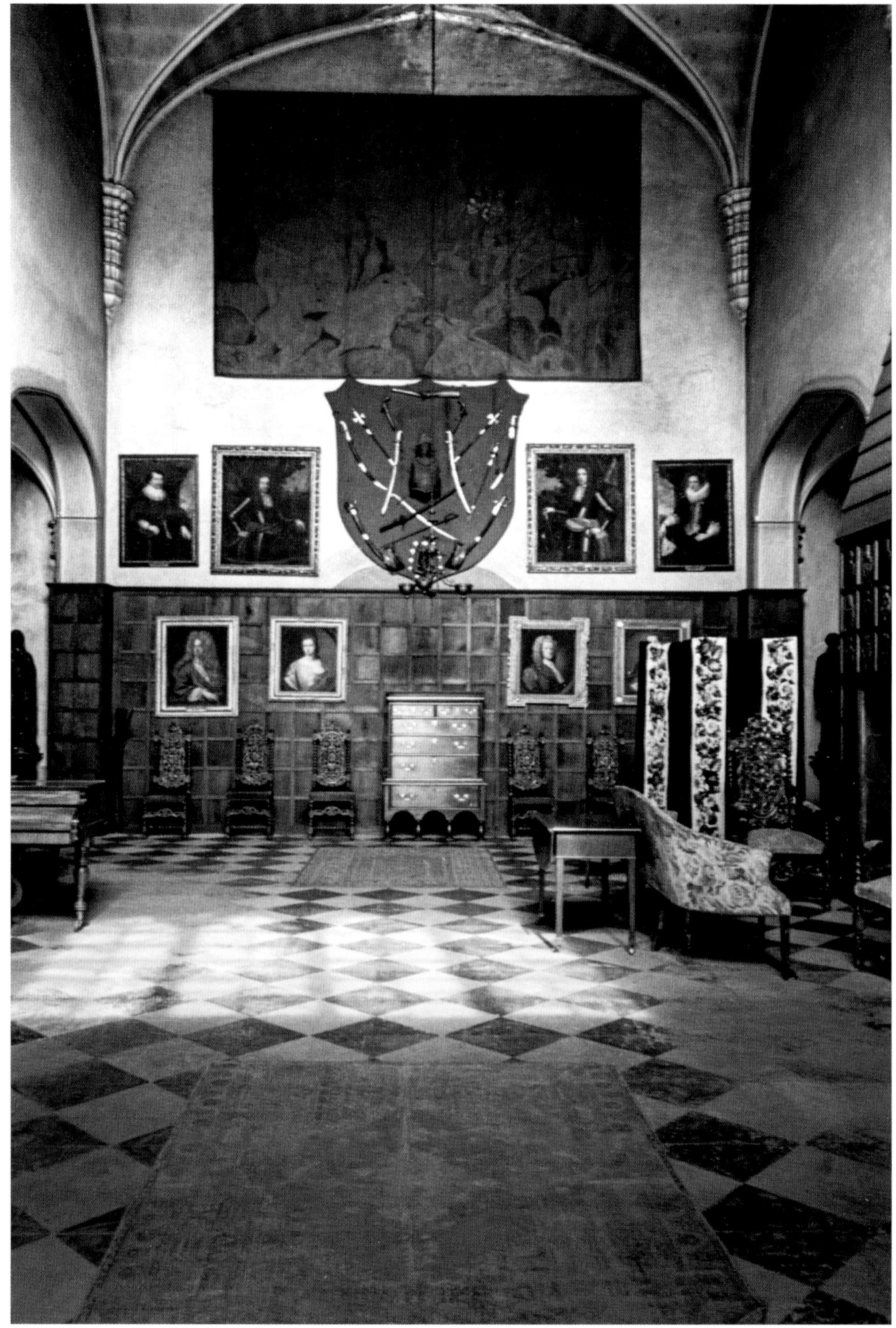

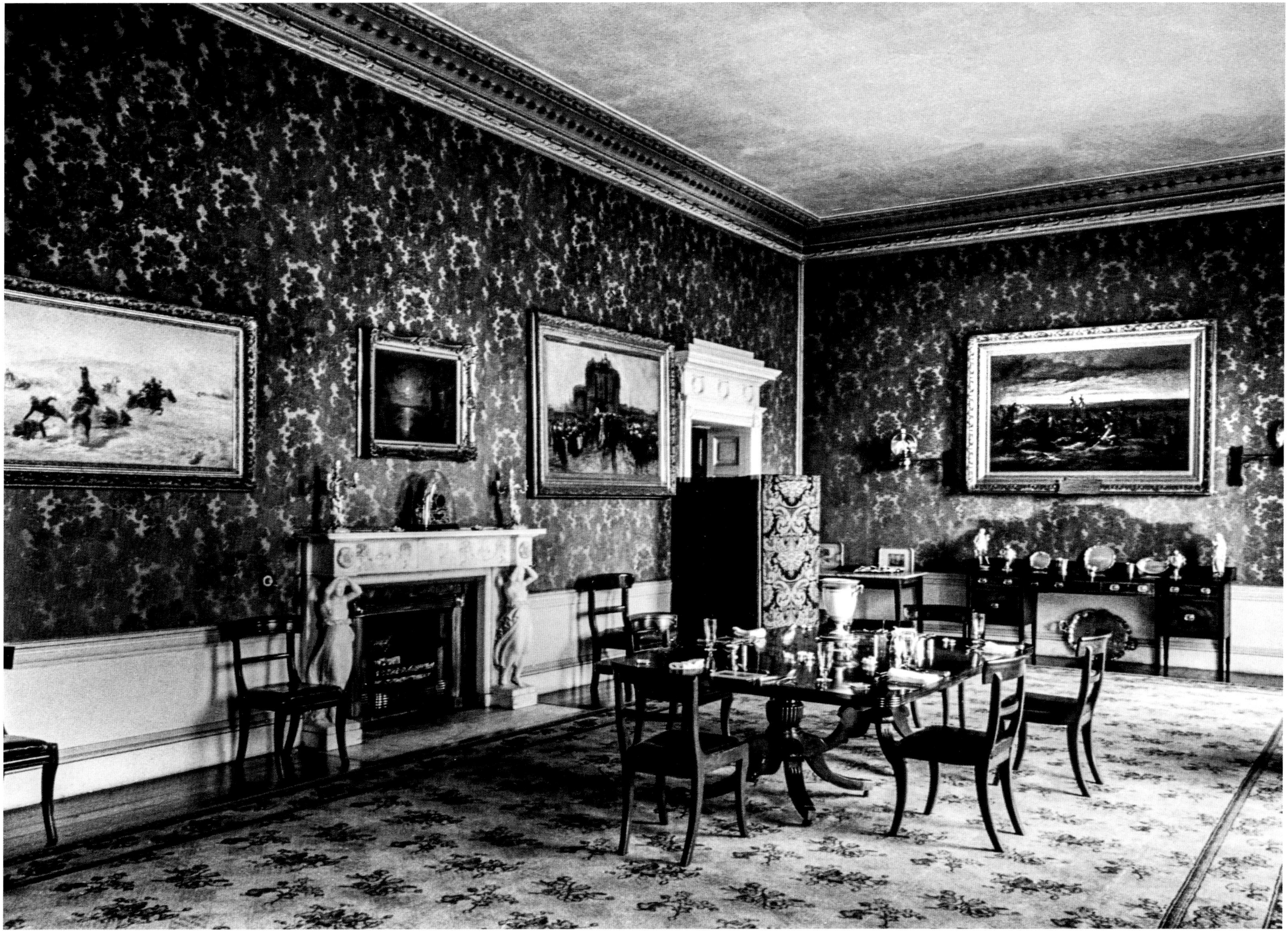

Killeen Castle
County Meath
12th July 1950

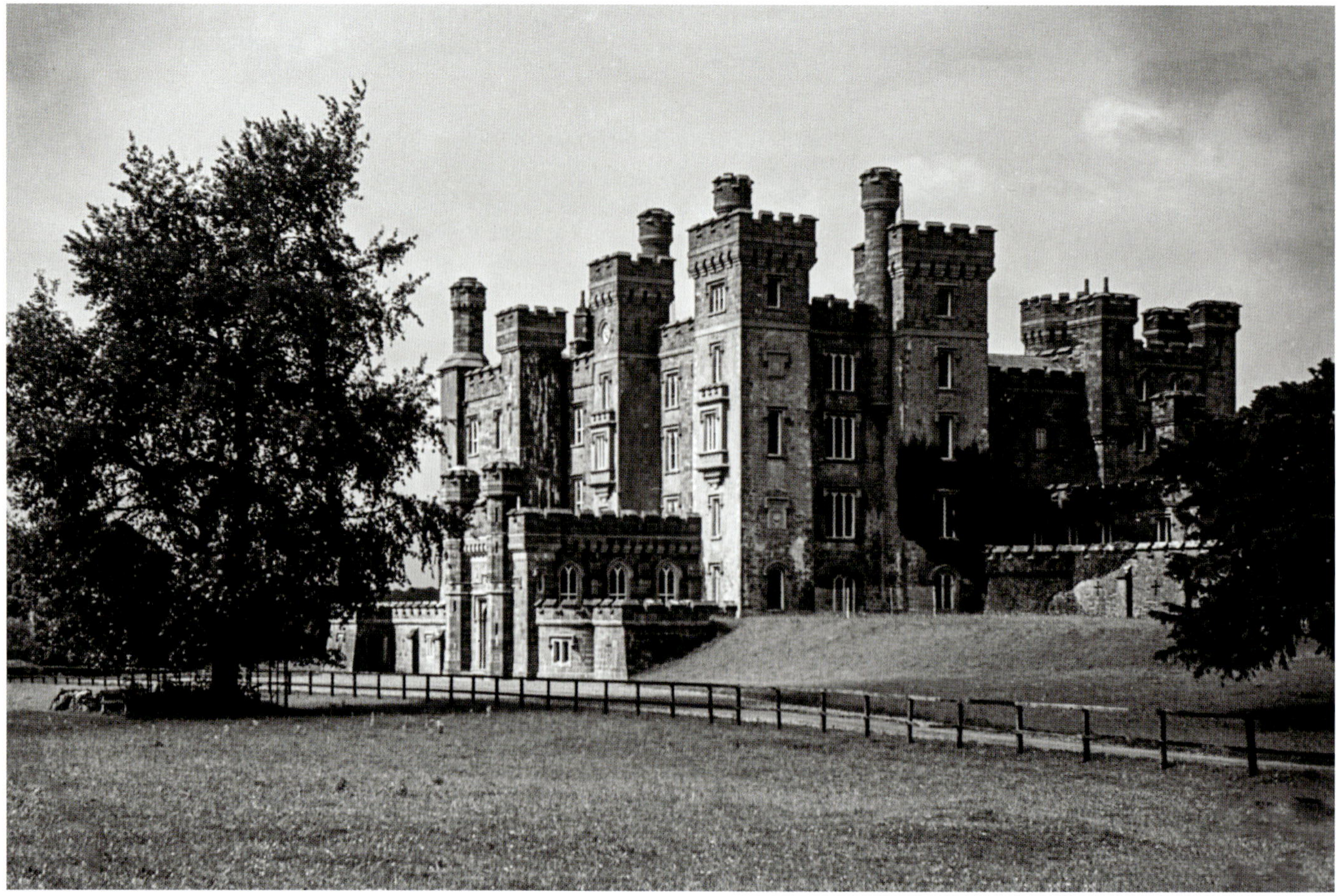

In her sprightly memoirs, *Seventy Years Young*, published in 1937, Daisy, Countess of Fingall, recalled how, during the Civil War, she and her husband, the 11th Earl, spent a night sitting in the library of Killeen Castle waiting for the IRA to arrive and set fire to the building. But no one turned up and in the morning the couple retired to bed, the castle safe, at least for the moment. Later, Daisy Fingall thought how often she had imagined the castle as a beautiful ruin: 'And I saw it in my mind, with the light falling through its empty window spaces and its battlemented walls lifted gauntly against the sky.'

Such is the case today, because although Killeen Castle survived the War of Independence and the Civil War, in May 1981 four men arrived at the then-empty property, poured petrol around the rooms and set the place alight. Since then, it has stood empty and gaunt, as Daisy Fingall had predicted, although the surrounding estate has been converted into a golf course, its perimeter speckled with holiday chalets. Today it all looks very different from July 1950 when Browne visited to photograph the building, just a year before Daisy's son, Major Oliver Plunkett, 12th (and last) Earl of Fingall, sold Killeen to Sir Victor Sassoon and auctioned the castle's contents over a period of five days. He then moved into another house nearby, while managing a stud on the estate owned by Sassoon.

The earl's forebears had arrived at Killeen in 1399, when Sir Christopher Plunkett married heiress Joan de Cusack. Their elder son, John, inherited the Killeen estate, while his younger brother, Christopher, was bequeathed neighbouring Dunsany. John Plunkett's son, yet another Christopher, was created 1st Baron Killeen, and in 1629 the 9th Baron, Luke Plunkett, became 1st Earl of Fingall.

Unlike their cousins at Dunsany, the Killeen Plunketts always remained Roman Catholic: a set of vestments owned by one of the family, St Oliver Plunkett, was preserved in the building. However, they were able to hold on to their property in County Meath even though they did not live in the castle for much of the eighteenth century. By 1763, the building was described as being 'a ruin for a great number of years' and 'not even capable of being made habitable for a family'. After Arthur Plunkett succeeded as 8th Earl in 1793, he decided to restore and enlarge the castle during the first years of the nineteenth century, employing Francis Johnston. Johnston added a

Above: The heavily battlemented and turreted exterior of Killeen Castle
Opposite: The 12th and last Earl of Fingall

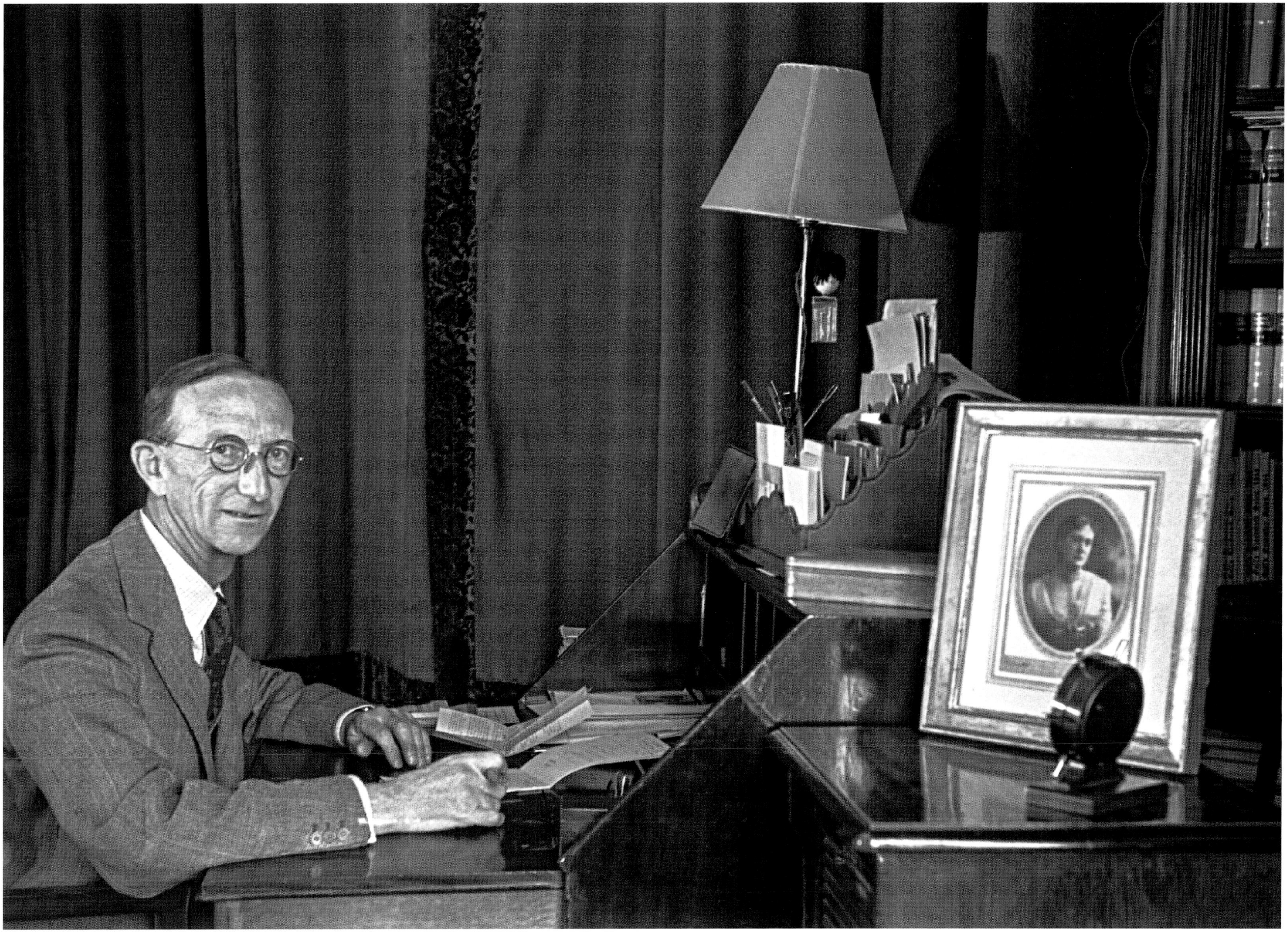

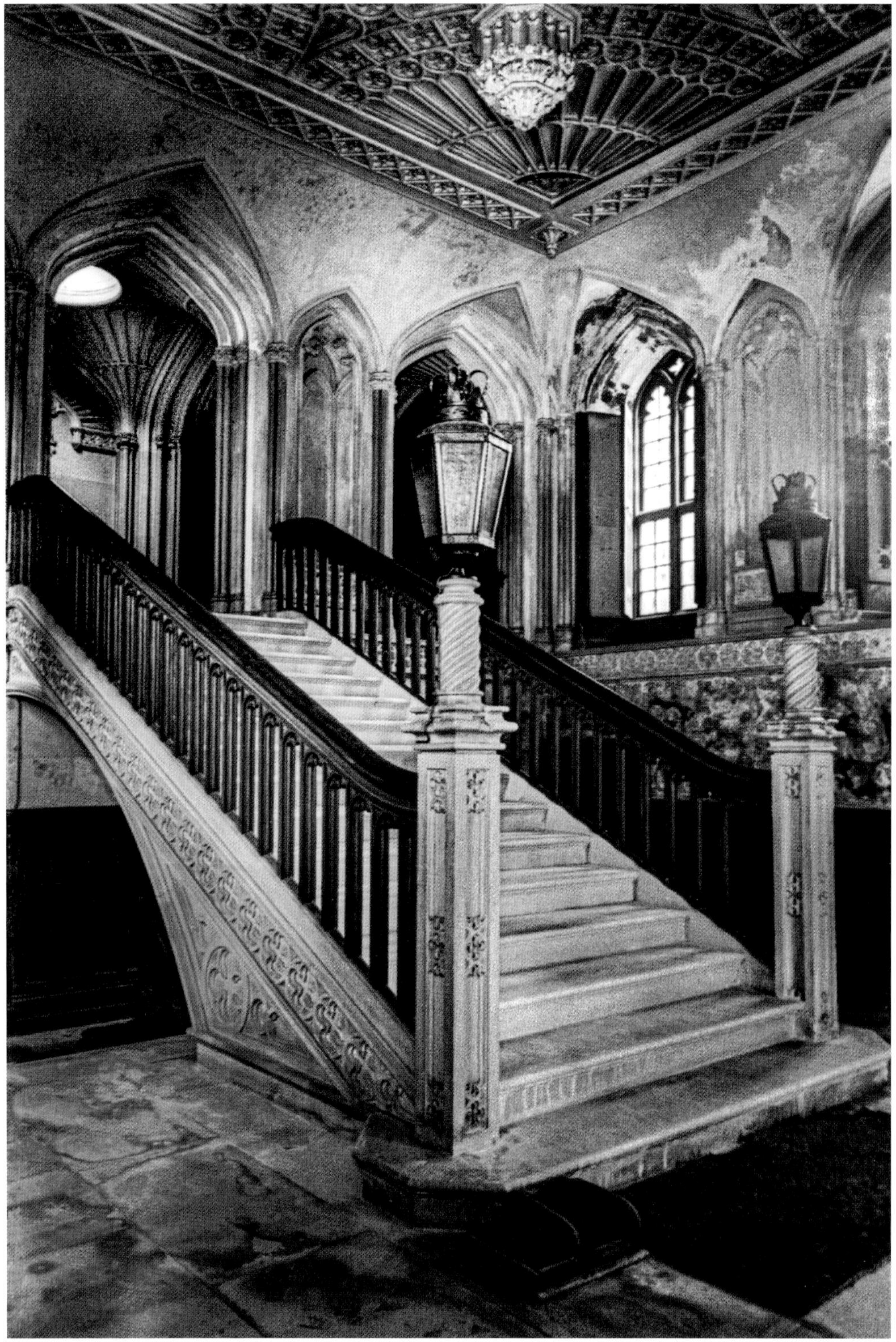
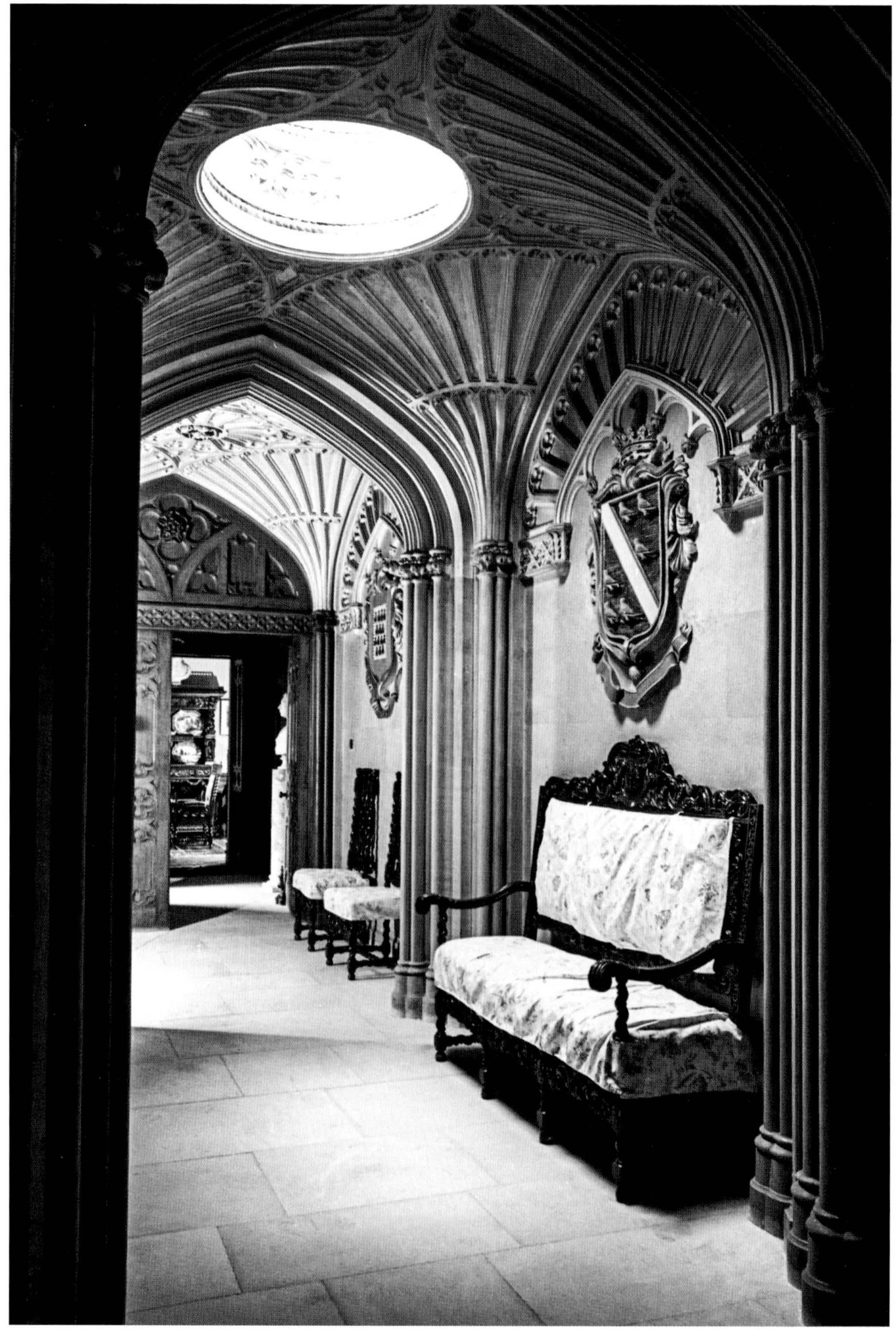

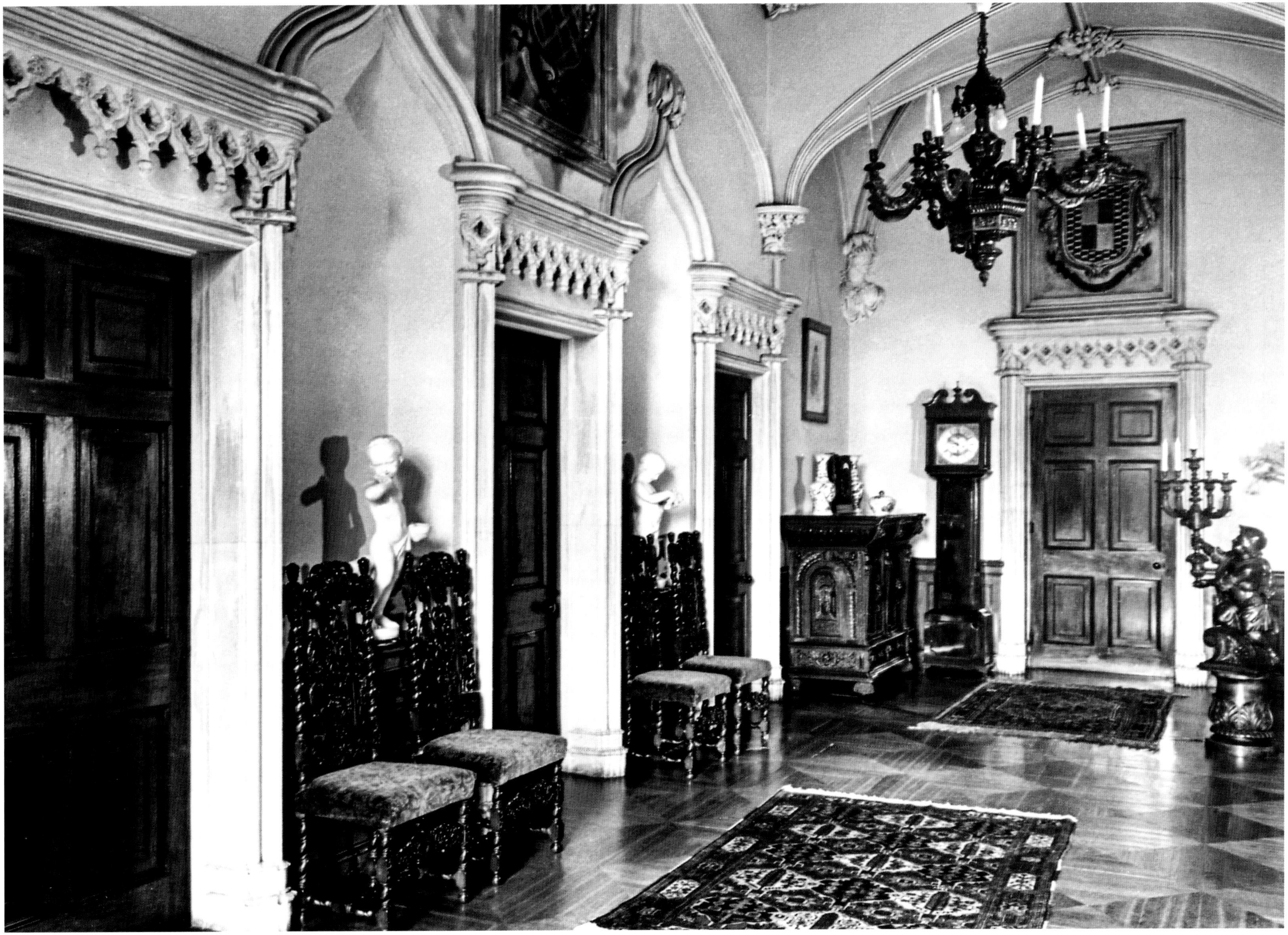

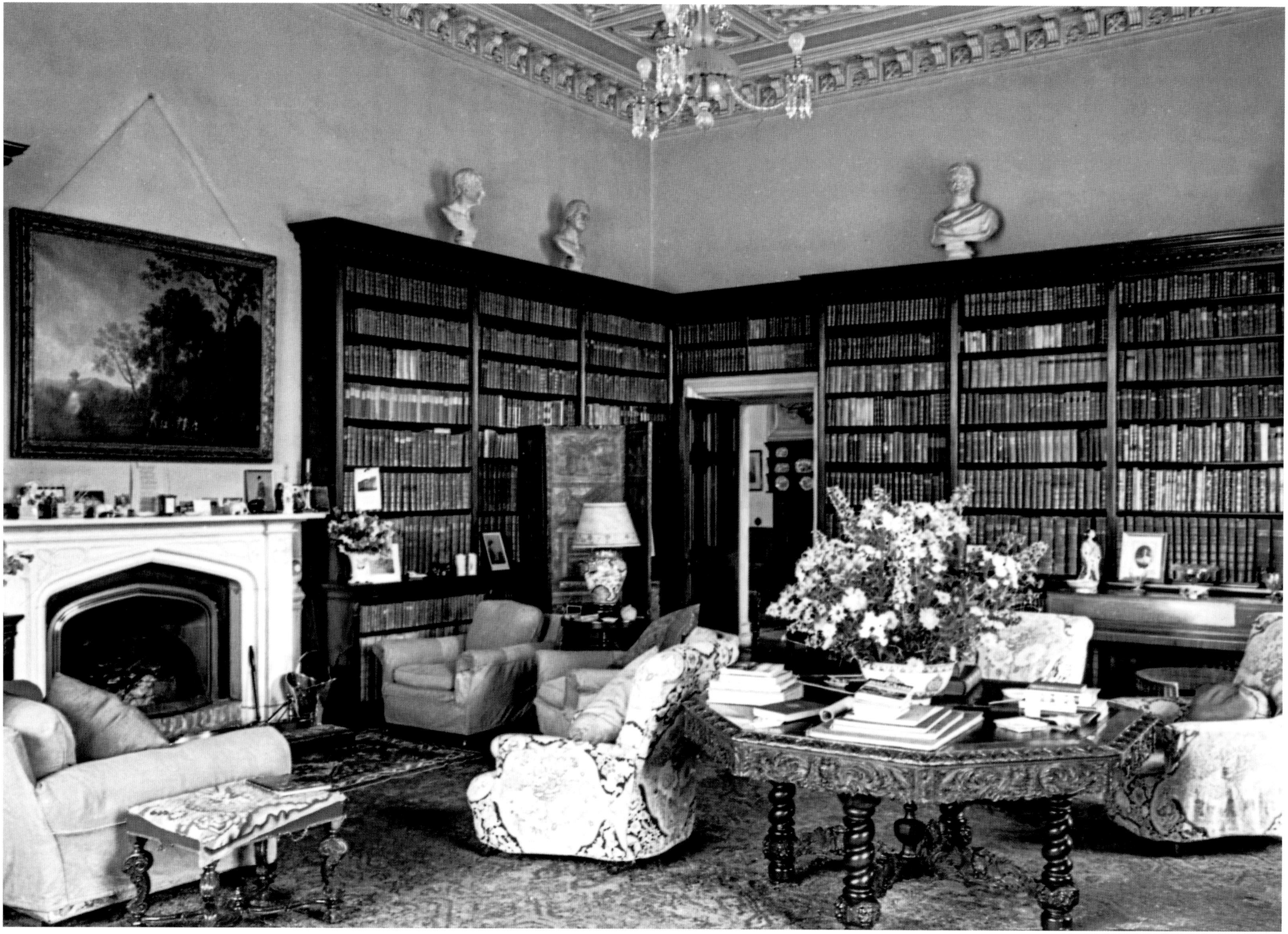

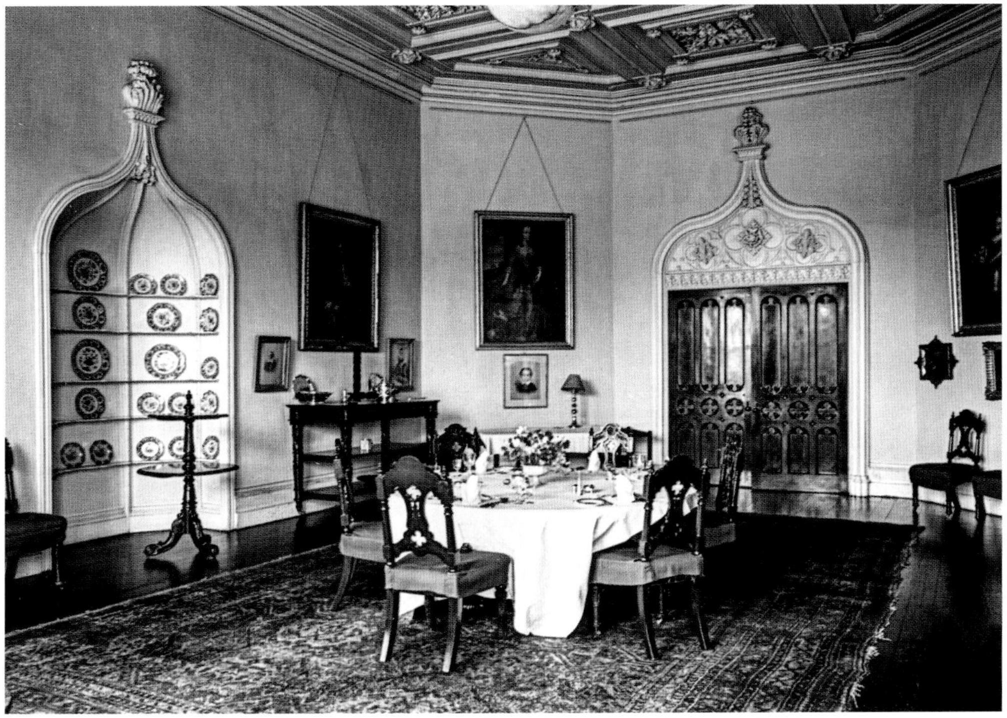

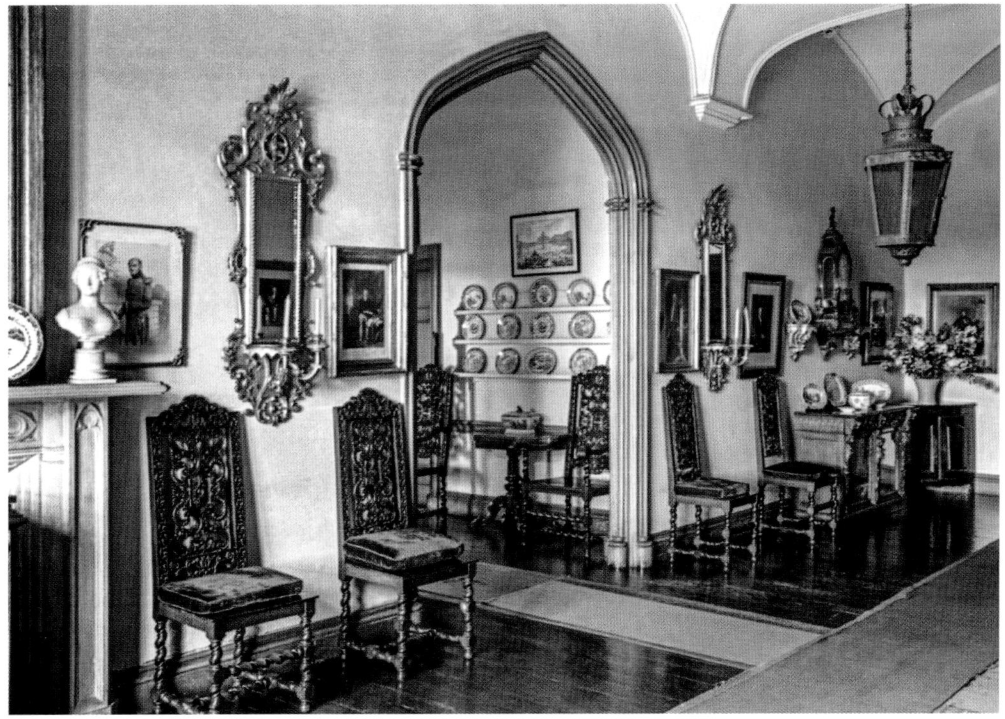

three-storey-over-basement extension to the south of the existing property. This held a new drawing and dining room, as well as lobby, hall and staircase.

The 9th Earl carried out further work: around 1841 architect James Shiel designed a new entrance front on the east side with a grand oak staircase hall rising 60 feet and leading to the main reception rooms. Those rooms were decorated in Perpendicular Gothic style, typically a long and narrow corridor on the principal floor, having a ceiling smothered in plaster fan-vaulting and pendants. The dining room took the form of an elongated octagon, while the library ceiling was again ornamented with delicate plaster tracery. The latter room was given its bookcases by Daisy Fingall at the beginning of the twentieth century when, following advice given to her by Sir Hugh Lane, they were made by Hicks, the Dublin cabinetmaker. All of this decoration was lost in the fire of 1981, making Browne's photographs, taken shortly before the castle was cleared of its contents, a precious record of the Plunkett family home.

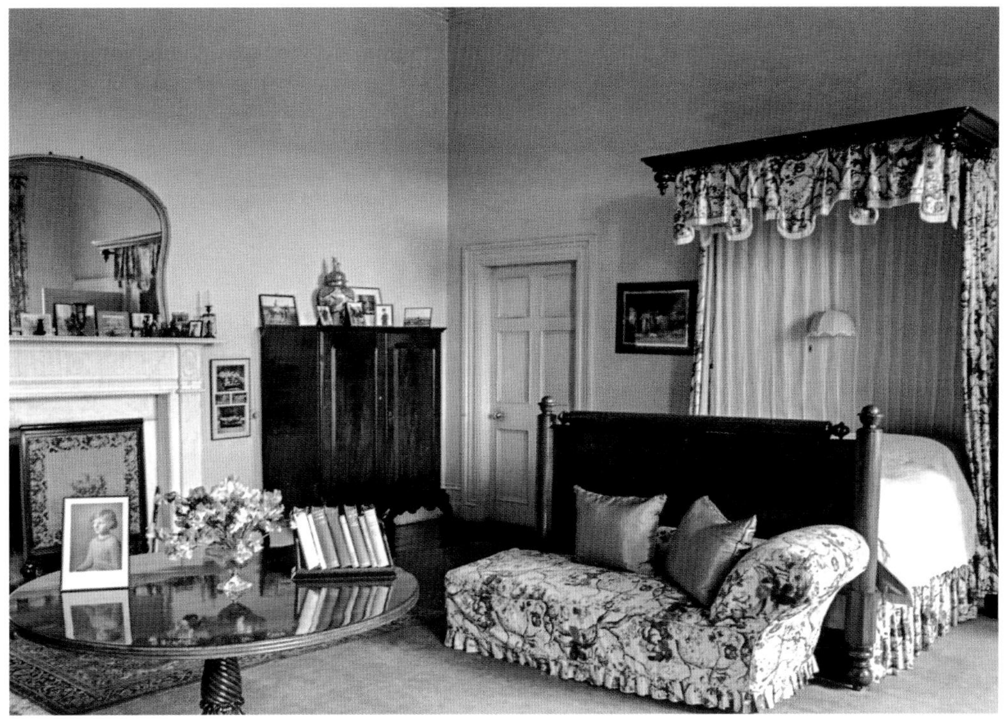

Page 60: The Entrance Hall and Lobby at the top of the stairs
Page 61: The Oak Hall, off which opened the main reception rooms

Opposite: The Library with bookcases designed by Sir Hugh Lane and made by James Hicks
Above: The Dining Room, like others decorated in Perpendicular Gothic style
Above Right: A View of the Picture Gallery. Right: The White Bedroom

KILLRUDDERY
COUNTY WICKLOW
28TH APRIL 1947

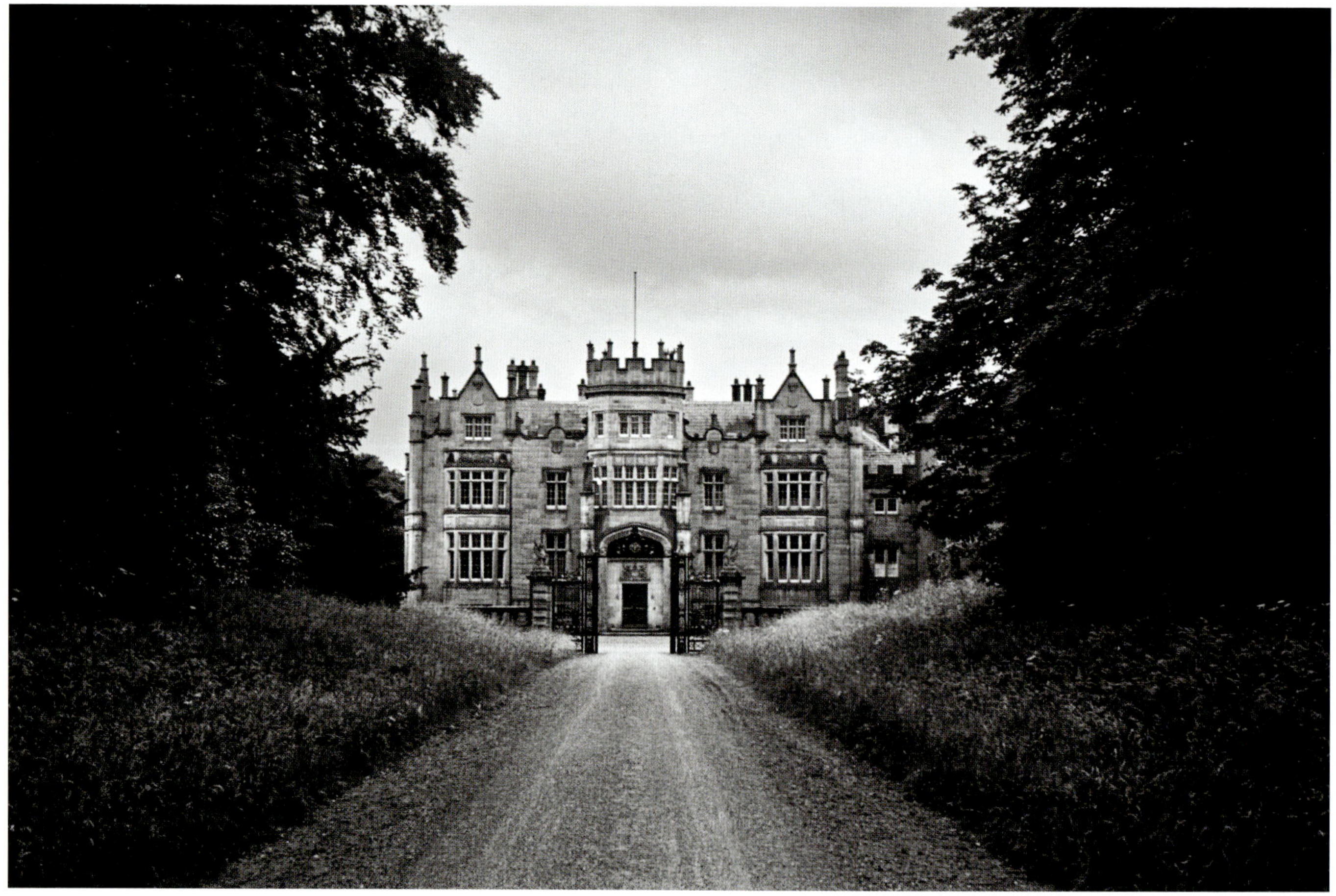

In 1822 John Preston Neale wrote of alterations that had recently been undertaken at Killruddery by father and son architects Richard and William Vitruvius Morrison, 'to whom much is due for the good taste of introducing into their native country a style of architecture before unknown to it, and which peculiarly harmonises with the picturesque nature of the country'. In fact, despite Neale publishing an engraving of the house in a finished state, Killruddery was then still very much a work in progress; it was not until 1829 that the Morrisons' improvements and additions to the building were completed.

Still owned by the same family, the lands of Killruddery were granted by James I to Sir William Brabazon in 1618 as a reward for services to the crown; nine years later, Sir William, already Baron Ardee, was created 1st Earl of Meath. It appears there was already some kind of castle on the site, and this was improved by Lord Meath. The building was destroyed during the Confederate Wars of the 1640s but restored, or rebuilt, by the second earl. Killruddery's justly famous gardens, designed by a Monsieur Bonet, who had supposedly trained at Versailles, date from the 1680s, during the lifetime of the 3rd Earl. With their lime walks, long canals and *patte d'oie* Angles, they are the finest surviving example of a baroque garden in Ireland and Britain.

Killruddery appears to have remained little changed in the eighteenth century, but after the 9th Earl was killed in a duel in 1797, his brother John Chambré Brabazon succeeded to the estate and title, and decided the family home required improvement. The old house was described by George Newenham Wright as 'very uninteresting' and 'unfit for the residence of a nobleman of taste and fortune'. Evidently the 10th Earl considered himself to be such a nobleman, and after first commissioning designs from Francis Johnston, in 1820 he entrusted the job of transforming Killruddery to the Morrisons; the eventual cost was £20,000.

The scheme involved moving the entrance from the east to the north side, which was given a two-storey Elizabethan Revival facade, centred on a polygonal battlemented tower concluding in an octagonal ogee dome. On either side of this were mullioned bays and a skyline densely lined with finials, pepperpots and Tudoresque chimneys. Inside, beneath a vaulted ceiling, a long flight of steps led up to the Great Hall, some 40 feet high. The room had a ceiling of carved beams resting

Above: The former entrance front to the house, demolished in the mid-1950s

Opposite: The Entrance Hall and Great Hall, also lost to demolition in the same period

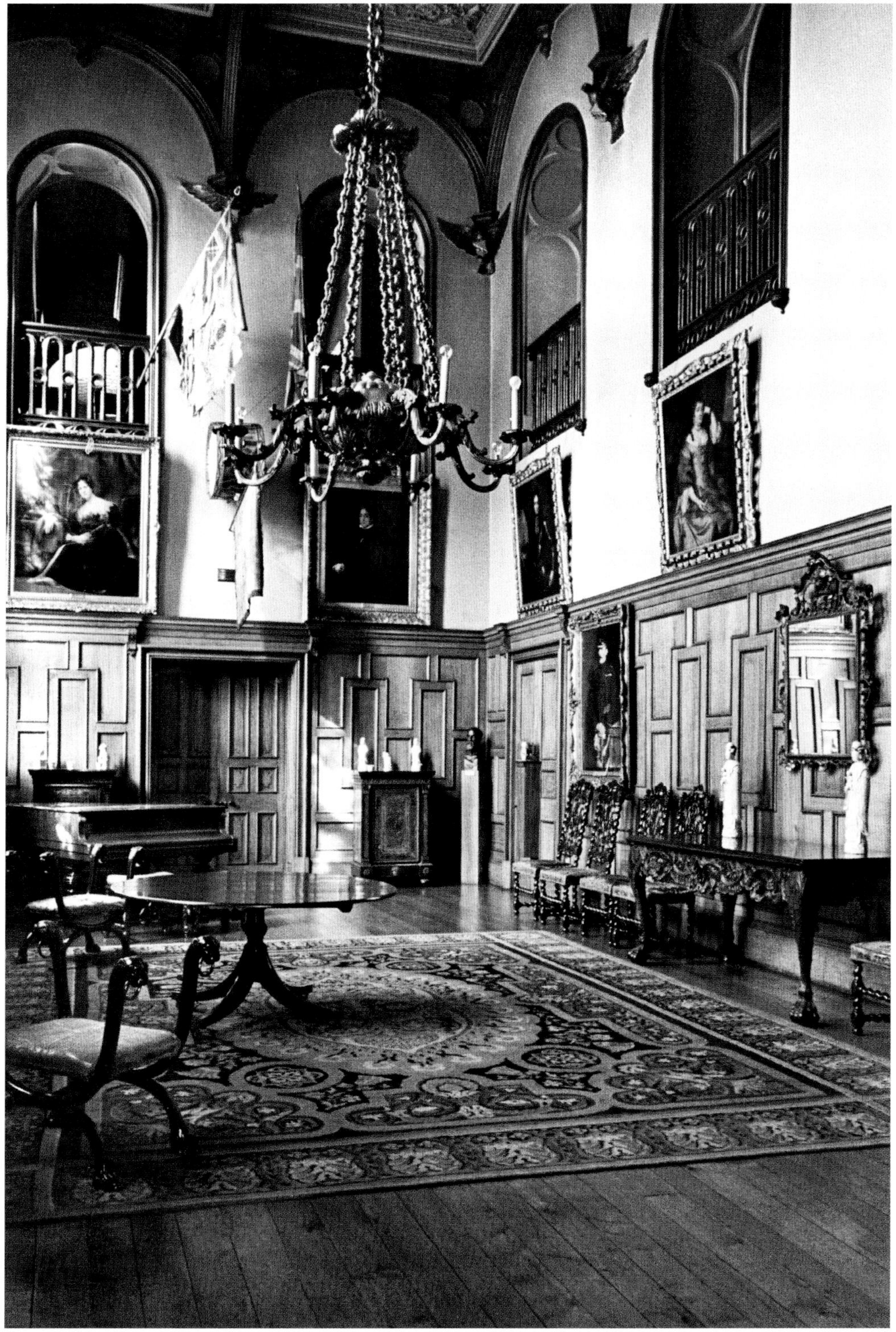

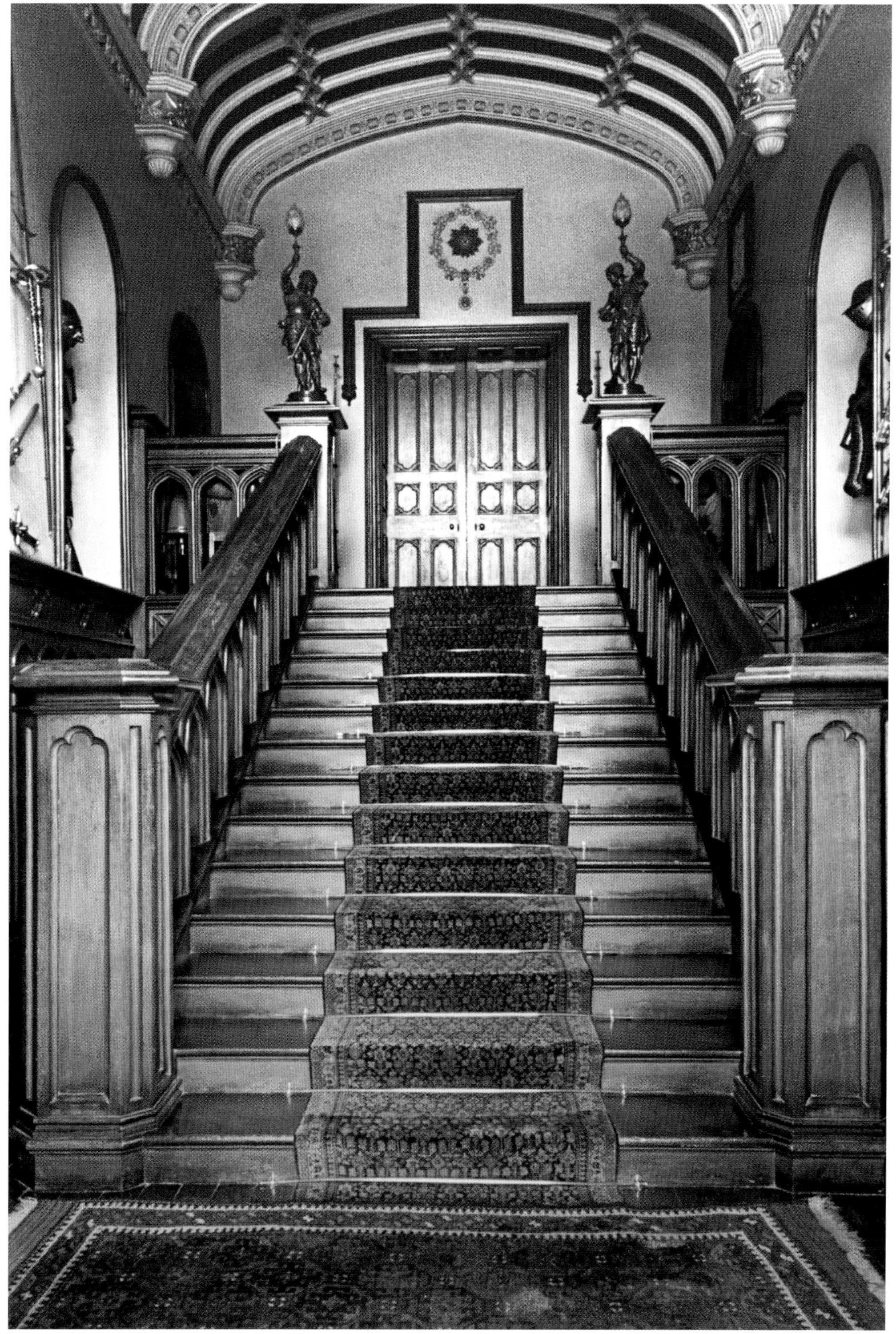

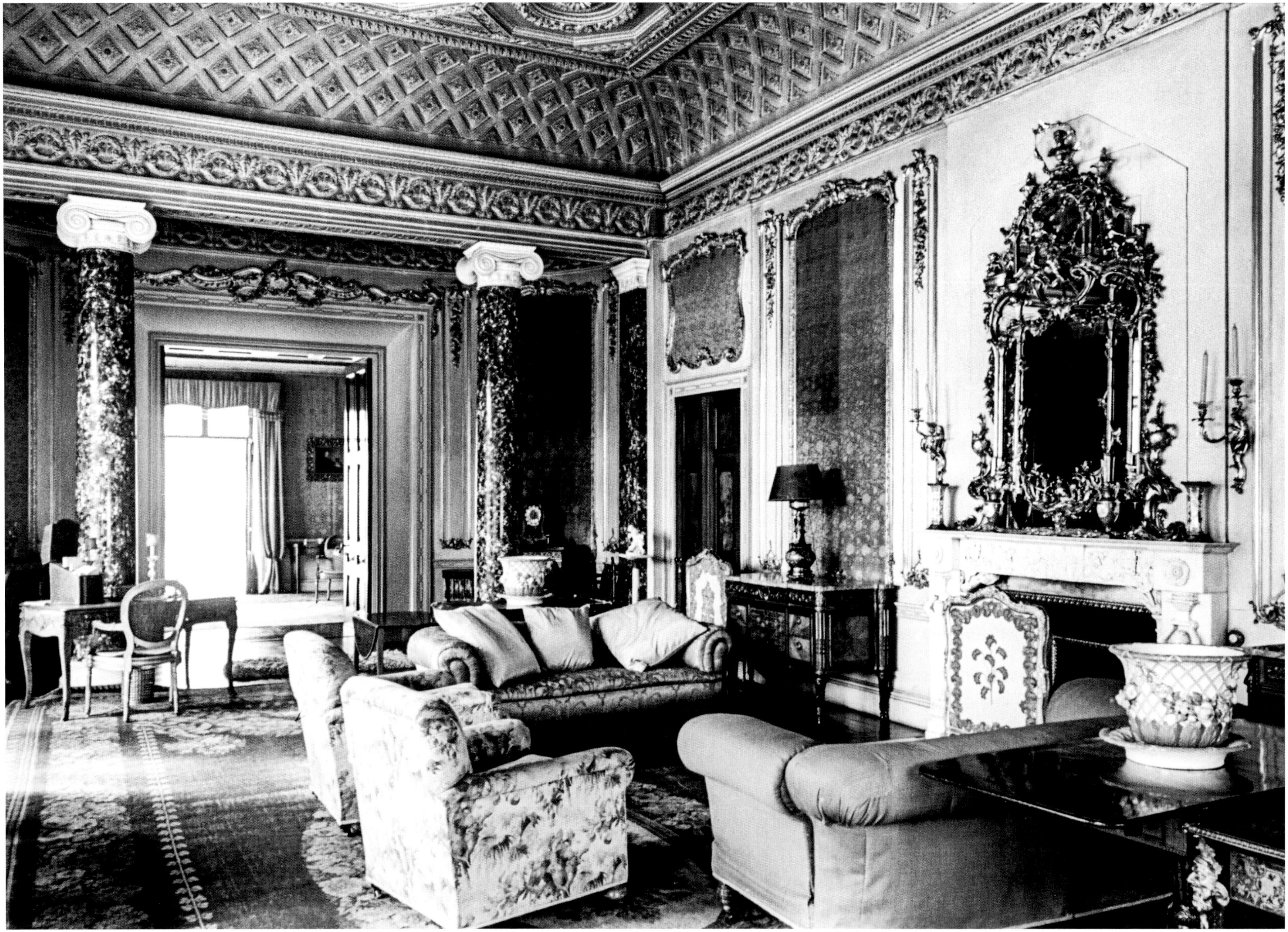

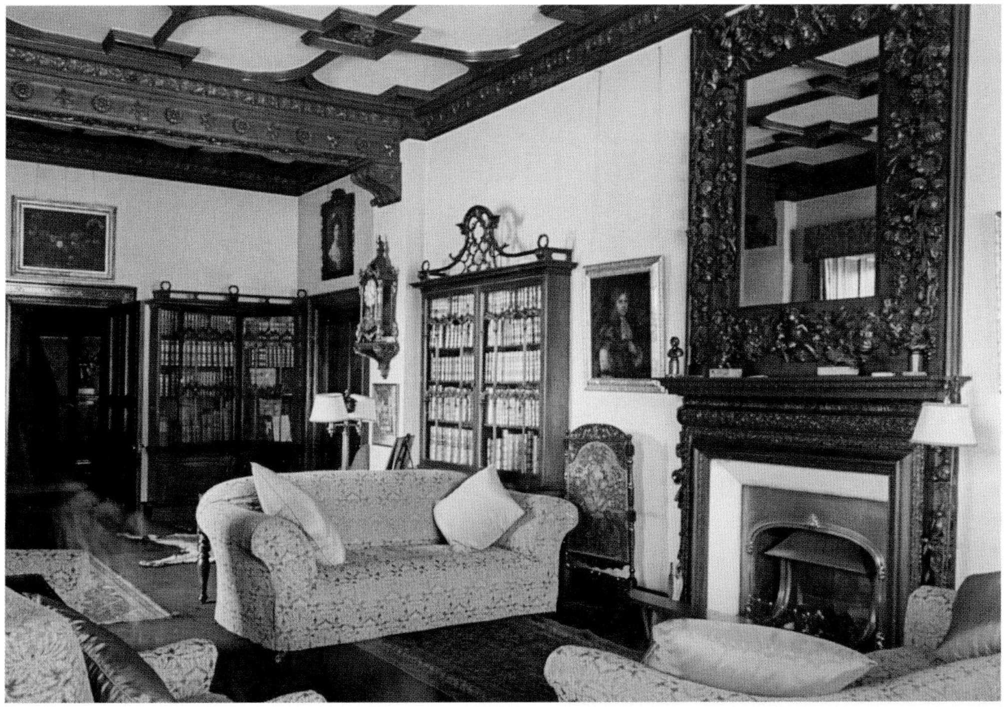

on corbels modelled as goshawks (which feature on the Brabazon crest), with plasterwork by Henry Pobje and a stained-glass window by John Milner.

Milner was also responsible for the glass in the dining room added by the Morrisons, while Pobje's talents were again on display in the coved and compartmentalised ceiling of the main drawing room. Later alterations made to the house included a large domed conservatory designed by William Burn and constructed in 1852.

All this was still in place when Browne photographed Killruddery in 1947. However, early in the following decade, the 14th Earl, who had inherited the estate in 1949, decided to reduce the size of his family home, requiring the demolition of a large part of the Morrison additions. Their great facade came down, along with the staircase inside the entrance and Great Hall beyond, as well as the dining room and a number of other rooms. This work was overseen by architect Claud Phillimore, who specialised in such reconfigurations. As a result, visitors to Killruddery today would not necessarily know that it was once much larger, as can be seen in these photographs.

Left: Killruddery's Saloon looking through the Small Drawing Room to the Conservatory

Above: The Library
Right: Looking from the Small Drawing Room (now Dining Room) into the Saloon

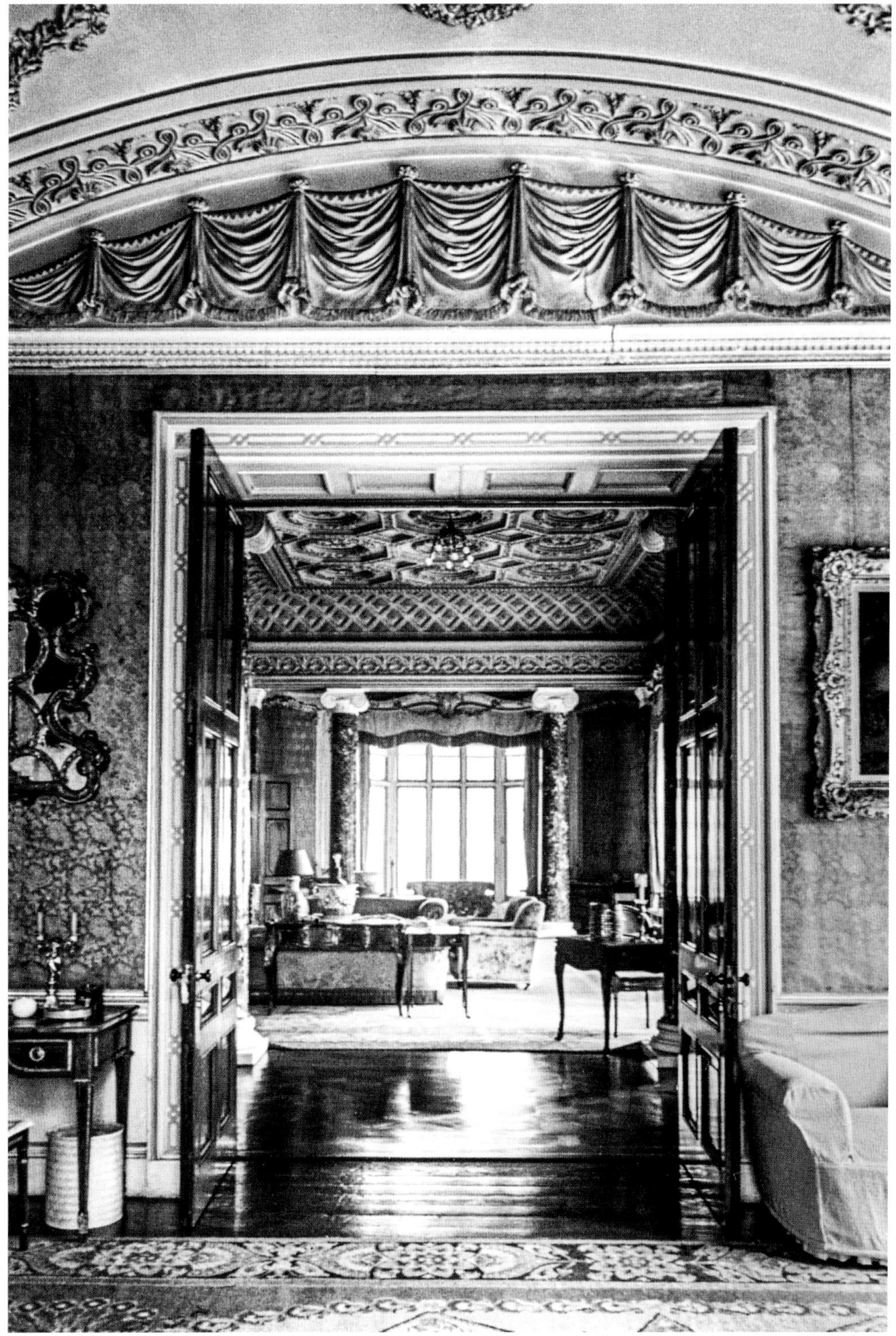

Howth Castle

County Dublin

14th July 1947

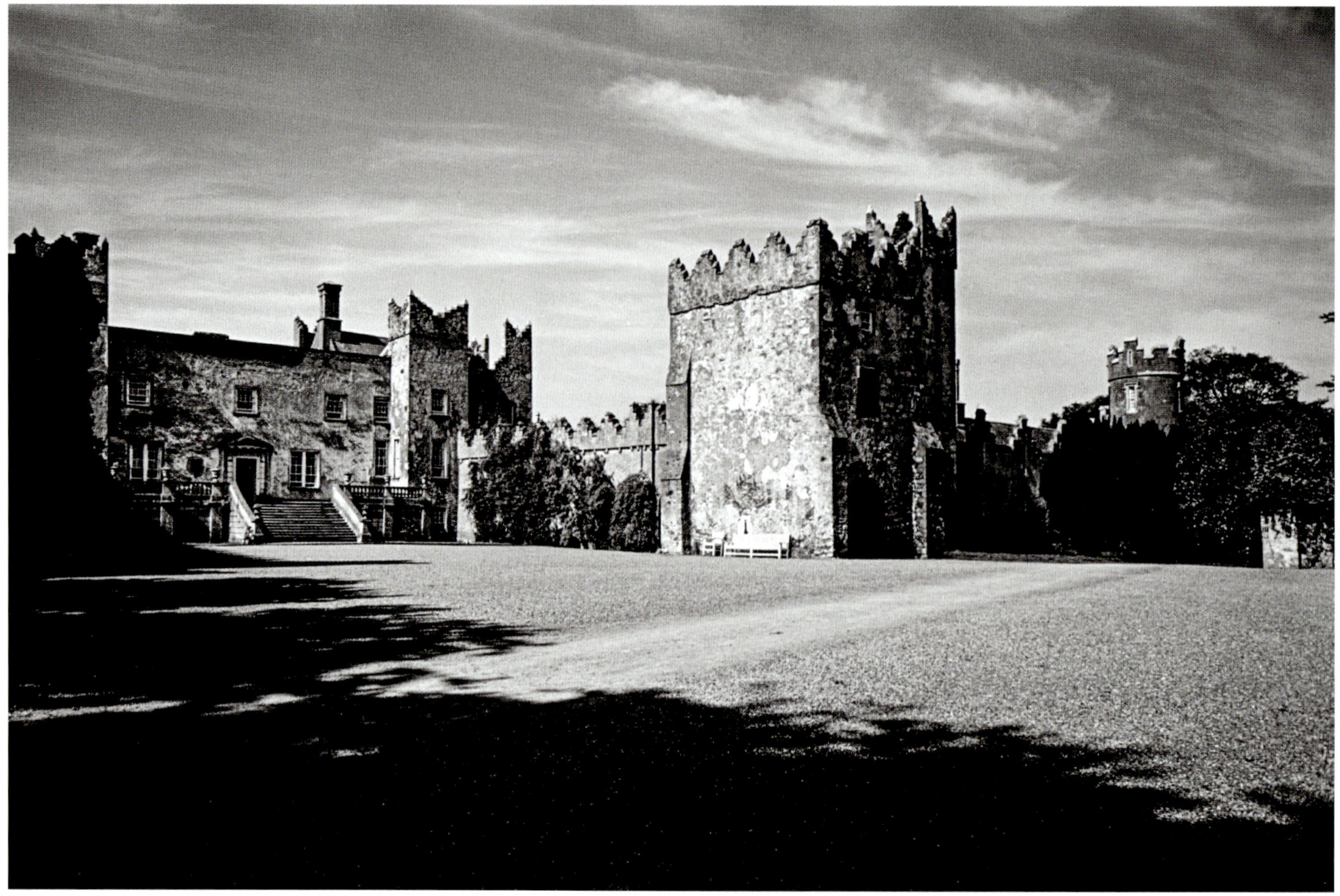

In October 2018 it was announced that Howth Castle and the surrounding 530 acres, until then home to the same family for some 840 years, had been sold to an Irish investment group; three years later, many of the property's contents were dispersed at public auction. The building dates back to the Middle Ages, its origins traced to one Almeric Tristram, who came to Ireland in 1176 with the Anglo-Norman knight John de Courcy. The following year, on 10 August, the feast day of St Lawrence, Almeric defeated a force of Hiberno-Norsemen at Evora Bridge in Howth and thereby gained possession of the peninsula. In gratitude for this victory, he took the surname St Lawrence, by which his descendants have been known ever since.

The original castle was probably constructed of wood and stood close to Howth's harbour. However, by 1235 the St Lawrences had moved to the present building's location, although once more their castle was made of wood; the earliest parts of the structure here now, the keep (the section to the left of the present front door) and gate tower (a little in front and to the right of the main building), date from the mid-fifteenth century and were erected by Christopher St Lawrence, 2nd Baron Howth. In the adjacent gardens, traces can be found of the walls and turrets that would once have enclosed these structures.

Additions were made to the building in 1558 by Christopher, 8th Baron Howth, known as the Blind Lord (although it is not known if he was wholly or partially blind). It was during his lifetime that Gráinne Ní Mháille, otherwise known as Granuaile, or the Pirate Queen, is said to have arrived at the gates of Howth Castle and found them locked as the family were at dinner. In retaliation, she kidnapped Lord Howth's grandson, the future tenth baron, and only released him after a promise was given that the gates would always remain open and that an extra place would be laid at every meal: this agreement was thereafter honoured by successive generations of the family.

At some date prior to 1641 Nicolas, 11th Baron, added another floor above the hall and then his son William, 12th Baron, built the castle's east wing, or Tower House, between 1660 and his death in 1671. However, Kenelm's Tower, at the end of this wing, was added by Thomas, 3rd Earl of Howth, in 1855. Long before then, further alterations had been made by William, 14th Baron, who modernised and enlarged the old keep, and laid out the terrace and flight of stone steps leading to a pedimented doorcase. An inscription beside this reads 'The castle was rebuilt by the Right Honourable William, Lord Baron of Howth, Anno Domini 1738.'

Above: The castle's forecourt reflecting centuries of change

Opposite: The Entrance Hall, with a map of Howth painted by MacDonald Gill above the chimneypiece

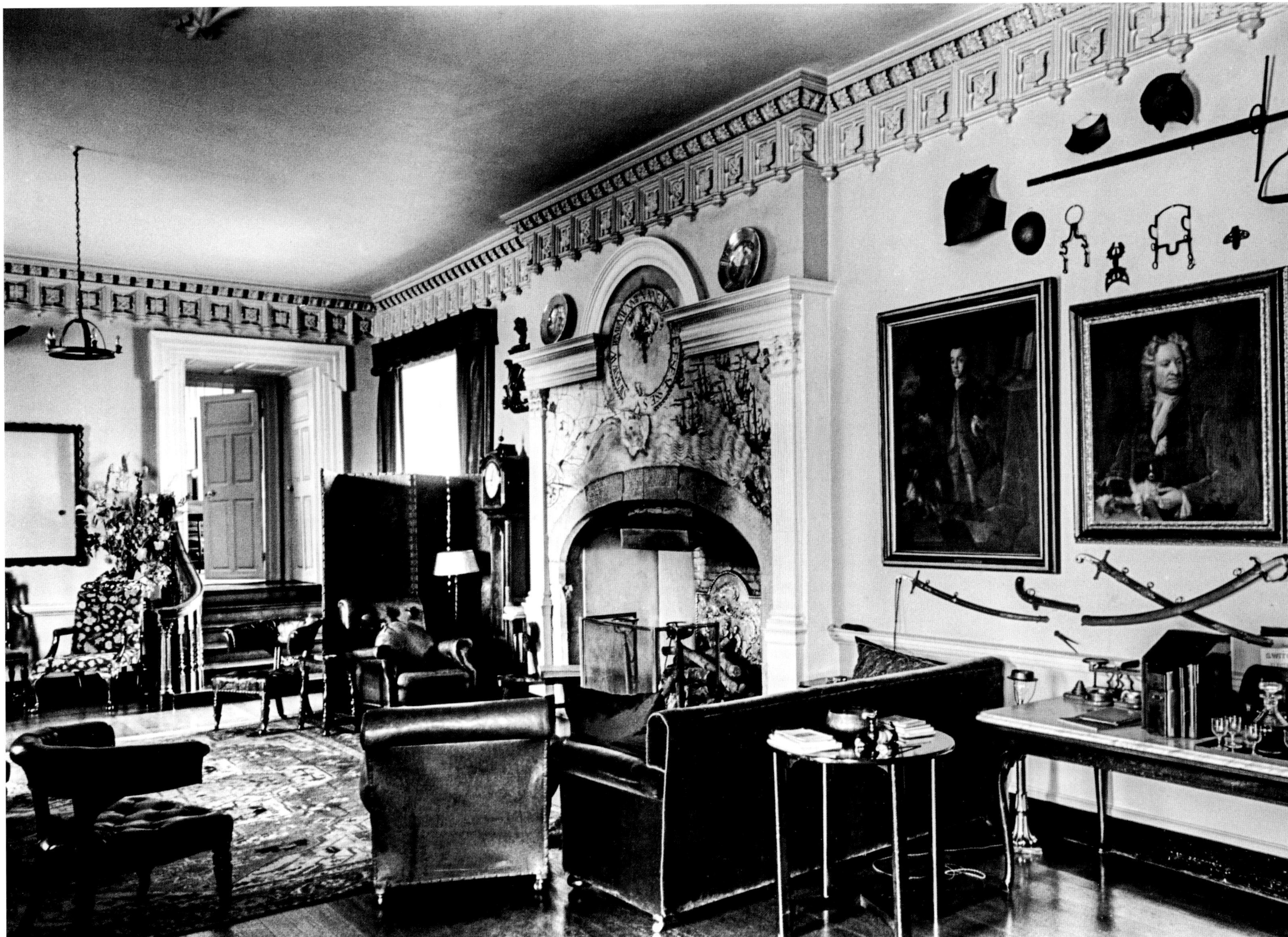

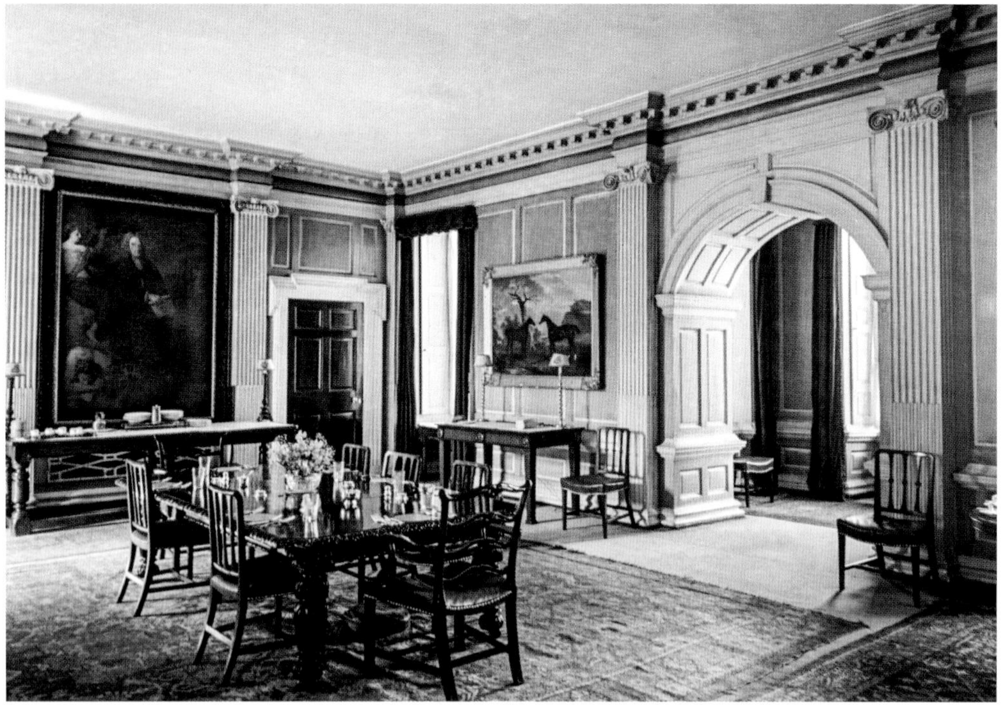

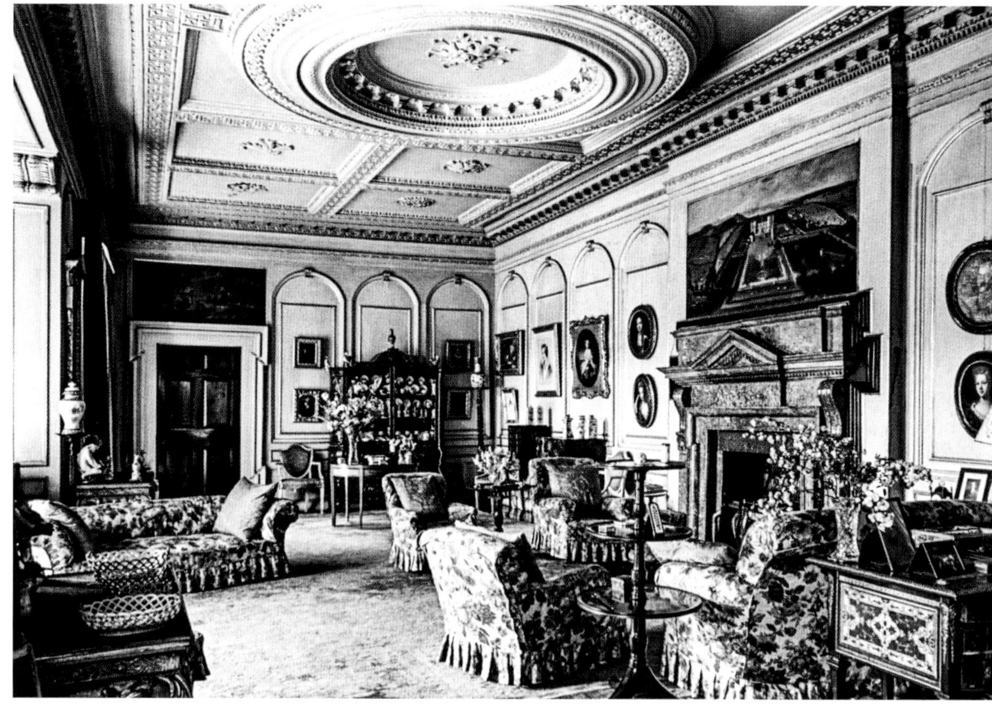

William's son, Thomas, 15th Baron, was created 1st Earl of Howth in 1767. Three more generations followed until 1909 when the 4th Earl died without leaving a son. Howth Castle and estate then passed to his sister's son, Julian Gaisford, who assumed the additional surname of St Lawrence by royal licence. He commissioned architect Edwin Lutyens to make substantial changes and additions to the old building. These include the Gaisford Tower at the end of the west wing, built to accommodate the family library, in which he incorporated an early eighteenth-century stone chimneypiece removed from an old house in Killester. The same building also provided a pilastered Venetian window that Lutyens converted into a frame above the entrance hall chimney; inside this the artist and cartographer MacDonald Gill painted a map of Howth. At the same time, Lutyens designed the steps to the east of the new tower, a loggia with bathrooms above between the old hall and the west wing, a chapel at the end of the east wing and a sunken garden.

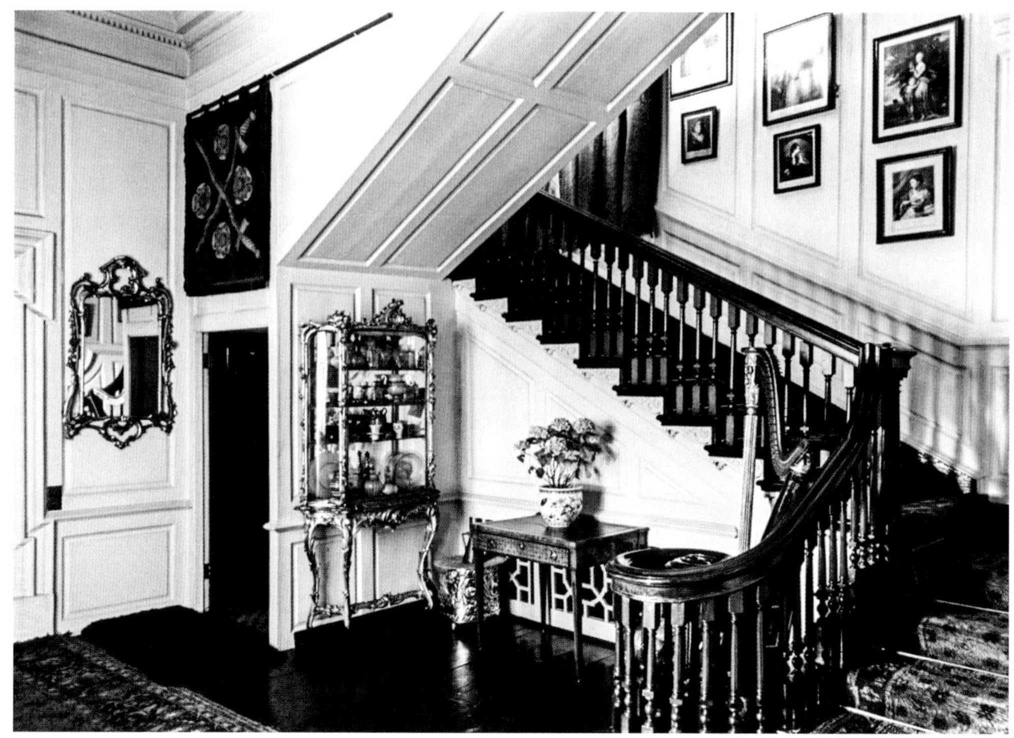

Above: The Dining Room created by Edwin Lutyens out of three small rooms off the hall
Top Right: The Drawing Room with an 18th century perspective painting of the castle and gardens over the chimneypiece
Bottom Right: The panelled principal staircase
Opposite Page: The Library, occupying the west tower added by Lutyens at the beginning of the last century

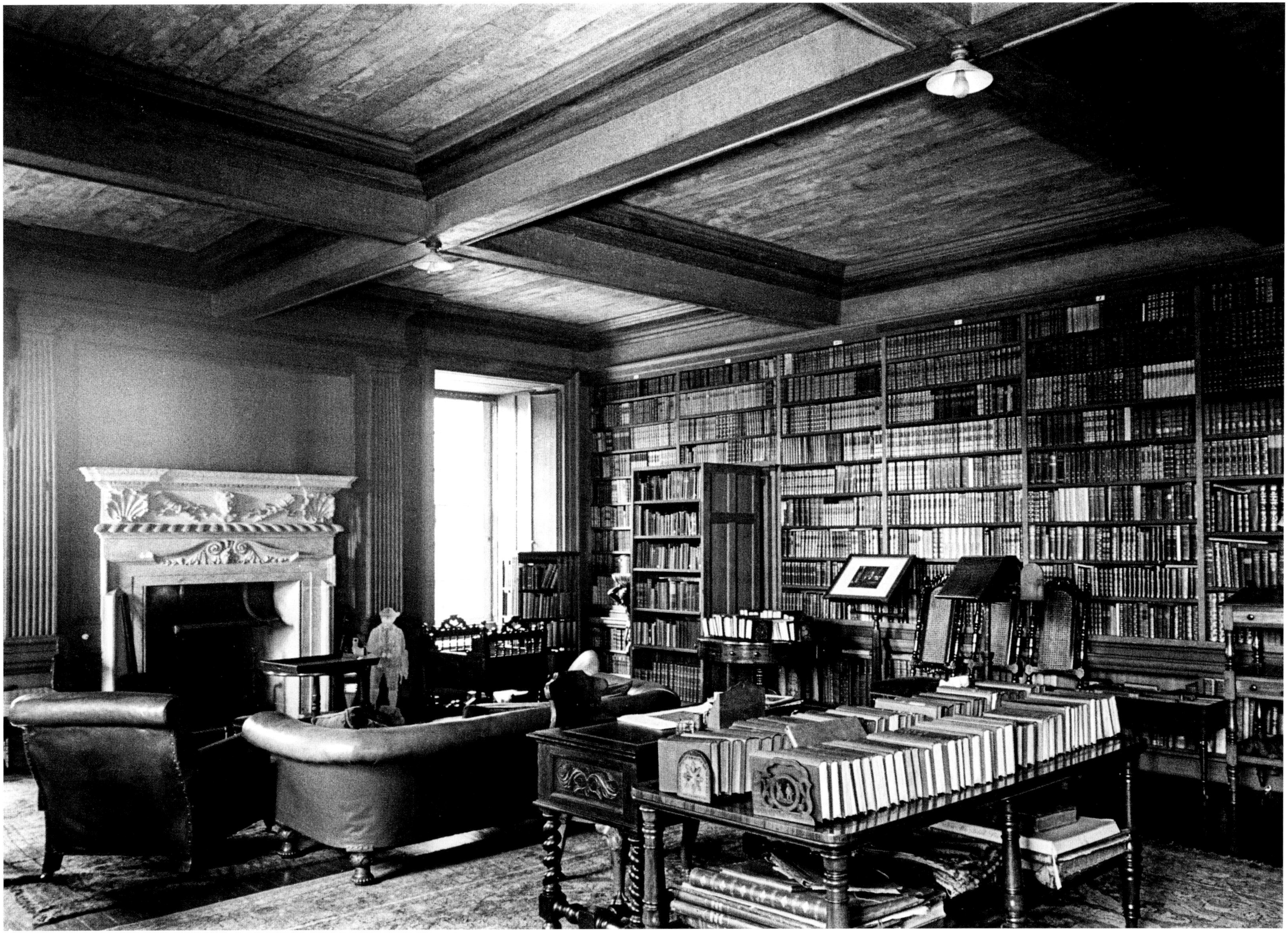

Dromoland Castle
County Clare
7th May 1948

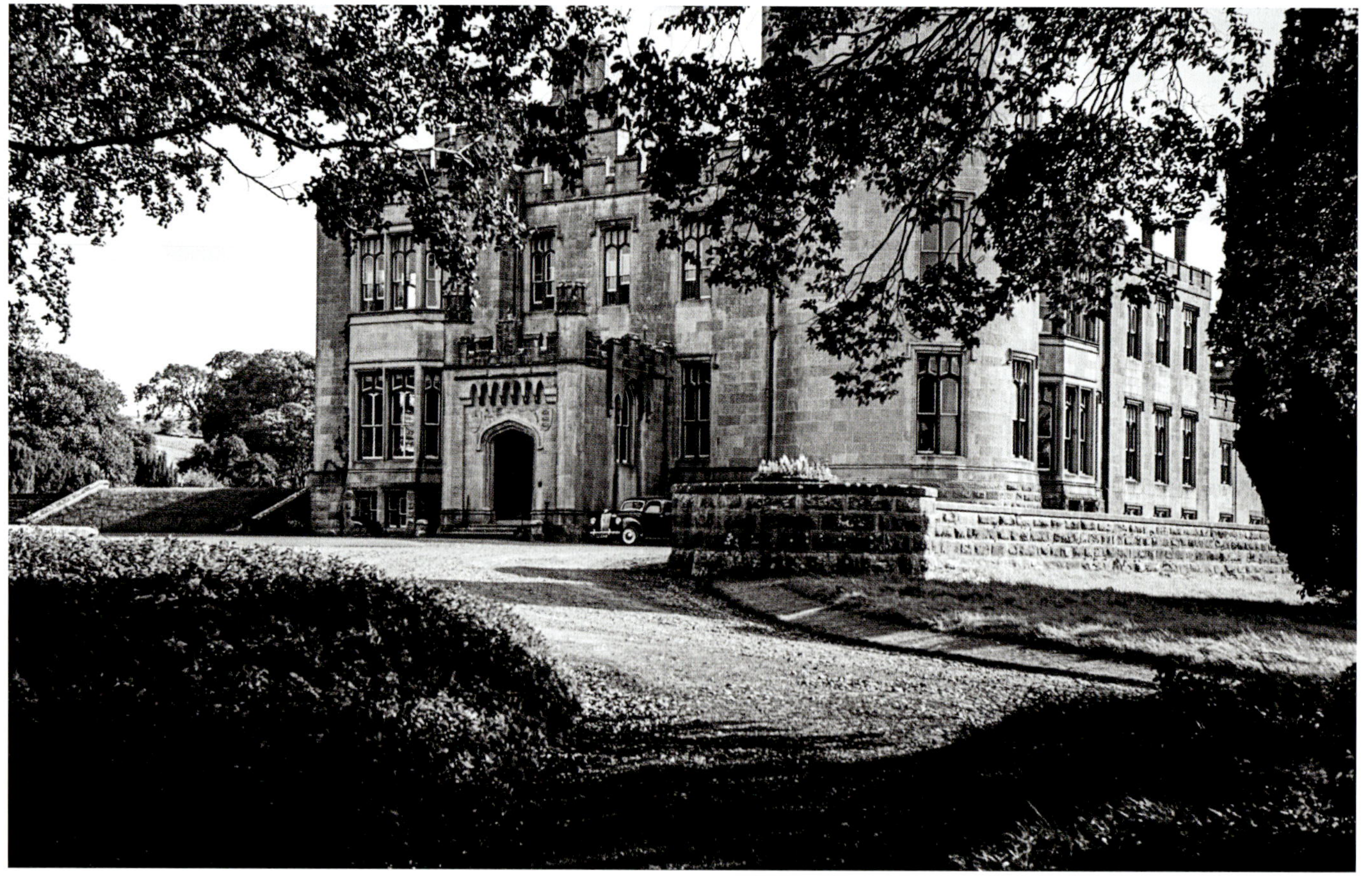

The O'Briens of Dromoland were descendants of Brian Boru, High King of Ireland, who defeated a force of Vikings at the Battle of Clontarf in April 1014. For many centuries, one branch of the family was based at Leamaneh Castle, but at the beginning of the eighteenth century Sir Donough O'Brien, reputedly the richest commoner in Ireland, turned his attention to another property, Dromoland, where a late fifteenth- or early sixteenth-century tower house already stood. Over the decade before his death in 1717, Sir Donough embarked on building a new residence next to the old one. This was still unfinished when the estate was inherited by his grandson, Sir Edward O'Brien, then a minor. Over the next few years, the boy's widowed mother, Catherine O'Brien, assumed responsibility for completing the project, for which both Thomas Burgh and John Aheron appear to have contributed designs, although Sir Edward may also have had a hand in the work. During his time, a number of other buildings were erected in the grounds of Dromoland, including an octagonal gazebo and a temple, both of which survive.

The eighteenth-century classical house, on the other hand, was demolished some hundred years later, when Sir Edward O'Brien, the fourth baronet, decided to commission a new residence from architect James Pain. Initially Pain proposed what was essentially an enlarged version of the existing building, but then he and his client settled on the idea of a romantic castle and this was the scheme followed. Probably for financial reasons, the construction of Dromoland Castle was a gradual affair, lasting almost twenty years from 1819 to 1838; a surviving watercolour shows the old house still standing while the new one was going up immediately beside it. But eventually the building created by Sir Edward's forebears was demolished, with just the castle remaining (although the eighteenth-century stable block still survives). Unfortunately, Sir Edward died in 1837 and didn't see the finished result. It was left to his eldest son, Sir Lucius O'Brien, later 13th Baron Inchiquin, to finish the job.

Writing in the year of Sir Edward's death, Samuel Lewis described Dromoland as 'a superb edifice in the castellated style, lately erected on the site of the ancient mansion, and surrounded by an extensive and richly wooded demesne, in which great improvements have recently been made'. Wonderfully picturesque in its lakeside setting, Dromoland Castle has long been considered Pain's most successful exercise in the Gothic

Above: The romantic castle designed by James Pain to replace an earlier classical house

Opposite: The Drawing Room hung with a series of 17th century portraits brought into the family by Catherine Keightley, daughter-in-law of the 1st Baronet

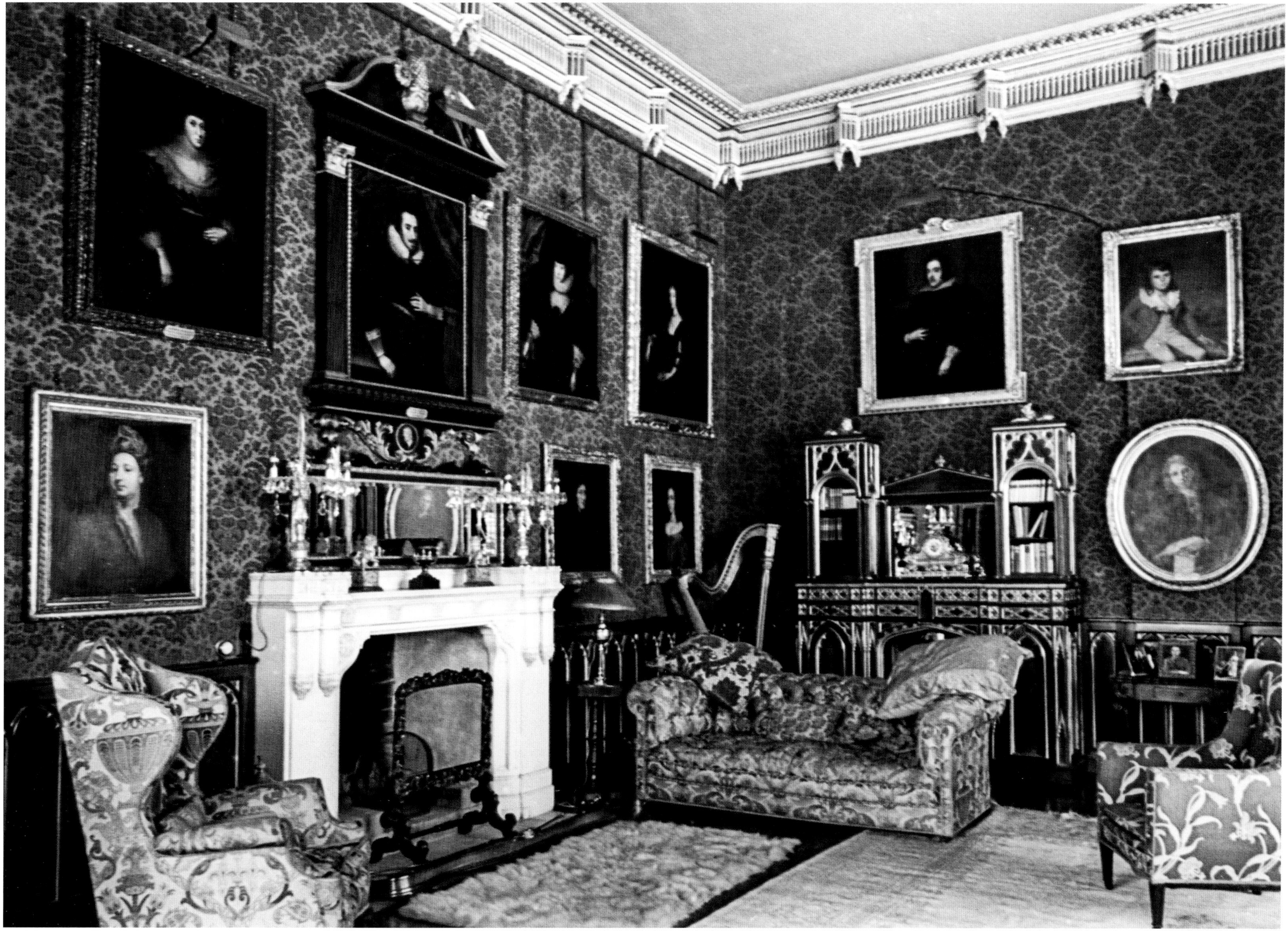

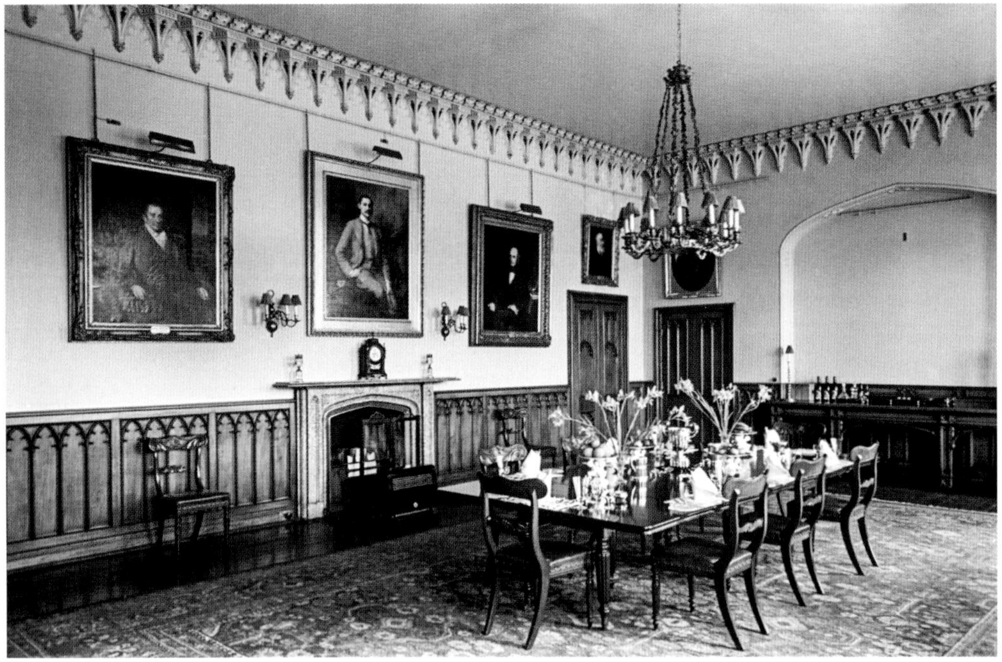

idiom, the many towers of varying dimensions and shapes producing a satisfying asymmetry in its exterior. The interiors are less fanciful, conforming to a familiar country house manor, with just the occasional door frame and some of the cornices hinting that this is supposed to be a castle.

Further generations of the family remained living at Dromoland until the second half of the last century. During the War of Independence there was talk of the IRA burning the building, until it was recalled that Sir Lucius O'Brien had taken care of his tenants during the years of the Great Famine in the 1840s. In 1948 Sir Donough O'Brien, 16th Baron Inchiquin, began to entertain paying guests in the castle, and it was around this time that Browne photographed the building. However, the income generated was insufficient and in 1962 Lord Inchiquin sold the castle, along with some 330 acres of surrounding land. Many of the contents were dispersed then or in later sales. Dromoland Castle is today a luxury hotel.

Above: The Dining Room with a portrait of the 15th Baron over the chimneypiece
Right: Another view of the Drawing Room
Opposite Page: The Library

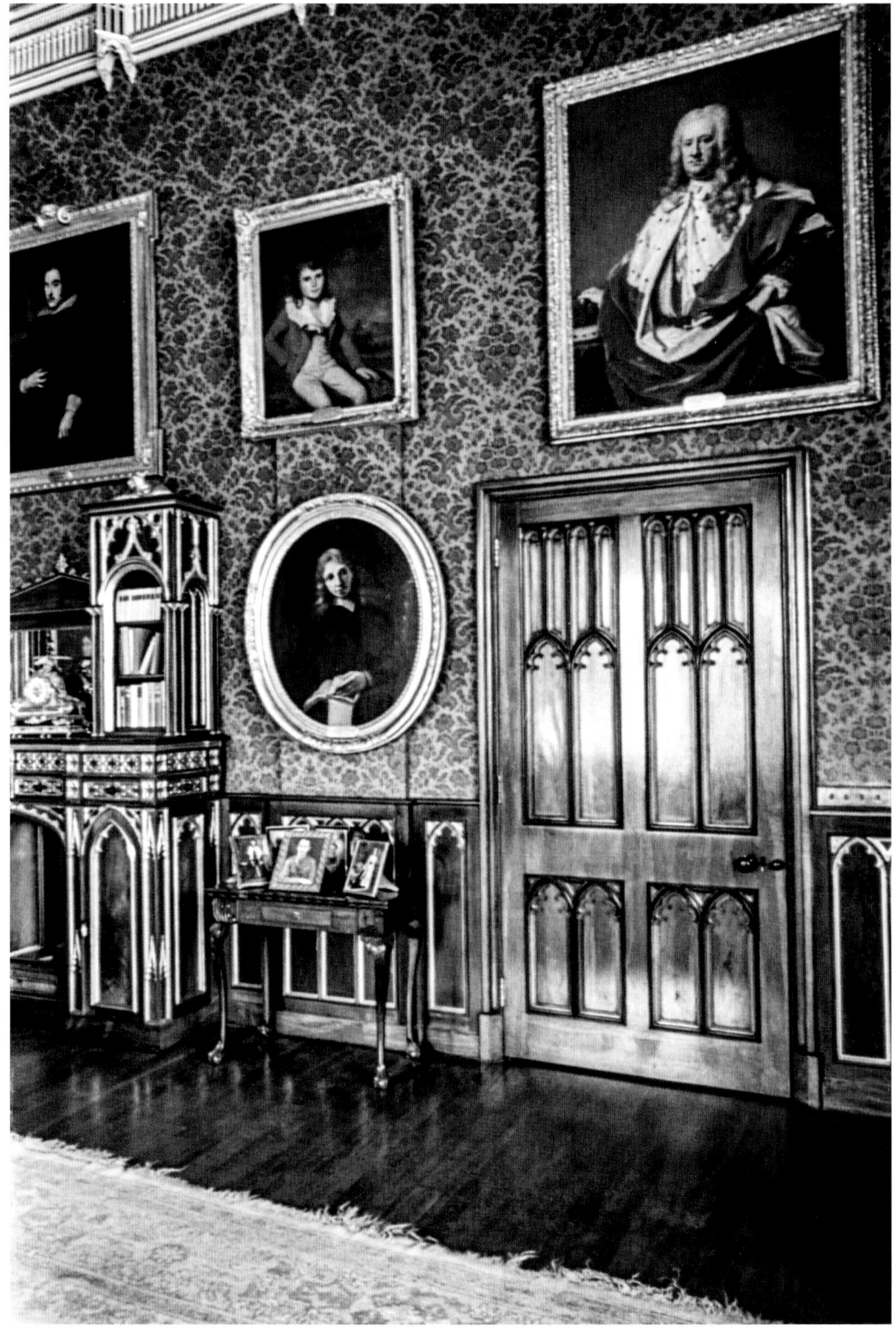

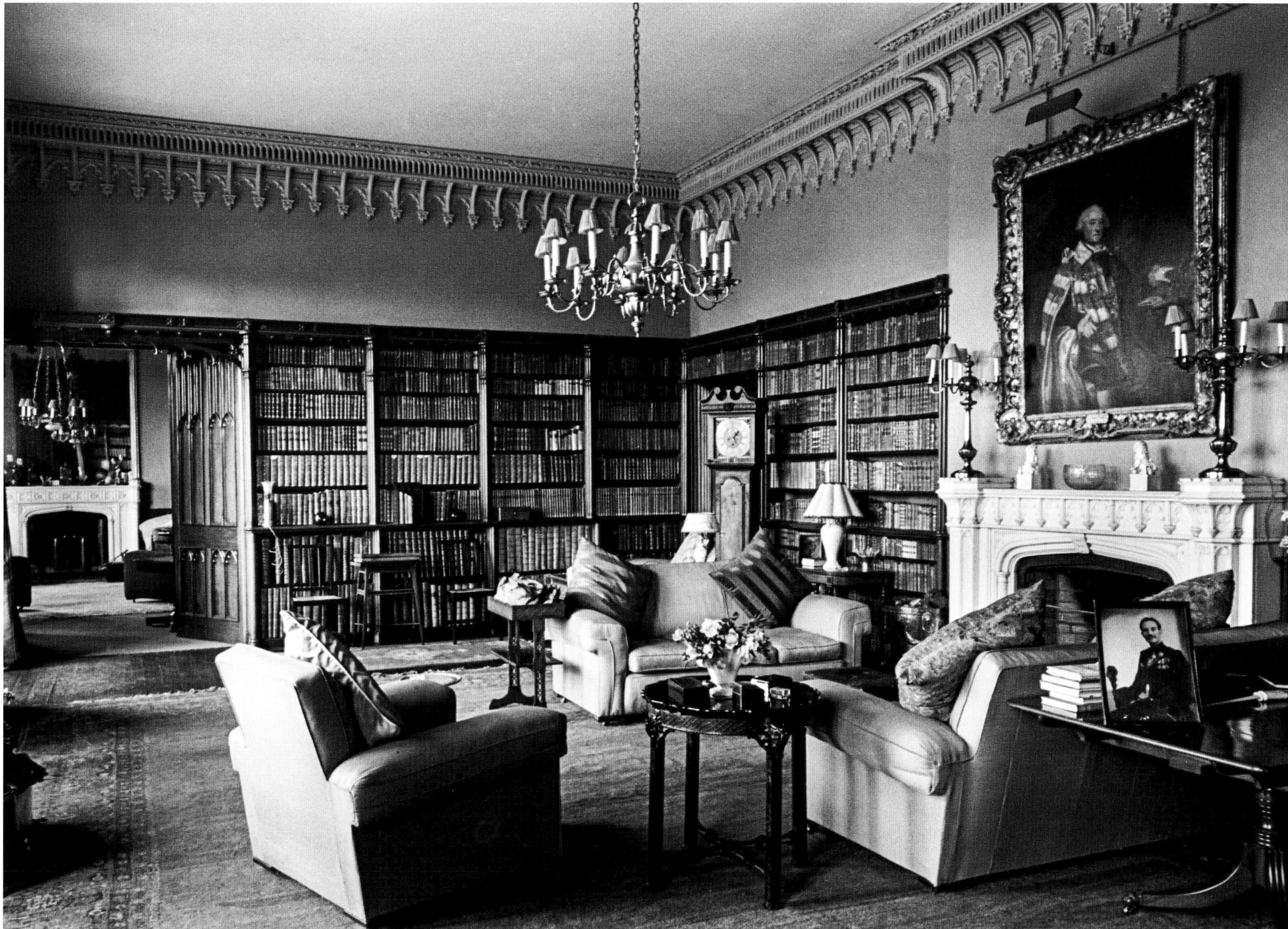

DUNSANY CASTLE
COUNTY MEATH

27TH AUGUST 1950

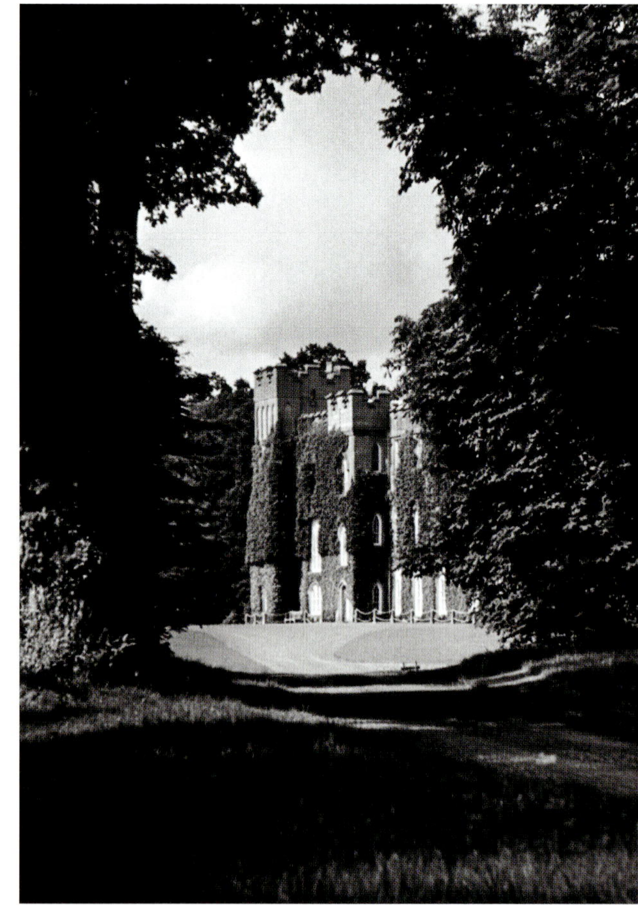

During the summer of 1950 Browne photographed two County Meath castles a short distance from each other and owned by branches of the Plunkett family. But whereas Killeen Castle is now a gutted ruin in the middle of a commercial golf course, Dunsany Castle remains a private home, little altered from when Browne paid his visit. The oldest part of the building is thought to date from c.1180, when its construction was ordered by the Anglo-Norman knight Hugh de Lacy, whose principal stronghold was nearby at Trim. Like that castle, Dunsany would have had four stone towers with defensive walls between them, and some of this work survives in the present building's foundations.

Both Dunsany Castle and its neighbour at Killeen were owned by the Cusack family. However, in 1399 Sir Christopher Plunkett married Joan de Cusack, heiress to Killeen and Dunsany. The couple had two sons, the elder, John, inheriting the Killeen estate and the younger, another Christopher, that of Dunsany. In due course, Christopher became the 1st Baron Dunsany, although the precise date of this creation is unclear. Meanwhile, the Dunsanys' cousins at Killeen Castle became 1st Barons Fingall and later Earls of Fingall. The last holder of this title died in 1984.

Above: The castle seen from the avenue
Opposite: The ground floor Dining Room overseen by the butler of the time, Mr T. Brookes

The most notable difference between the two families was that while the Killeen Plunketts always remained Roman Catholic, the Dunsany Plunketts became members of the Church of Ireland in the eighteenth century. Given that they almost lost their castle and estate during the upheavals of the previous century, this change of religious loyalty is understandable, but stable times post-1700 allowed the 13th Lord Dunsany to carry out improvements to the old building. The courtyard between towers was filled in to create a staircase hall and some of the main reception room ceilings were decorated with neo-classical plasterwork. In the past, this work has been attributed to both Michael Stapleton and James Wyatt but is now considered to be by an unknown hand.

Further alterations and additions were made by the 14th Baron in the early 1840s, notably to the dining room and library. It is thought that on this occasion architect James Shiel was responsible, not least because he was then working at nearby Killeen Castle. The library was fitted with grained Gothic bookcases and a ribbed ceiling, all still in place. Little changed until the beginning of the last century when the 18th Lord Dunsany, well-known as an author and playwright, asked the American-born architect George Jack to design an extension holding a billiard room.

When Browne visited, Dunsany Castle was occupied by Randall Plunkett, 19th Baron Dunsany, and his second wife Sheila Phillips, both of whom were photographed on the main staircase. The building is now home to his grandson, also called Randall Plunkett.

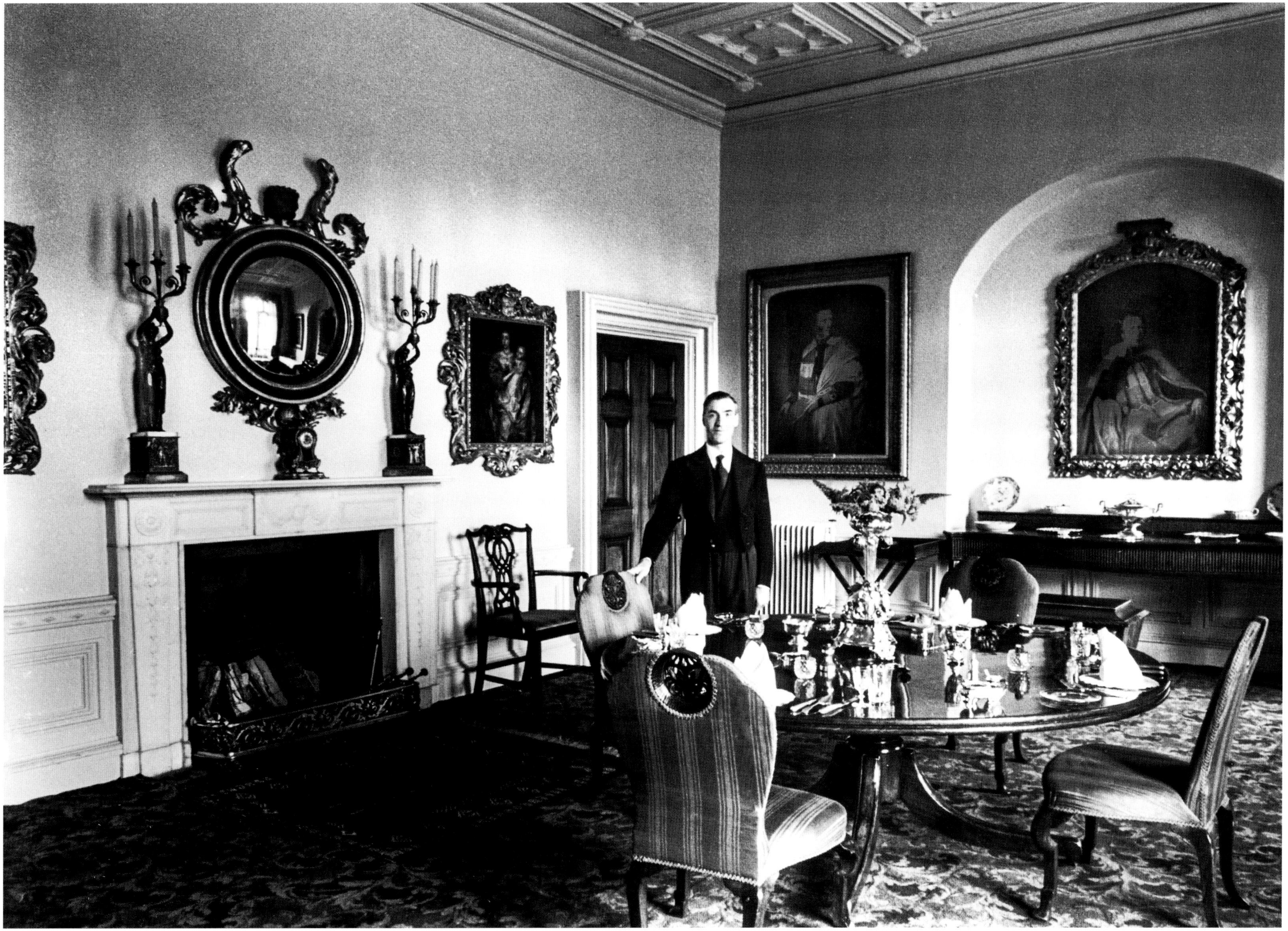

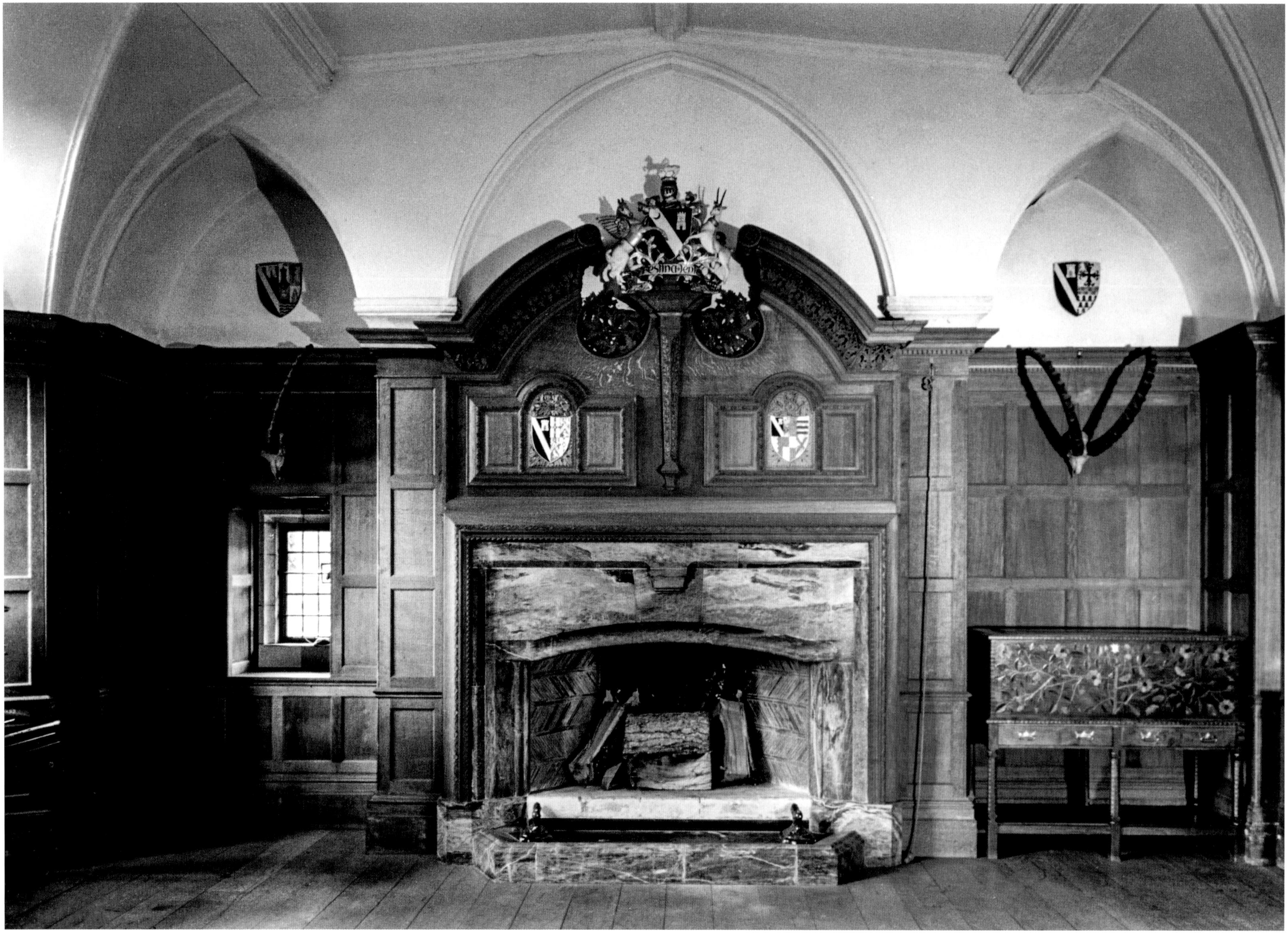

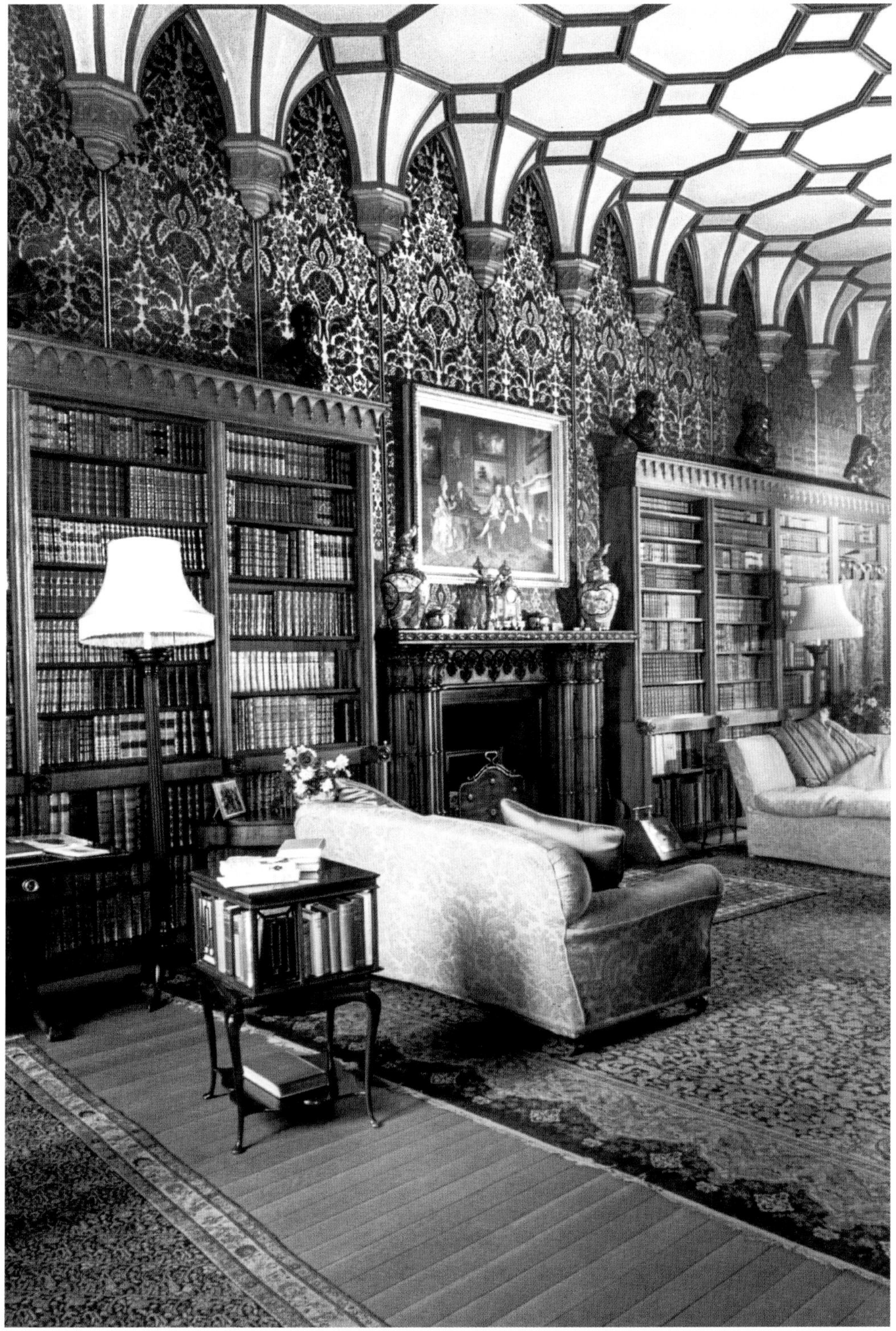

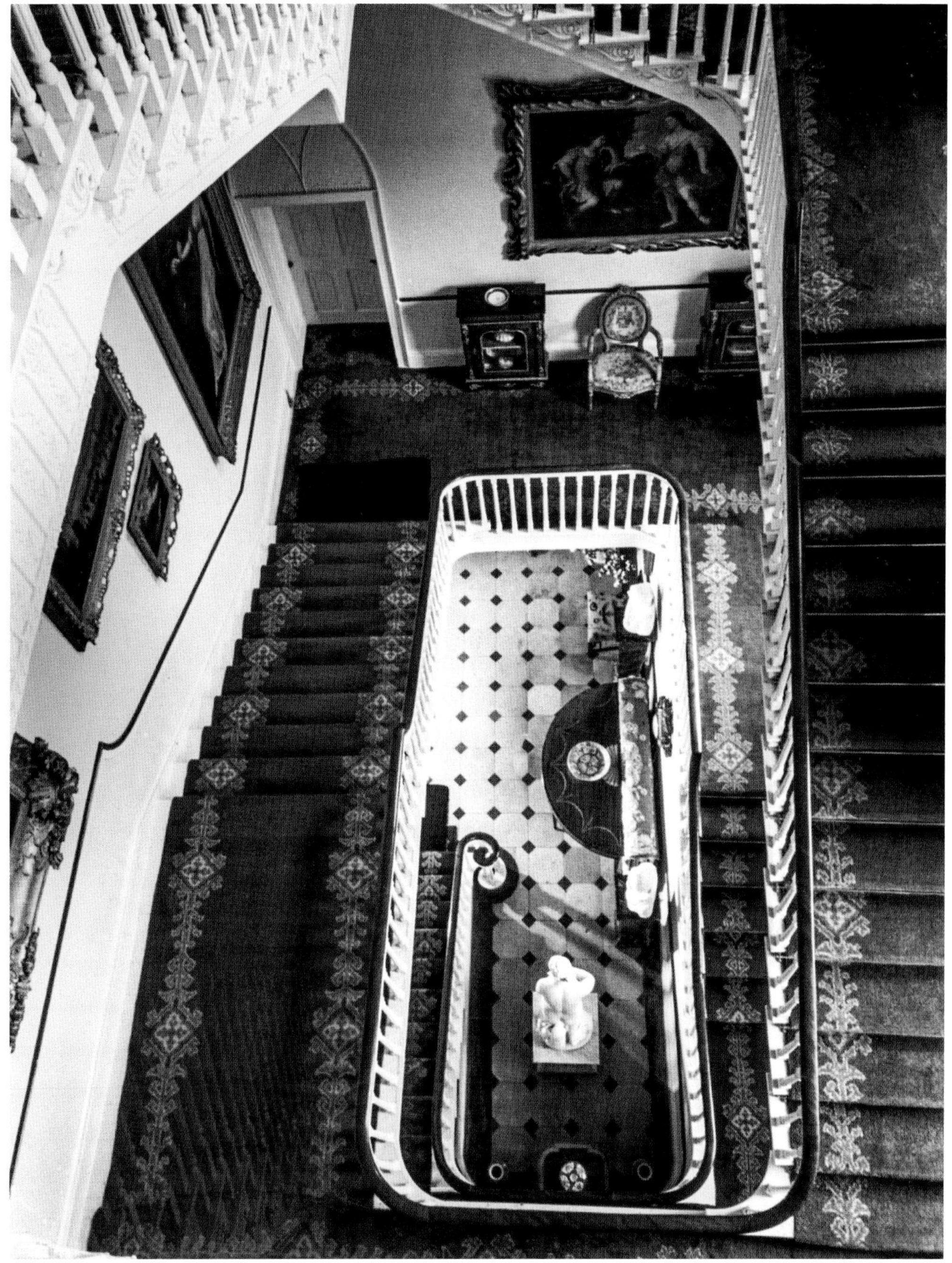

Opposite: A chimney piece in the panelled Billiard Room
Left: The Library with its grained bookcases
Above: The main staircase looking down to the ground floor

Knocklofty
County Tipperary
24th July 1948

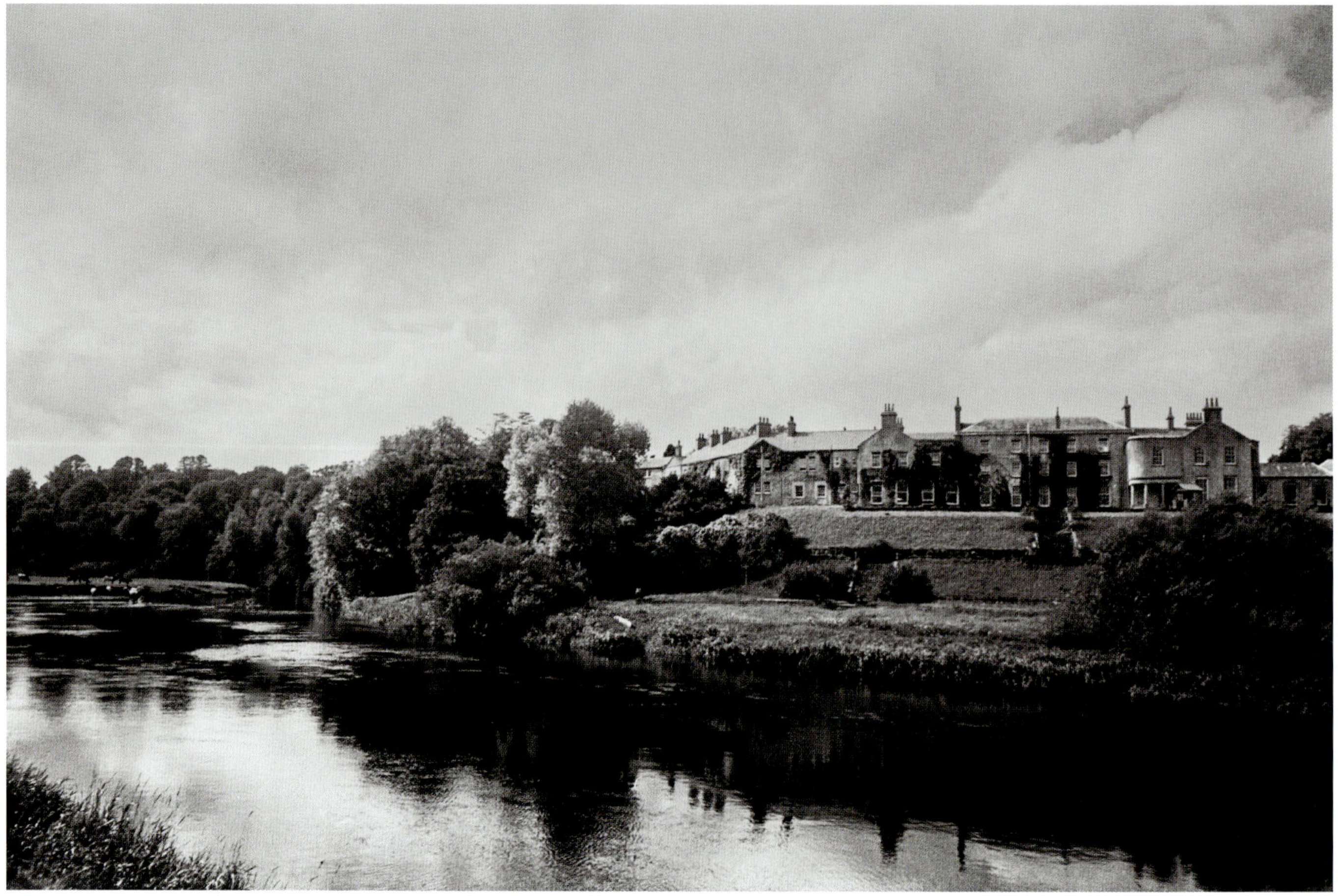

Around 11pm on 4 June 1974, John Hely-Hutchinson, 7th Earl of Donoughmore, and his wife Dorothy returned to their home, Knocklofty, County Tipperary, having been out to dinner. As the couple left the car, a number of men ran towards them waving guns. They seized the elderly pair, and when Lord Donoughmore, then aged seventy-one, resisted, he was struck on the head several times. He and his wife were forced into a car and driven away to an unknown destination. The kidnap made international headlines, not least because there appeared to be no motive for the crime. In fact, the Donoughmores had been picked almost at random, their captors being members of a maverick IRA unit who sought to influence official policy towards a hunger strike in British jails by five IRA prisoners, including the Price sisters. Ongoing mediation led to the hunger strike being called off, and after four days the Donoughmores were driven to Dublin and released in the middle of Phoenix Park in the early hours of the morning.

The Hely-Hutchinsons can be traced back to the Ó hÉalaighthe or O'Healy clan in County Cork, based around Donoughmore, some 12 miles south-west of Mallow. Like so many other families, they lost much of their territory and power during the seventeenth century, However, by the early eighteenth century, one Francis Hely, described in contemporary reports as a gentleman, was living in Gortroe, to the west of Mallow. In 1724 he and his wife Prudence had a son, John Hely, who, after studying at Trinity College Dublin, was called to the Bar and rose to become one of the most notable lawyers and politicians of the period.

In 1751 Hely married Christiana Nickson of Wicklow, great-niece and heiress of one Richard Hutchinson, whose own forebear had been granted by the English crown some 1,200 acres of land around Knocklofty in County Tipperary: the married couple duly changed their name to Hely-Hutchinson. Despite his brilliant career, John Hely-Hutchinson declined a peerage, but his wife was created Baroness Donoughmore, a recollection of her husband's family background. Their eldest son Richard inherited that peerage on his mother's death, before in turn being created Viscount Donoughmore and, in 1800, Earl of Donoughmore. He commissioned the construction of the present house at Knocklofty, the

Above: The garden front of Knocklofty viewed across the river Suir
Opposite: The panelled Dining Room in the south wing of the house

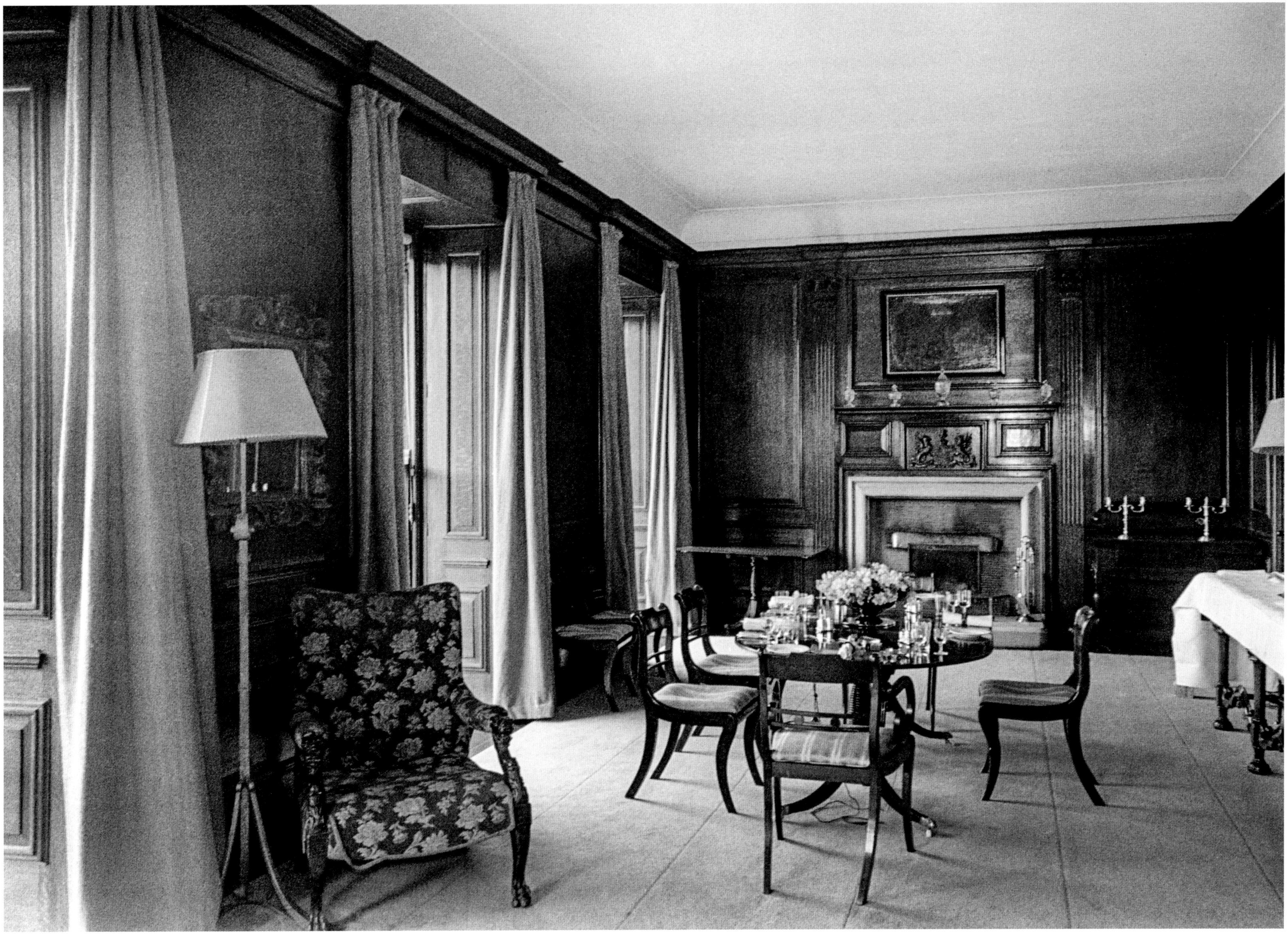

entrance front of which had a central block of seven bays and three storeys flanked by gable-ended two-storey wings that come forward to create a forecourt. At some point, a third inner bay was added to these wings, while in the early nineteenth century, along the front of the house, a single-storey corridor was created, with a three-bay domed projection at its centre. Other extensions were made to the building later in the same century, resulting in a very substantial house, along with several adjacent service wings. Inside, curiously, the largest reception space is not the drawing room but, at the centre of the house overlooking the gardens, a double-height library with a wrought-iron gallery running around three sides. Some of this work was presumably undertaken by the 2nd Earl, who inherited the title and estate from his unmarried elder brother.

Lord Donoughmore died in 1981, seven years after being kidnapped, and soon afterwards Knocklofty was placed on the market. Over the following years, it changed hands a number of times, for a period becoming a hotel. In the aftermath of the economic recession of 2009, the property was offered for sale but then became enmeshed in a legal dispute for more than a decade, during which time the house fell into serious disrepair. In September 2023 it was announced that Knocklofty had been bought and the new owner intended to carry out a full restoration of the building.

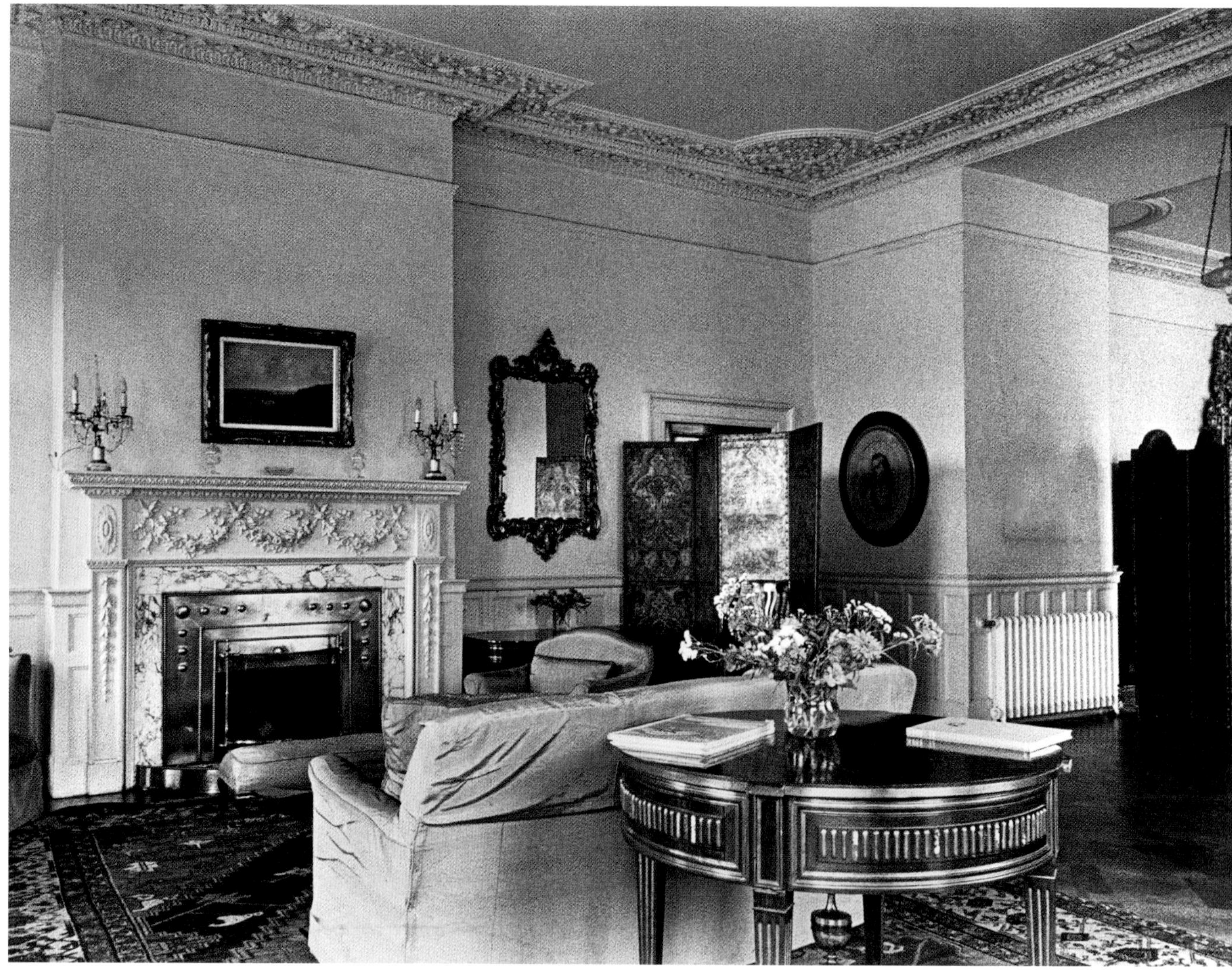

Above: A Drawing Room in the north wing of the house
Opposite Page Left: A bookcase-lined corridor
Opposite Page Right: Looking into the double-height Library

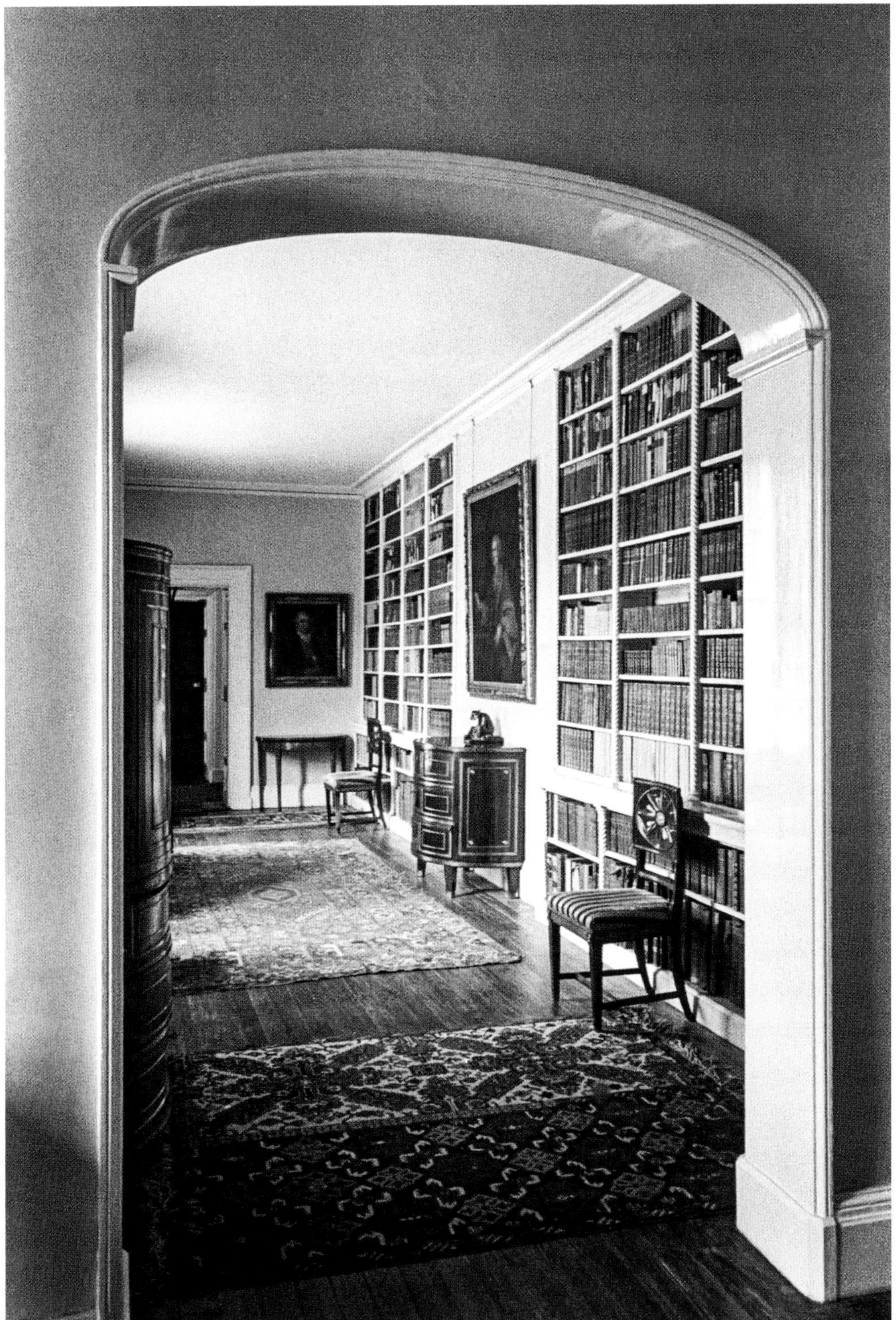

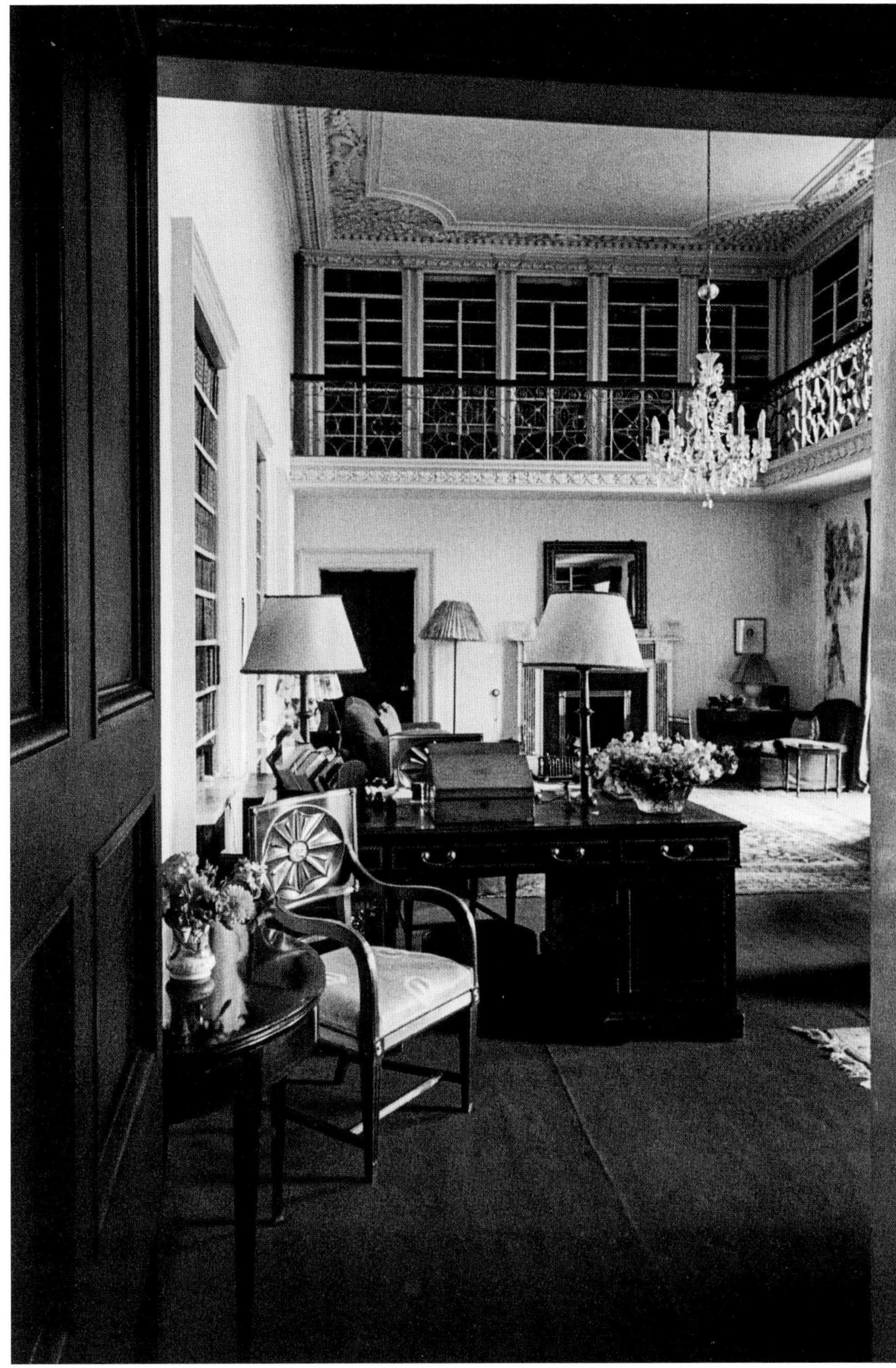

ROCKINGHAM
COUNTY ROSCOMMON
26TH APRIL 1948

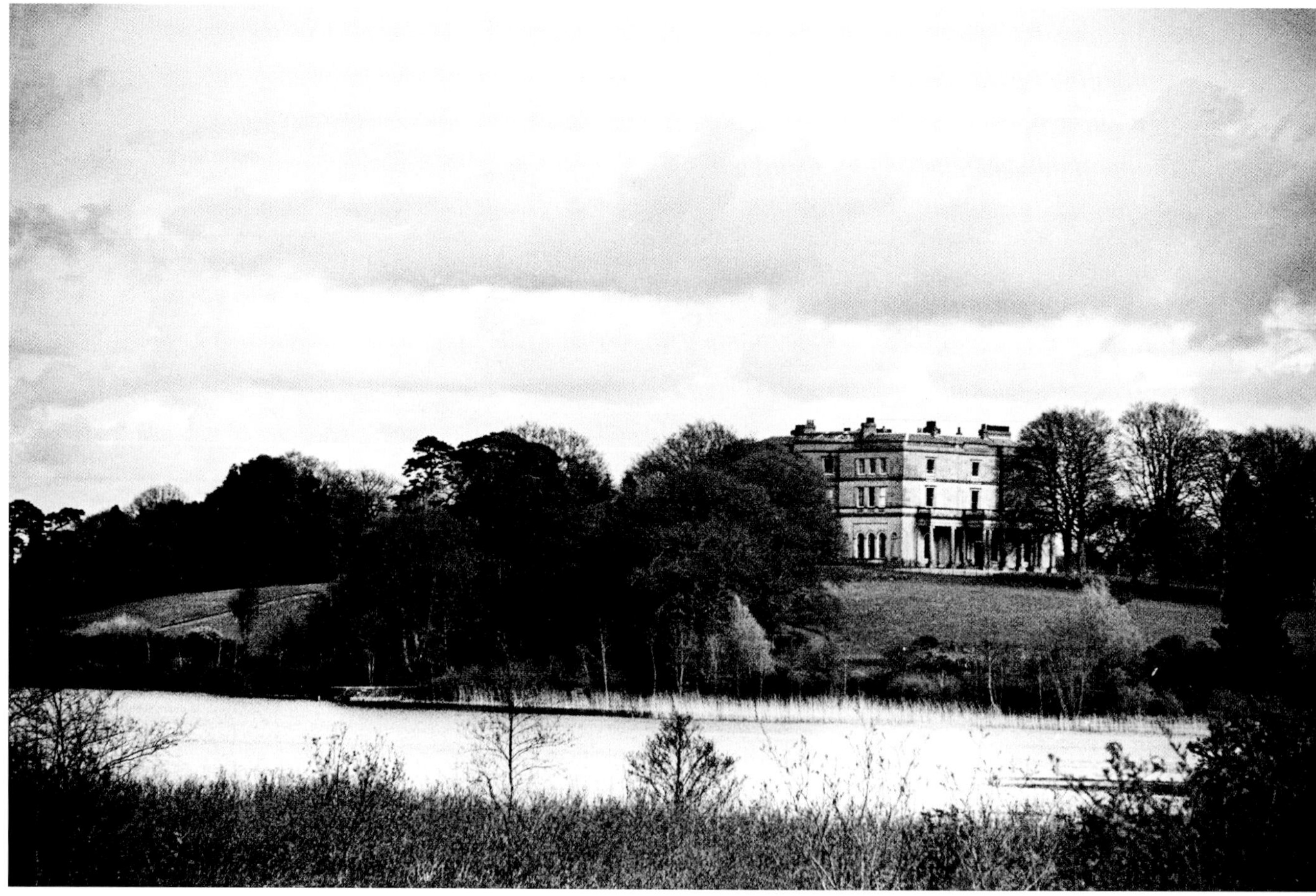

In the closing days of Queen Elizabeth I's reign she granted Sir John King – a soldier originally from Yorkshire – a lease on the former Cistercian abbey in Boyle. King was an exceptionally able and loyal servant of the crown, and this grant was confirmed by James I in 1617, along with surrounding land running to some 4,000 acres; by the time of his death in 1636, King owned land in twenty-one different counties.

Originally King and his descendants lived in the converted abbey, but at some time after 1720, Sir Henry King commissioned a large house in the centre of Boyle, and barely half a century later his son Edward King, 1st Earl of Kingston, chose to build a new residence, Kingston Hall, on an estate north-east of the town. King House in the town was first leased and then sold to the War Office in London, and served as a barracks until the second half of the last century; it is now a museum.

Before long Kingston Hall was superseded by yet another house, Rockingham. Constructed on the shores of Lough Key for General Robert King, 1st Viscount Lorton, this was designed in 1809–10 by English architect John Nash, and was originally of two storeys with an underground basement. The garden front had a curved central bow fronted by a semi-circular Ionic colonnade and surmounted by a great dome, with three-bay wings on either side. Owing to the project's spiralling costs – by 1817 more than £52,000 had been spent on the house – Nash was dismissed by Lord Lorton, and his Clerk of Works, John Lynn, was given responsibility for finishing the work. Landscape architect John Sutherland was tasked with designing Rockingham's demesne.

Twelve years after its completion, the need for extra bedrooms meant another storey was added to the building, which led to the loss of the great dome and, as Mark Bence-Jones has pointed out, 'making the house ungainly, where it had previously been of graceful proportions'. Further changes were made in 1863 after a fire destroyed much of the interior, following which a full restoration was required. Nevertheless, the interior of the house was impressive, not least the top-lit inner hall which led, via a screen of Corinthian columns, to a splendid imperial staircase with iron balustrade. There was a round drawing room (above which formerly rose Nash's dome), a fine dining room with three arched windows overlooking the demesne, and a great pilastered orangery.

By this time, despite large land holdings across

Above: Rockingham seen from Lorton Bridge
Opposite: The top-lit central hall with imperial staircase to one side

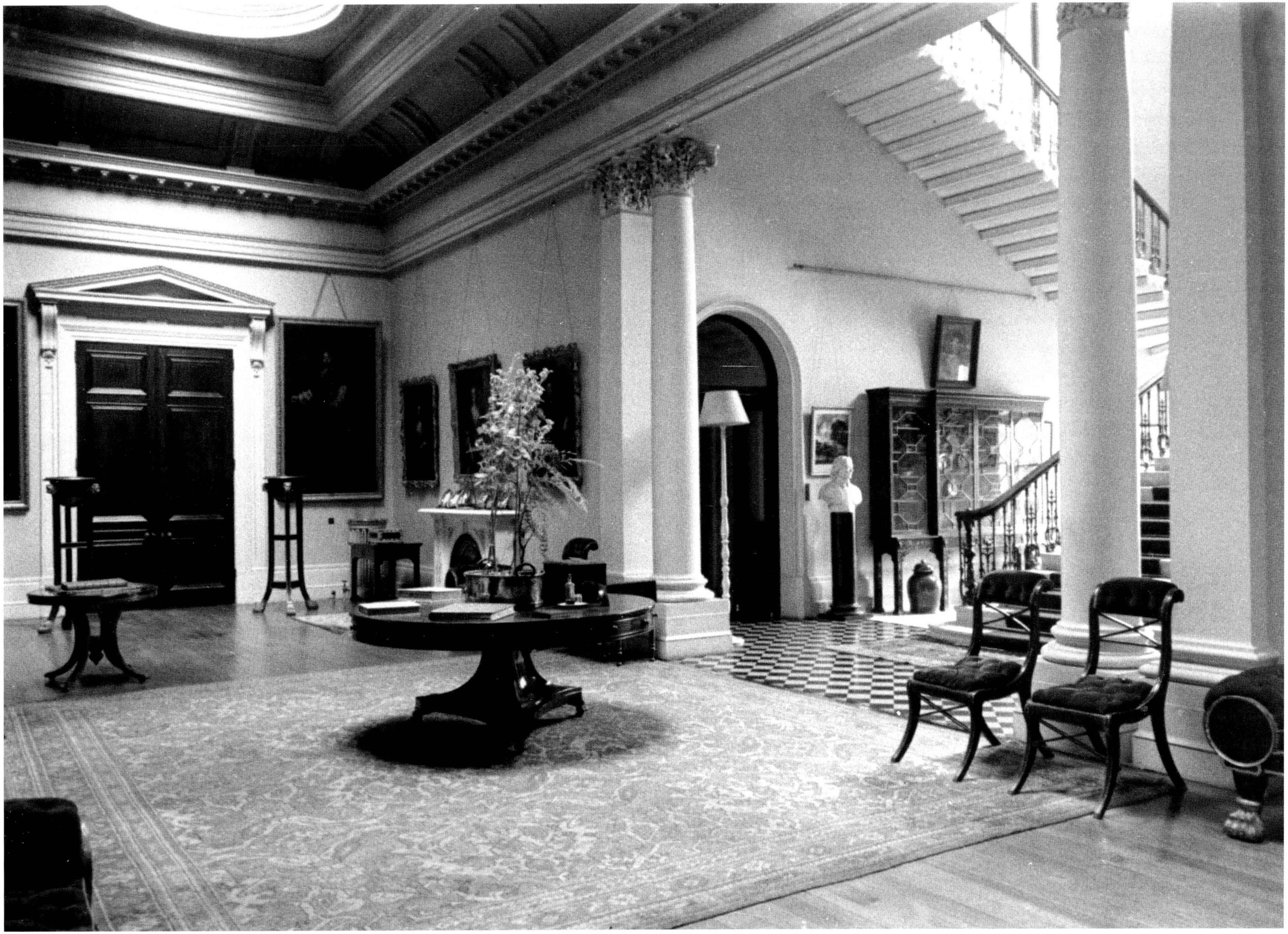

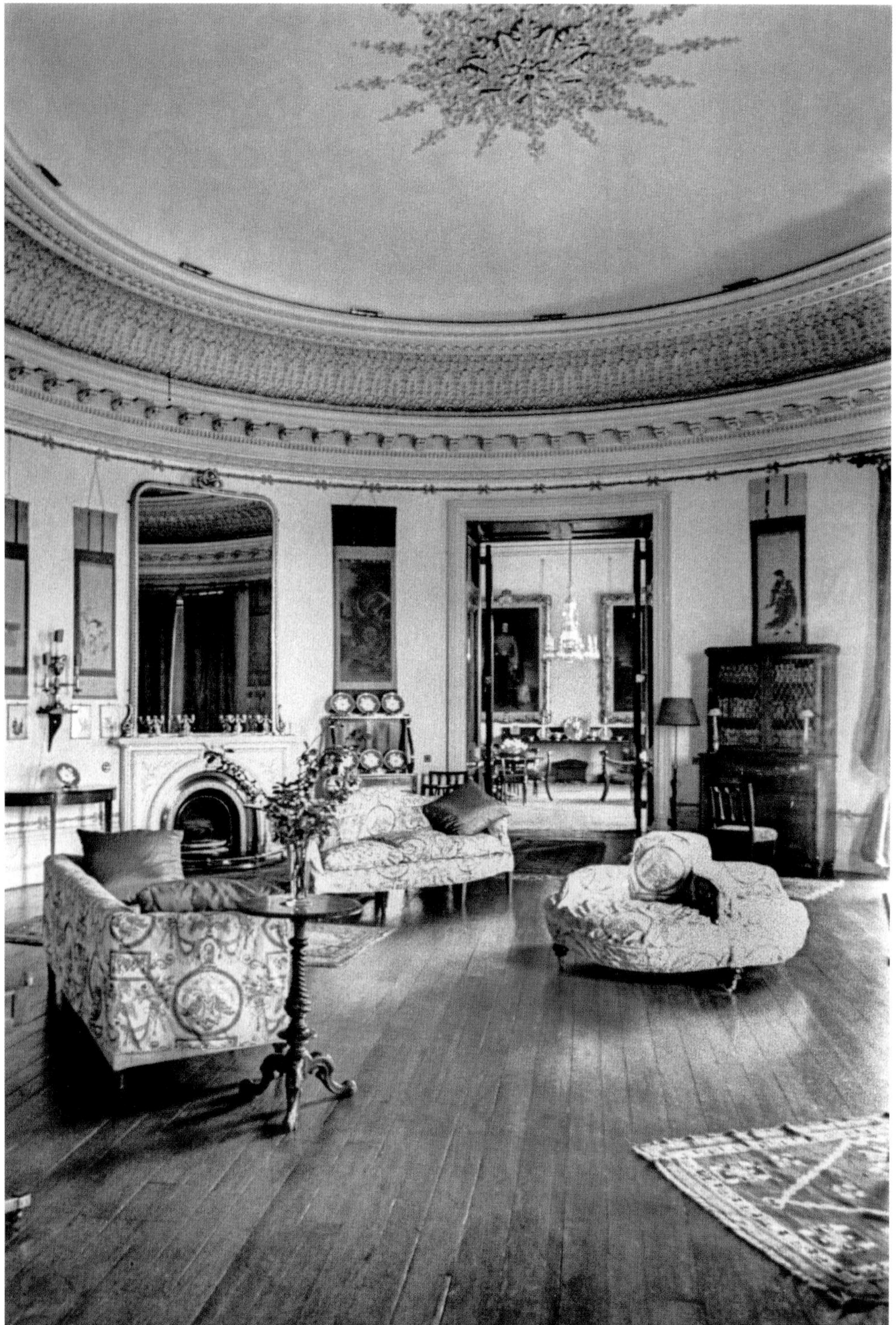

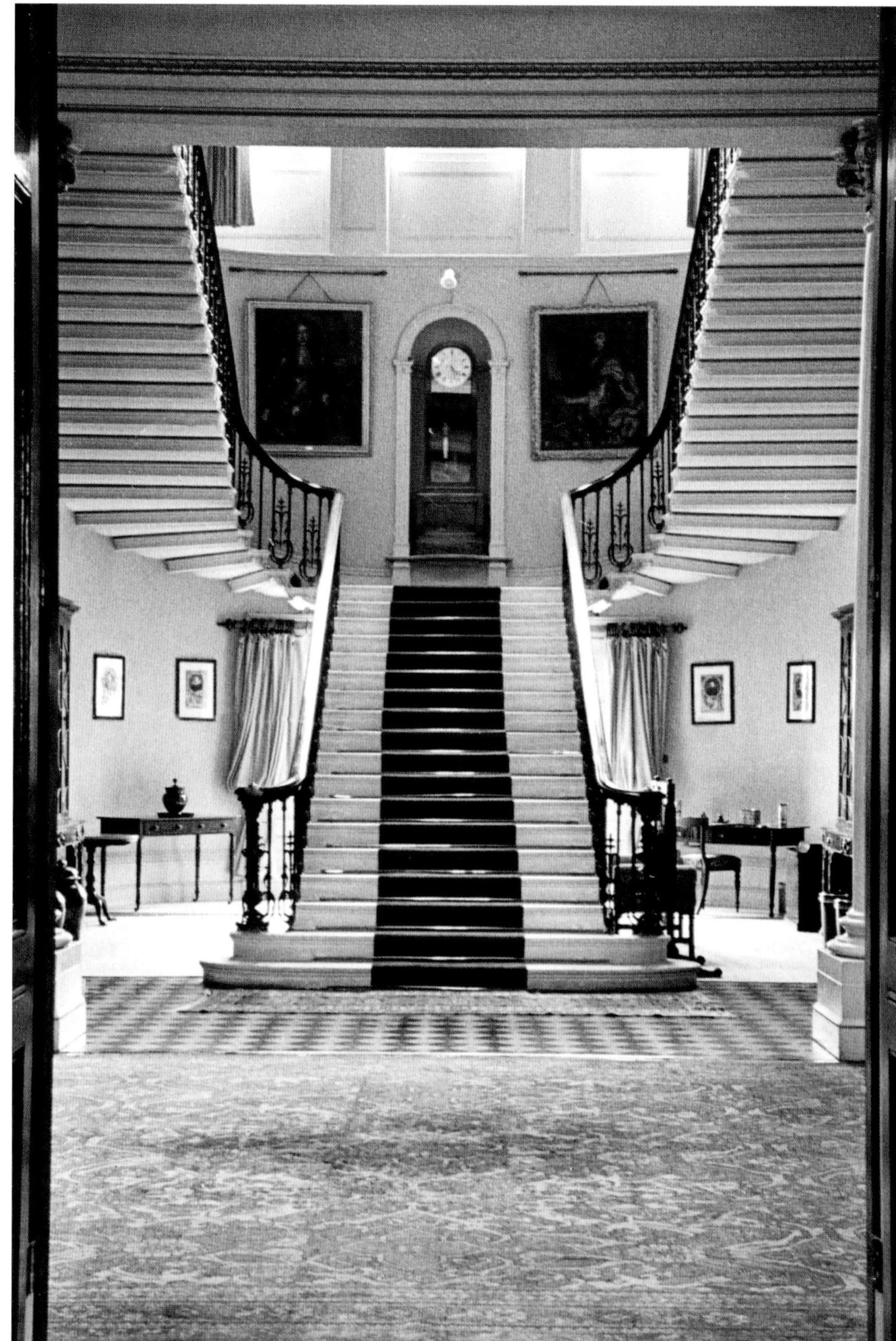

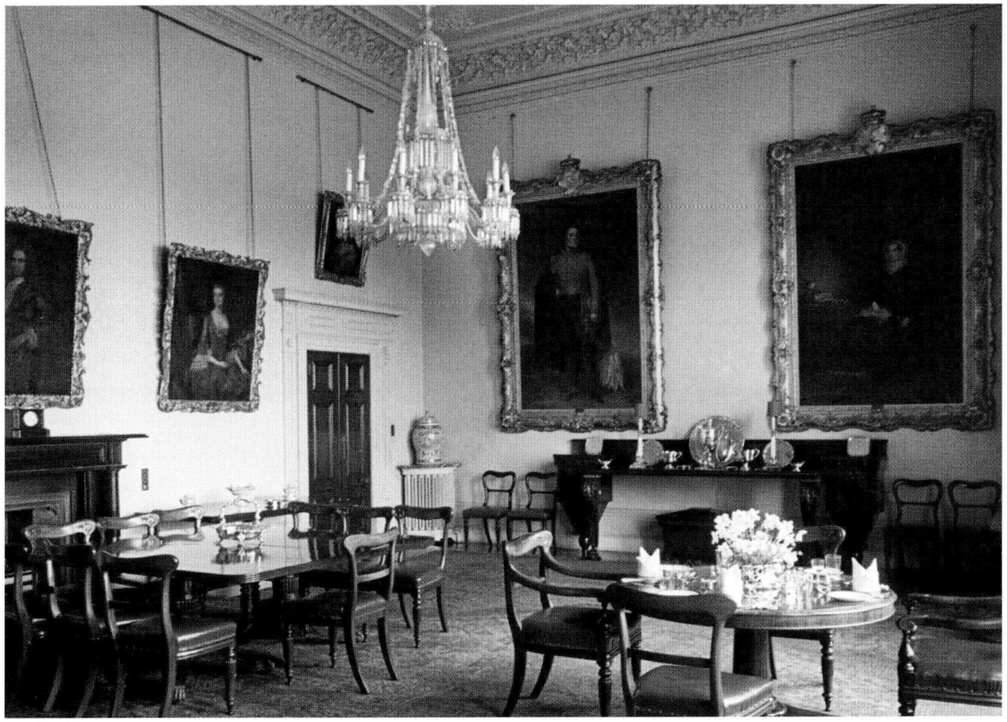

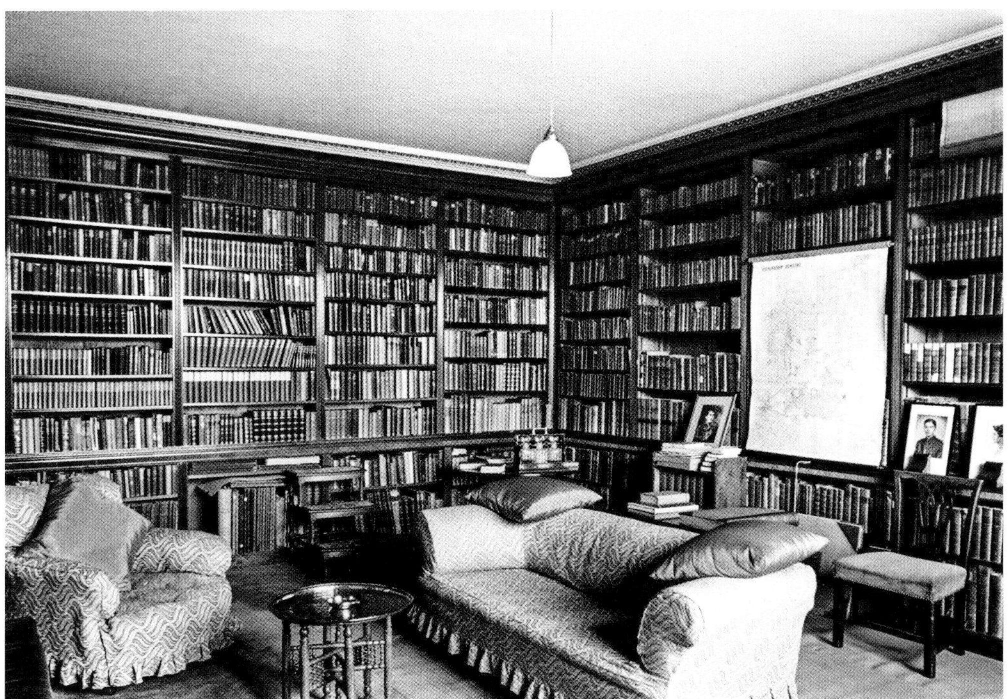

several counties, the family was suffering serious financial difficulty and on occasion Rockingham had to be let; in the early twentieth century, it was taken by Lord Dudley, then serving as Lord Lieutenant of Ireland. In 1888 Rockingham had been inherited by the Stafford-King-Harman family who lost their heirs in both the First and Second World Wars. Browne visited the house in 1948 and, just a few years later, advised by architect Philip Tilden, Sir Cecil Stafford-King-Harman rearranged the interior of the house to make it more manageable. Unfortunately, in September 1957 another fire left the building an empty shell. Sir Cecil considered rebuilding Rockingham as it had been designed by John Nash, but the cost was too great and so the house and its demesne were bought by the Land Commission. The shell of Rockingham survived until 1971 when it was demolished and replaced by a concrete viewing tower. Today the land around this site is a forest and activity park jointly managed by Roscommon County Council and Coillte.

Opposite Page Left: The Round Drawing Room with the Dining Room beyond
Opposite Page Right: The imperial staircase seen from the Drawing Room

Above: The Dining Room
Left: The Library

MALAHIDE CASTLE

COUNTY DUBLIN

26TH JULY 1947

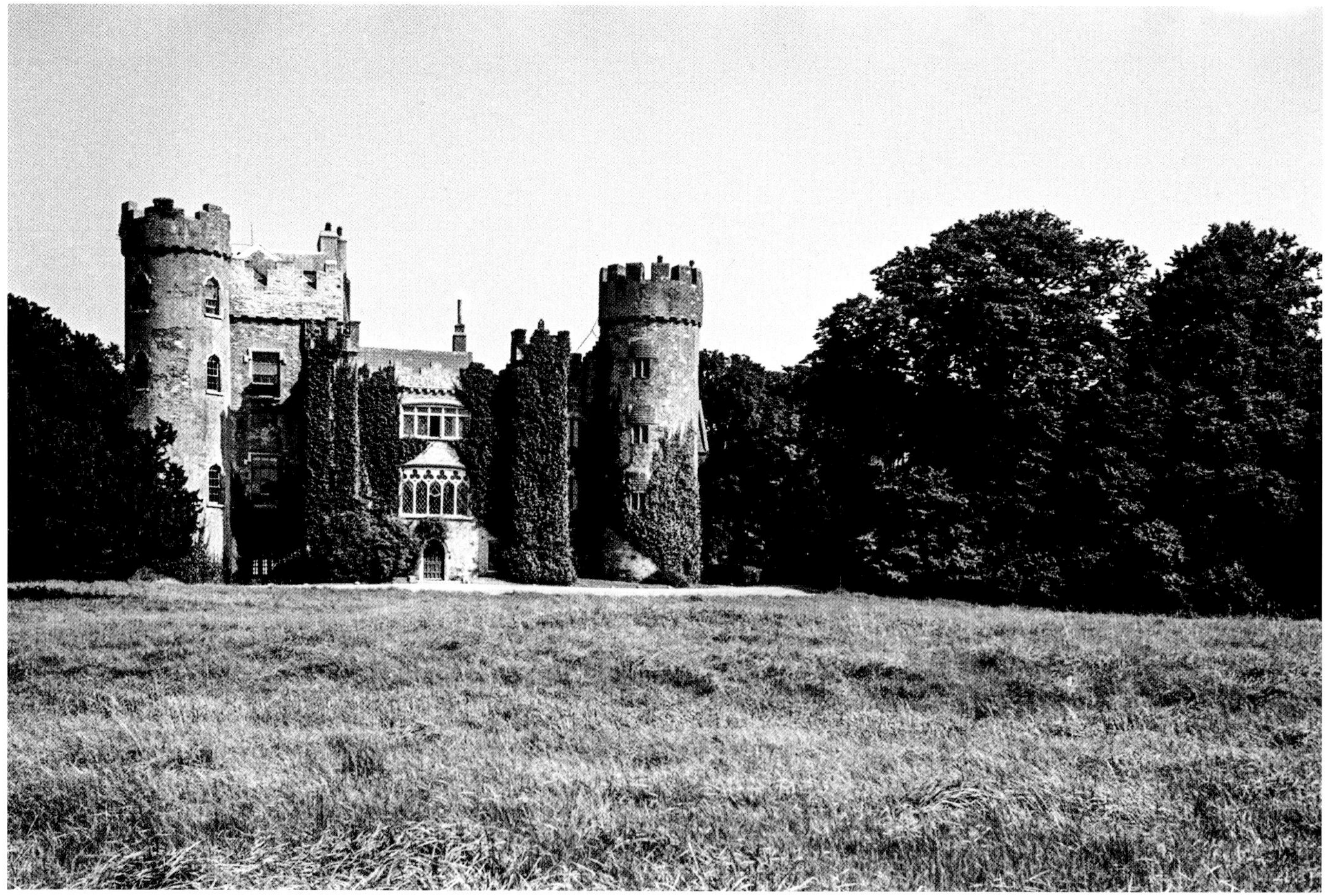

The history of Malahide Castle, County Dublin, dates back to 1185, when the land on which it stands was given by King Henry II to one of his knights, Richard Talbot. His descendants lived there until 1976, with only a brief absence during the years 1649–60 when the Talbots' property was granted to the Cromwellian regicide Myles Corbet; it was returned to them following the Restoration of Charles II (Corbet was hanged in 1662). Remaining Roman Catholic until 1774, the Talbots supported James II during the Williamite Wars. Famously, on the morning of 1 July 1690, fourteen male members of the family sat down to breakfast; that evening, after participating in the Battle of the Boyne, only one of them remained alive.

The original building on the site would have been a wooden structure and the oldest part of the present castle is a keep-like rectangular tower of three storeys, built c.1400 and incorporating the Great Hall, which dates to around 1475. The largest room in the castle, it measures 42 by 22 feet and is overlooked by a minstrel's gallery. The walls here are covered with Jacobite portraits connected to the Talbot family.

Some seventy-five years after the Great Hall's creation, the building was extended, and this area now holds the Oak Room. Located directly above the entrance hall, it is a rare surviving example in Ireland of a sixteenth-century panelled room, centred on a set of six carved panels, believed to be of Flemish origin, depicting biblical scenes. According to legend, another panel, showing the coronation of the Virgin, which today sits above the chimneypiece, vanished while the castle was occupied by the Myles Corbet, and then reappeared when the Talbot family returned to the castle. The Oak Room was enlarged in 1820 when a large latticed window was added.

Elsewhere, the interior of Malahide Castle reflects the evolution of the house over several centuries. Between 1765 and 1782, the west wing was extensively reconstructed following a disastrous fire, and the present two drawing rooms made out of what had previously been four smaller rooms hung with tapestries. During the same period, alterations were made to the bedrooms, while various floors and ceilings were raised and two circular turret rooms added off the drawing rooms.

Above: The castle's entrance front facing south-west across the demesne
Opposite: The 15th century Great Hall, its walls thickly hung with generations of family portraits

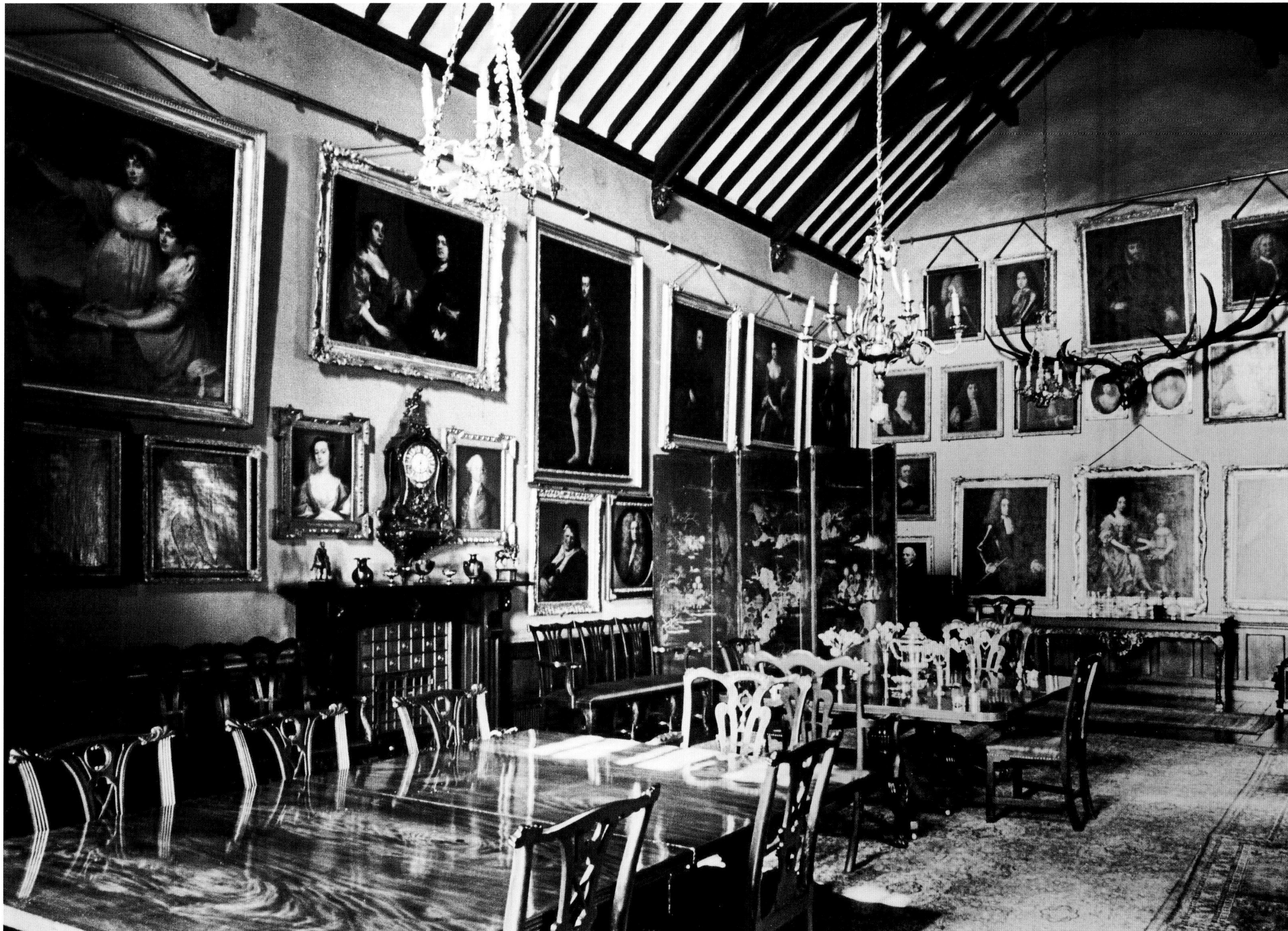

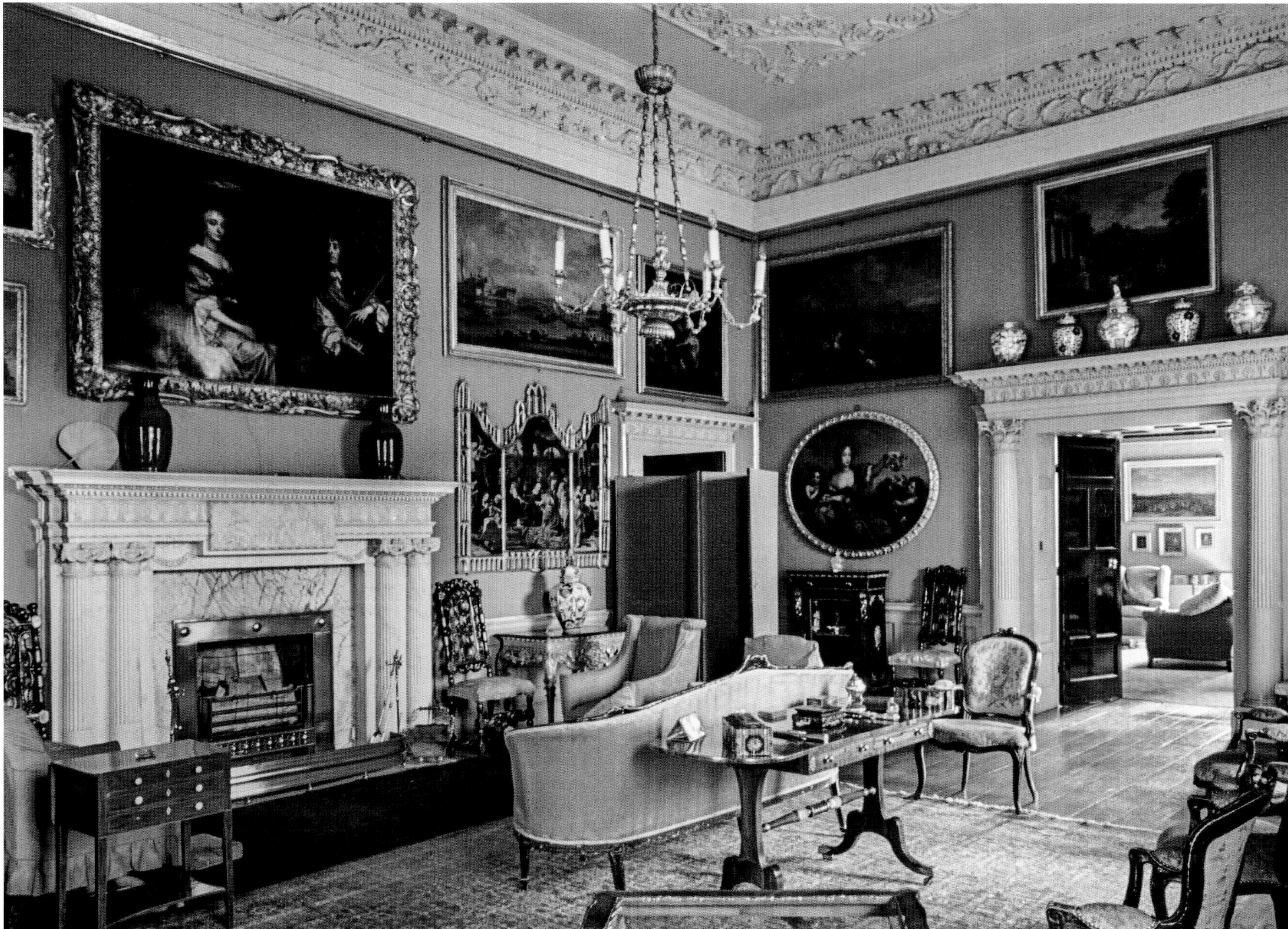

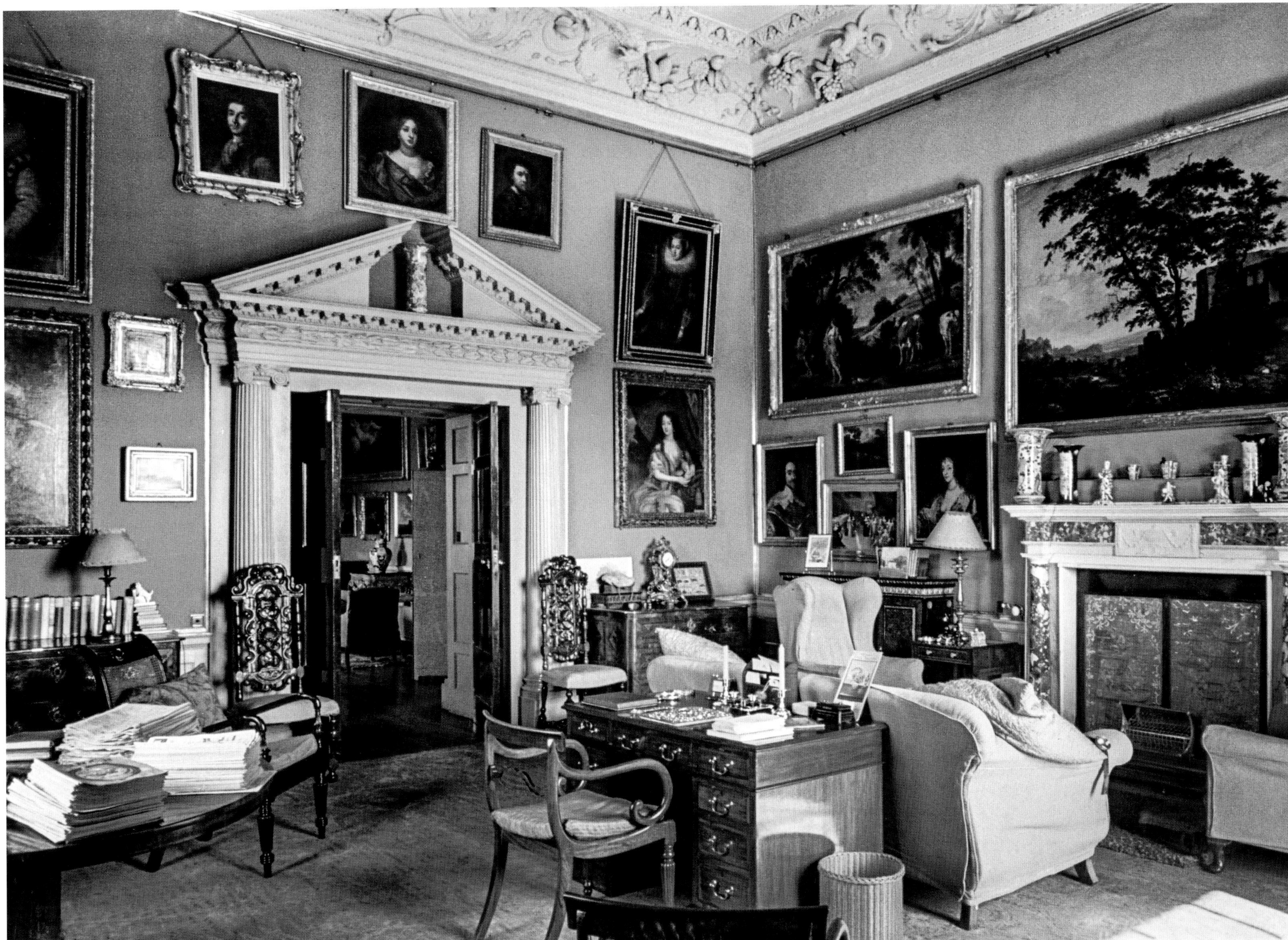

Another notable room in the castle is the Library, its walls hung with leather covered in silver leaf, lacquer made of resin before being adorned with tooled embossing and, finally, painted by hand with flower and insect motifs, each length of the leather different from the others.

Malahide Castle remained the home of the Talbots until the death of Milo Talbot, 7th Baron Talbot de Malahide in 1973. At the time, he had been negotiating to hand over Malahide Castle and its demesne to the Irish state. His sister and heir, the Hon. Rose Talbot, offered valuables from the building in lieu of death duties but this was refused, and a great sale of the castle's contents was held by Christie's over several days in May 1976, in consequence of which Dublin County Council, which had acquired the castle and grounds, found itself forced to bid against international dealers and collectors for many lots, only some of which it could afford to acquire.

Browne's photographs, taken the year before the death of the 6th Baron, show the castle still replete with furniture, paintings and bibelots collected by generations of Talbots, most of them forever dispersed at the Christie's sale.

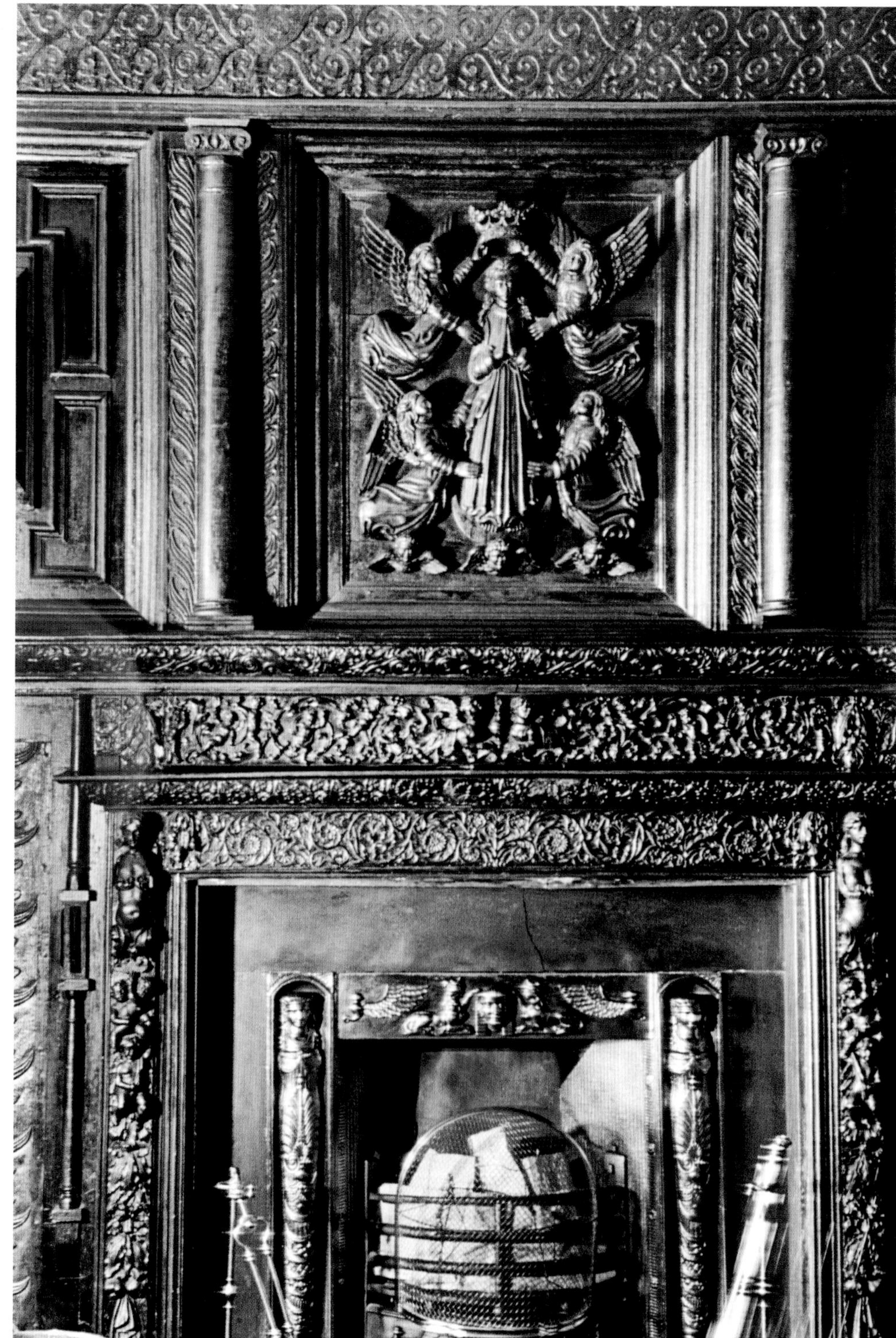

Pages 90–91:
Malahide Castle's interconnected Drawing Rooms, the contents of which were dispersed in the sale held here in 1976
Right: A carving depicting the Coronation of the Virgin in the Oak Room

Opposite: The Library, its walls hung with embossed leather

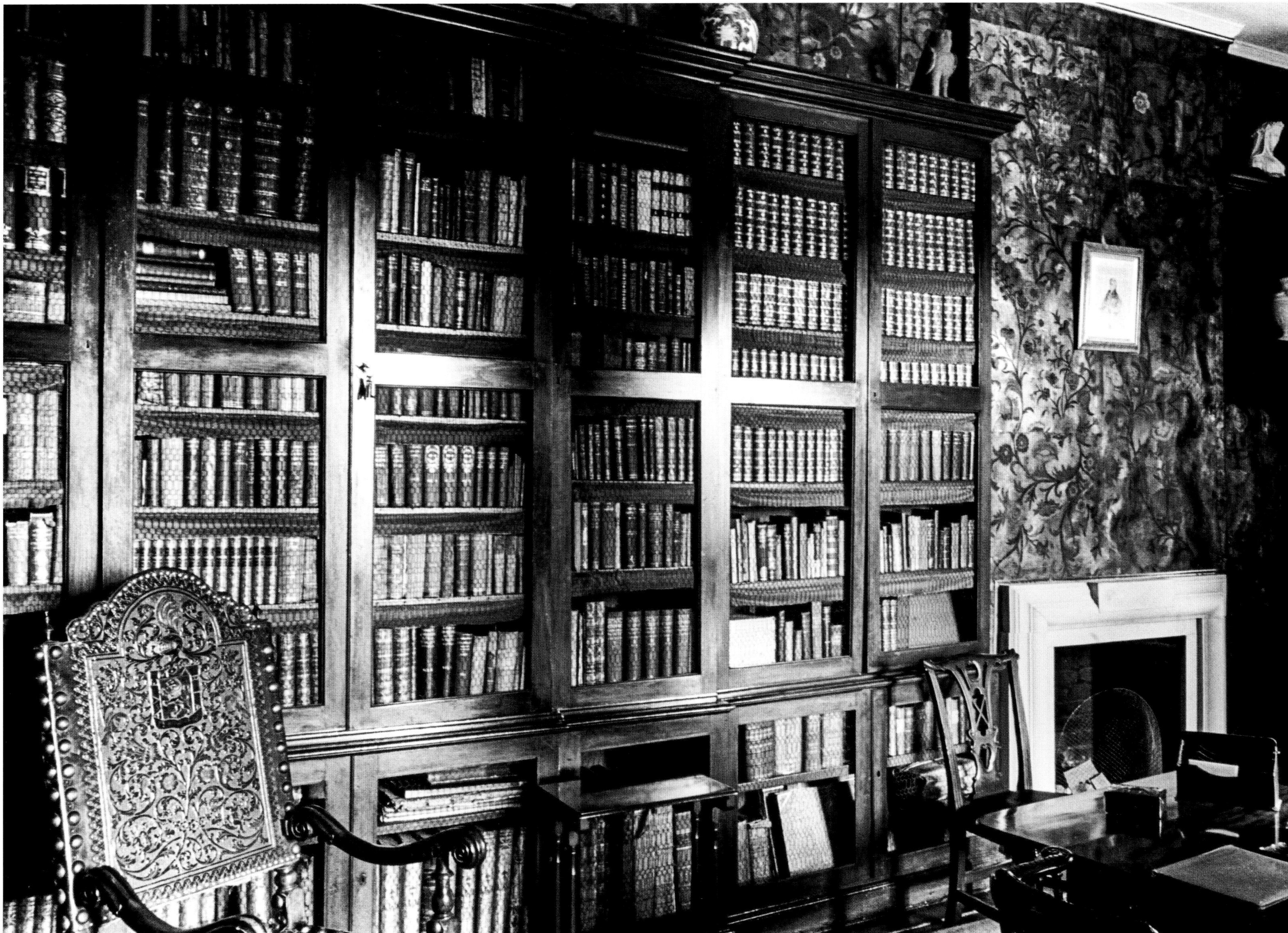

SHELTON ABBEY
COUNTY WICKLOW
9TH NOVEMBER 1946

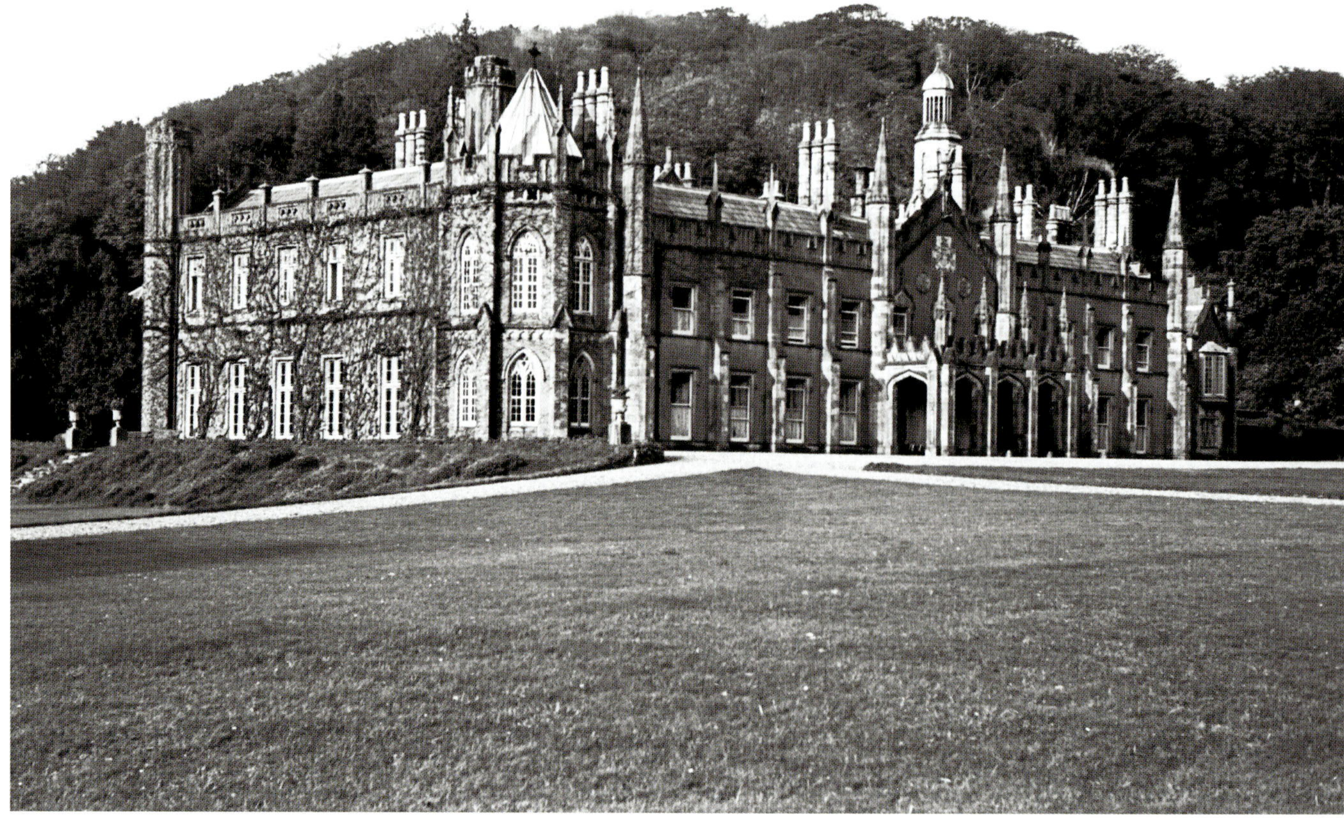

Shelton Abbey was originally built in the mid-1750s for Ralph Howard, future 1st Viscount Wicklow: a number of architects seem to have had a hand in its design, including Englishman Matthew Brettingham. However, the Georgian house was made over into something altogether more romantic at the instigation of the 4th Earl of Wicklow. In 1819 he commissioned the father and son practice of Richard and William Vitruvius Morrison to transform his country seat so that it gave the impression of being 'an Abbey erected during the fourteenth century, and with considerable additions, formed into a baronial residence shortly after the Reformation'.

The main facade was dressed up with a multiplicity of crenellations, pinnacles and polygonal turrets, the three centre bays dominated by a single-storey Tudoresque porte cochère, while at the south-east corner rose a two-storey octagonal tower with conical roof. Set back on the north side is a slightly later wing, likewise thought to have been designed by Richard Morrison and to date from the 1840s. Known as the 'Nunnery', it was built, seemingly, to house the 4th Earl's unmarried daughters. Inside the main block, some of the rooms retained their classical decoration, while others were made to suggest a similar age as the exterior. A cloister-like gallery, for example, ran around two sides of the central courtyard, and the two drawing rooms were given Gothic ceilings with fan vaulting and pendants.

Generations of the Howard family had married heiresses and were thus able to maintain the splendour of the Shelton Abbey. By the last century, however, this practice had died out and, after inheriting the property following his father's death in 1946, the 8th (and last) Earl of Wicklow was obliged to open the house as an hotel. Shortly before doing so, he invited Browne to come and photograph the place while it was still a private residence. Writing in 1822, John Preston Neale had advised that the building's principal rooms 'are adorned with a valuable collection of paintings of the Italian, French, and Flemish Schools; and the Library contains an extensive collection of scarce and valuable books, medals, drawings and engravings'. An inventory taken of Shelton Abbey's contents in 1914 shows that this remained the case, and many of the items listed therein are visible in Browne's pictures. We are fortunate to have this record, because Lord Wicklow's attempt to

Above: The early 19th century Tudoresque exterior of Shelton Abbey
Opposite: The Entrance Hall: almost all the decorative plasterwork has since been destroyed

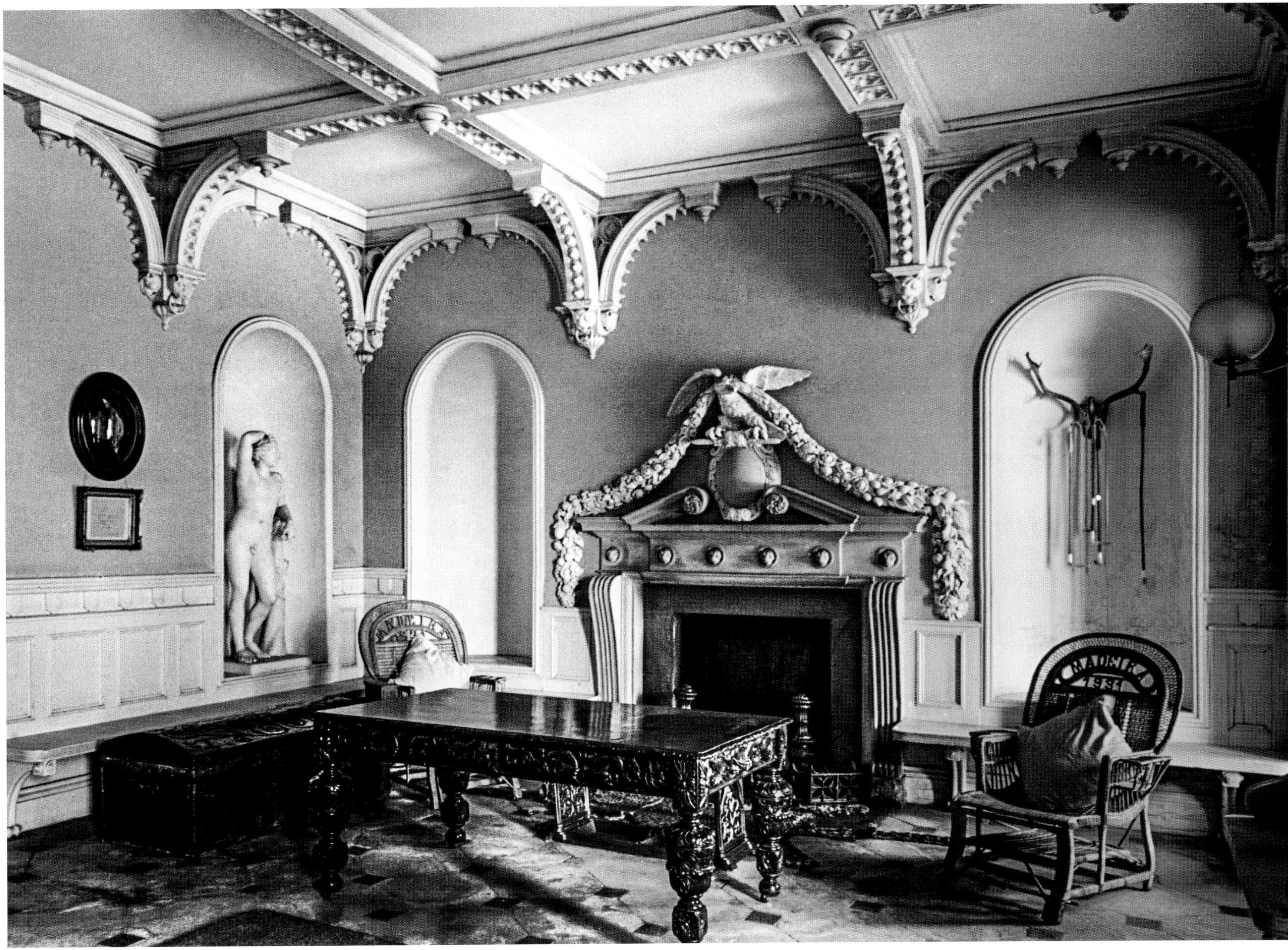

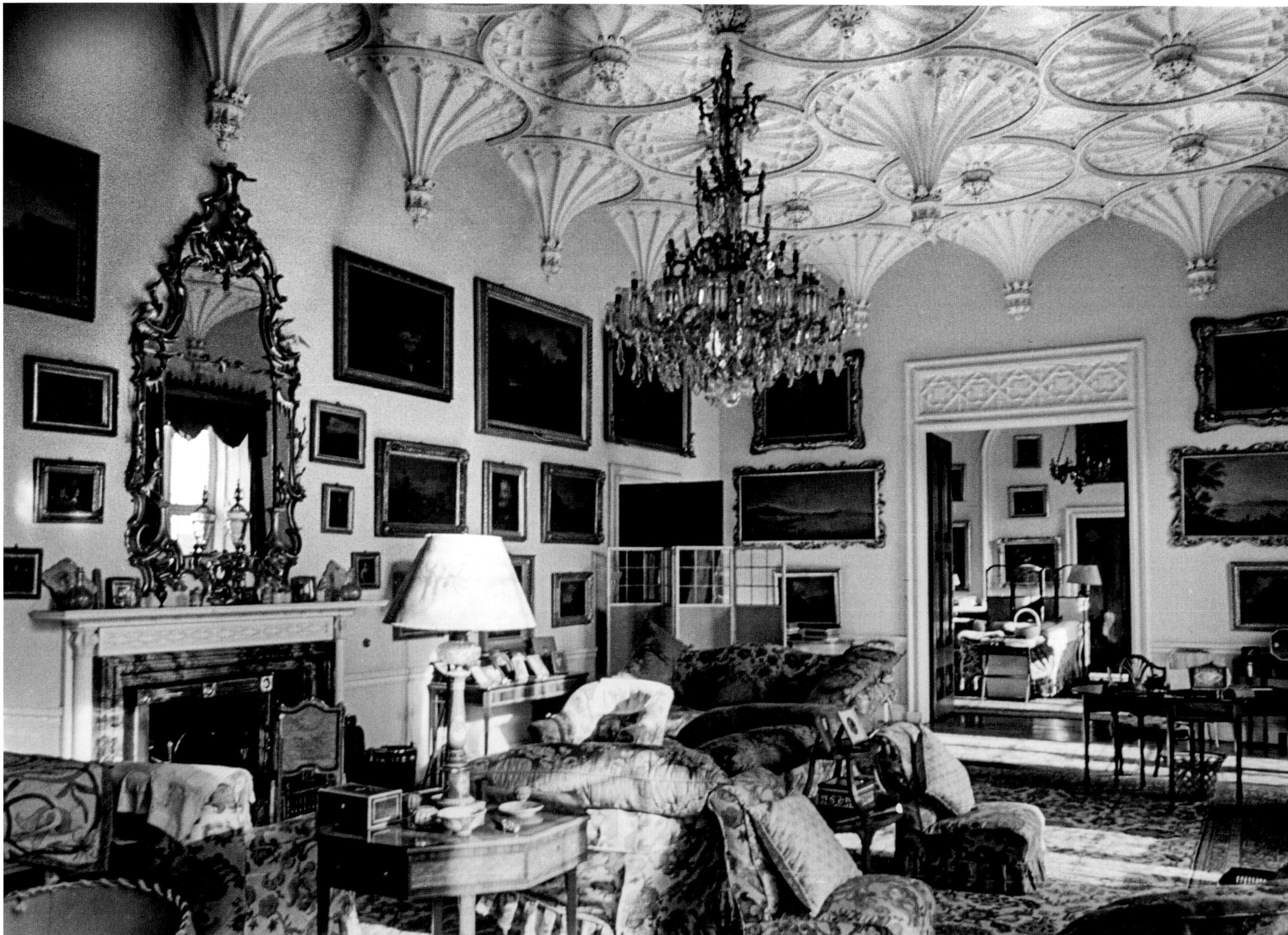

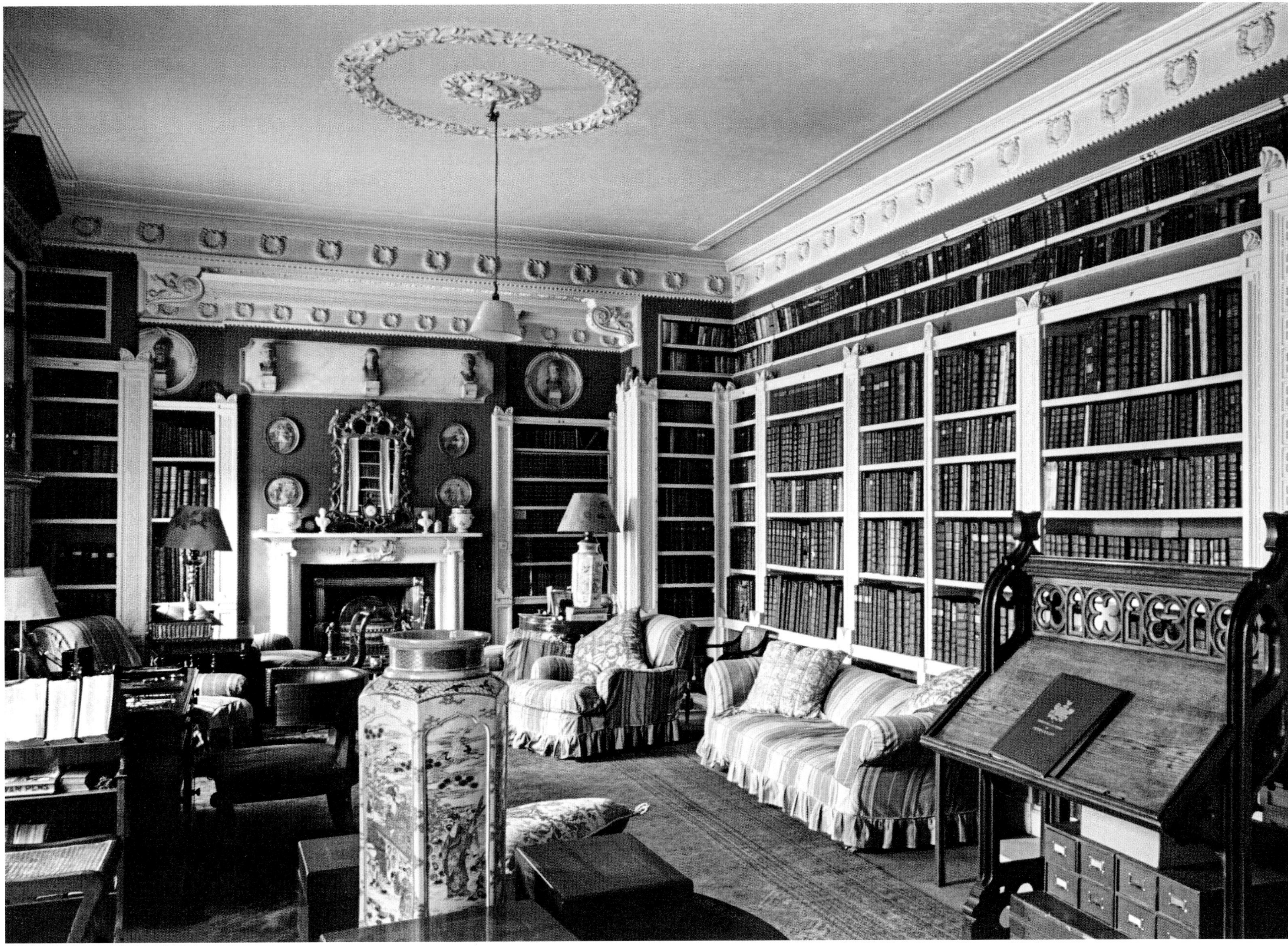

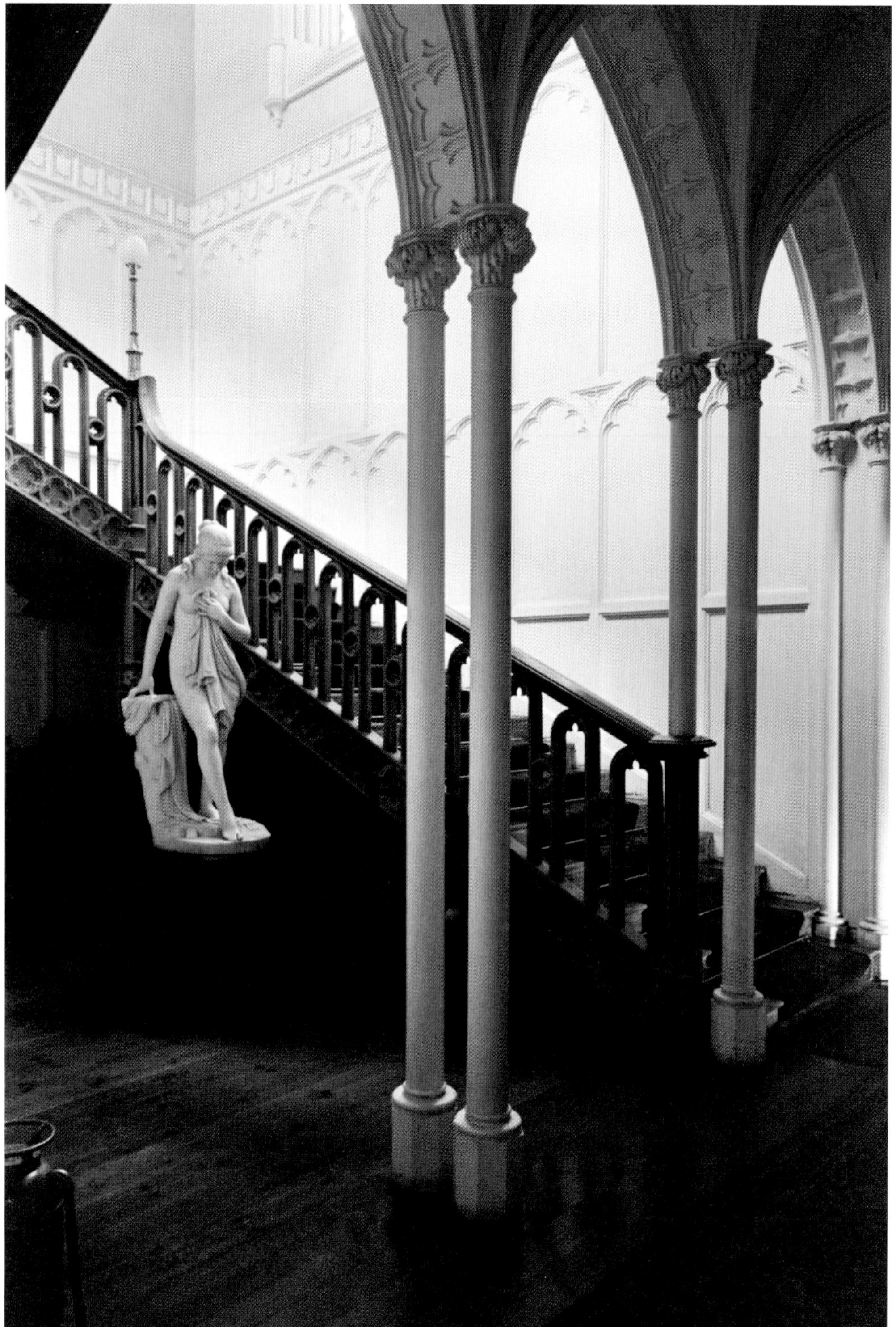

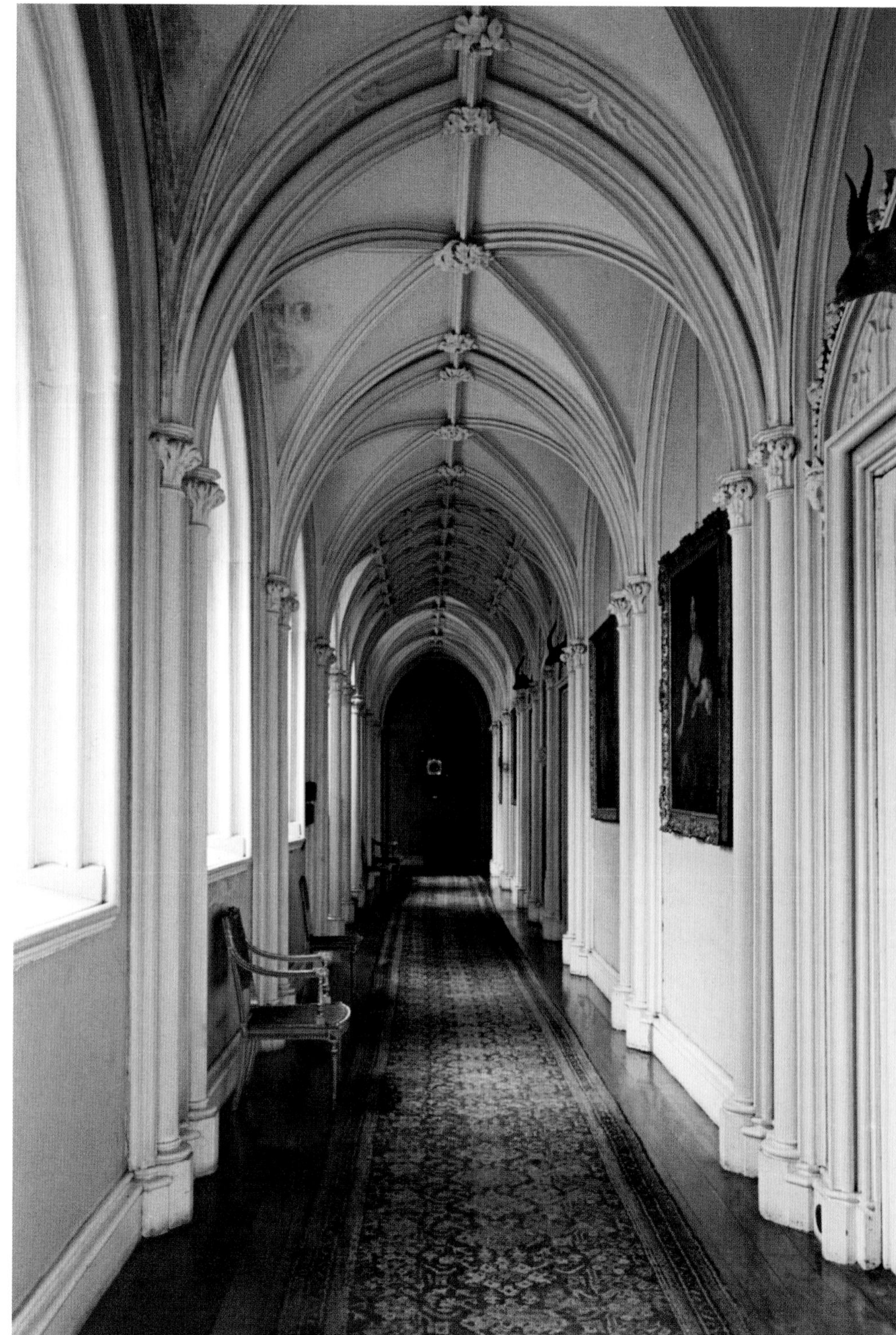

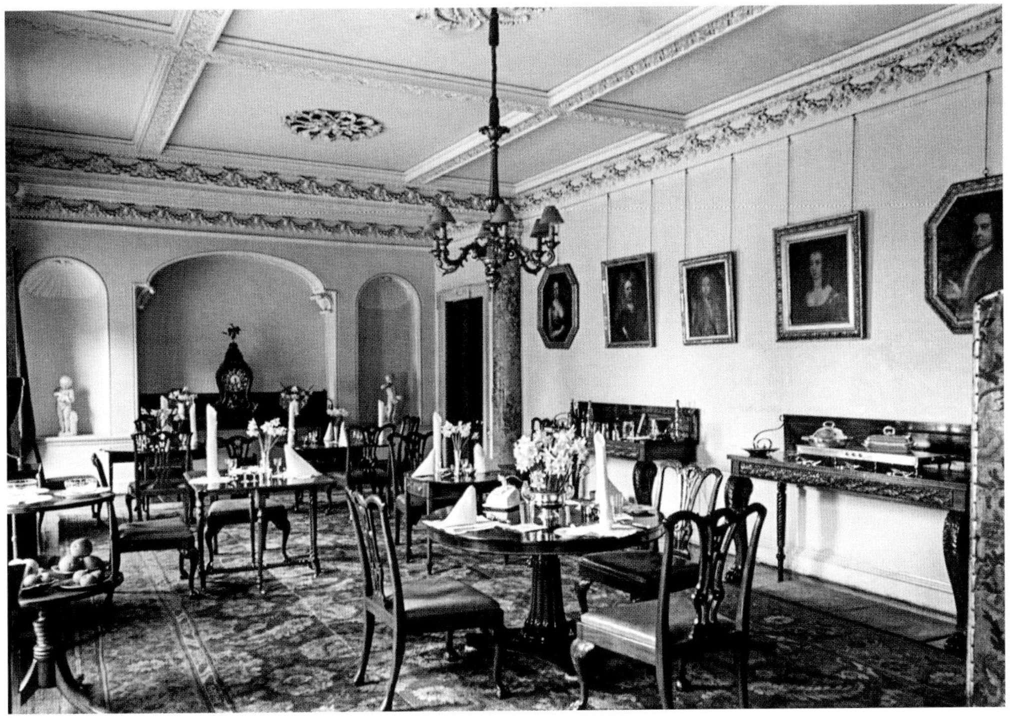

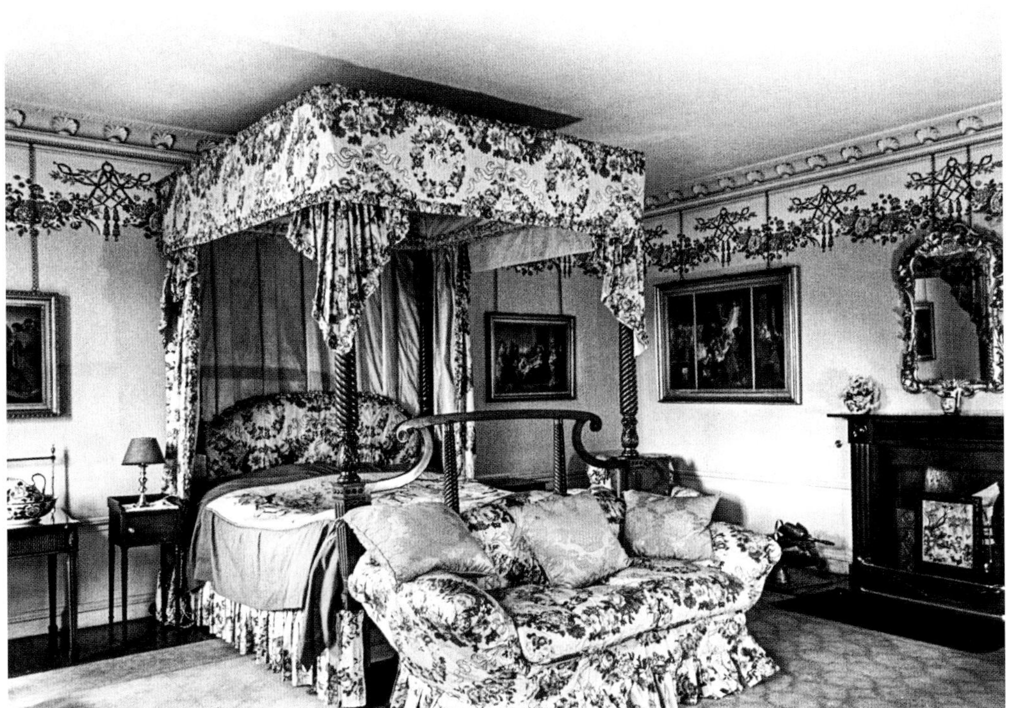

become a hotelier was not successful, and in May 1950 the house's contents were sold in a spectacular auction that lasted for thirteen days, the great majority of lots leaving the country, never to return.

After the sale Lord Wicklow wrote a rather poignant history of his family home, which opened with the words, 'Shelton Abbey is now a shut and empty house, and awaiting sale; as many readers may be aware, the reason why I have been compelled to take the step which I have done, is owing to the overwhelming burden of taxation … '.The house and demesne were later bought by the state, the buildings serving for a time as a forestry school and, more recently, as an open prison, with the consequence that much of the decorative detail seen in Browne's pictures has also been lost or badly mutilated. Meanwhile, Shelton Abbey's celebrated setting in the Vale of Avoca was likewise despoiled when a chemical plant was constructed on the lower park directly in front of the house.

Page 96: The Drawing Room with its extraordinary Perpendicular Gothic ceiling
Page 97: The Library, which has since lost its plasterwork and bookcases

Opposite Page left: The main staircase
Opposite Page right: A first floor bedroom corridor

Above: The Dining Room, decorated in the classical rather than Gothic style
Left: The Grand Bedroom

GLANANEA
COUNTY WESTMEATH

20TH AUGUST 1952

Glananea is one of a number of houses in County Westmeath built by branches of the Smyth family, although none of these properties is now occupied by their descendants. Believed to date from the last decade of the eighteenth century, the place was originally called Ralphsdale after the man responsible for commissioning the building, Ralph Smyth (similarly, a neighbouring Smyth house, Barbavilla, had been named after its owner's wife, Barbara Ingoldsby).

Of six bays and two storeys over basement, Glananea, as it came to be known towards the end of the nineteenth century, exemplifies the chaste neo-classicism of the period. The east-facing facade has a handsome stone doorcase with fan- and sidelights, approached by a short flight of steps. The garden front is of seven bays, those on the ground floor of the three-bay central breakfront being arched. Inside, most of the reception rooms have ceilings decorated with plaster garlands, ovals and medallions, although the drawing room ceiling is more elaborately ornamented, the inclusion of dancing figures carrying food and drink suggesting this may originally have been intended to serve as the dining room.

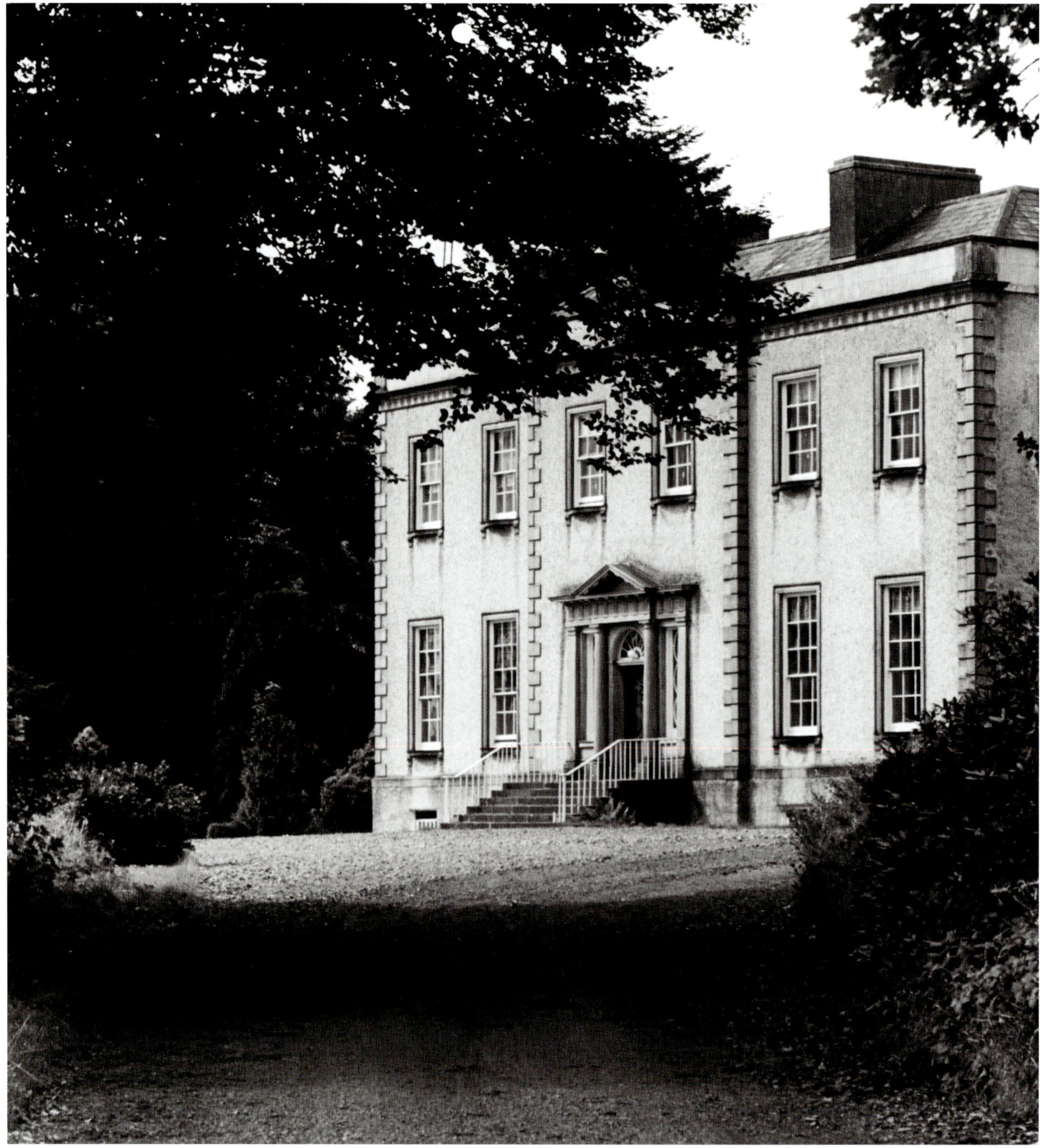

Right: The house's east-facing façade
Opposite: The Entrance Hall with its delicate neo-classical plasterwork

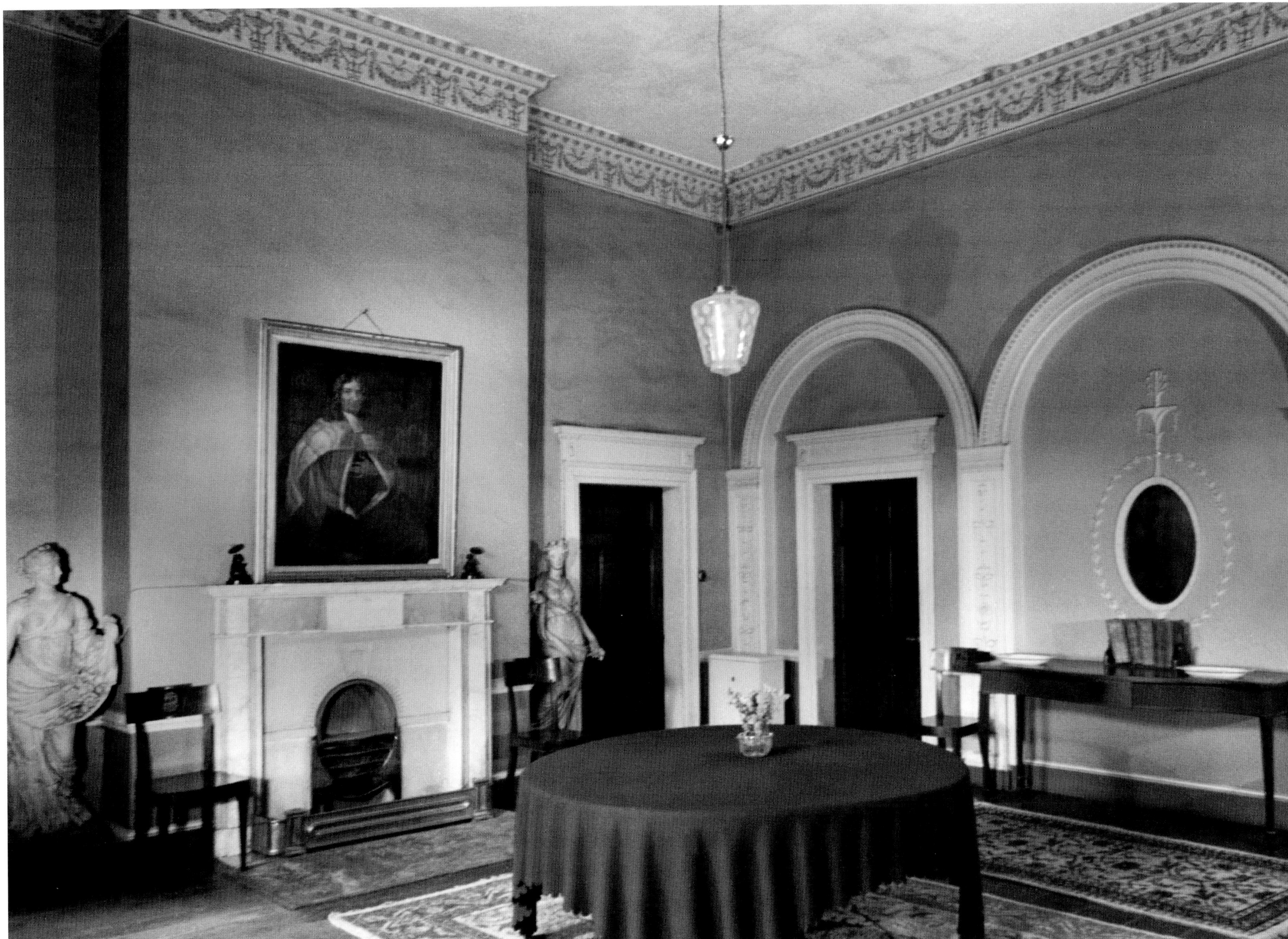

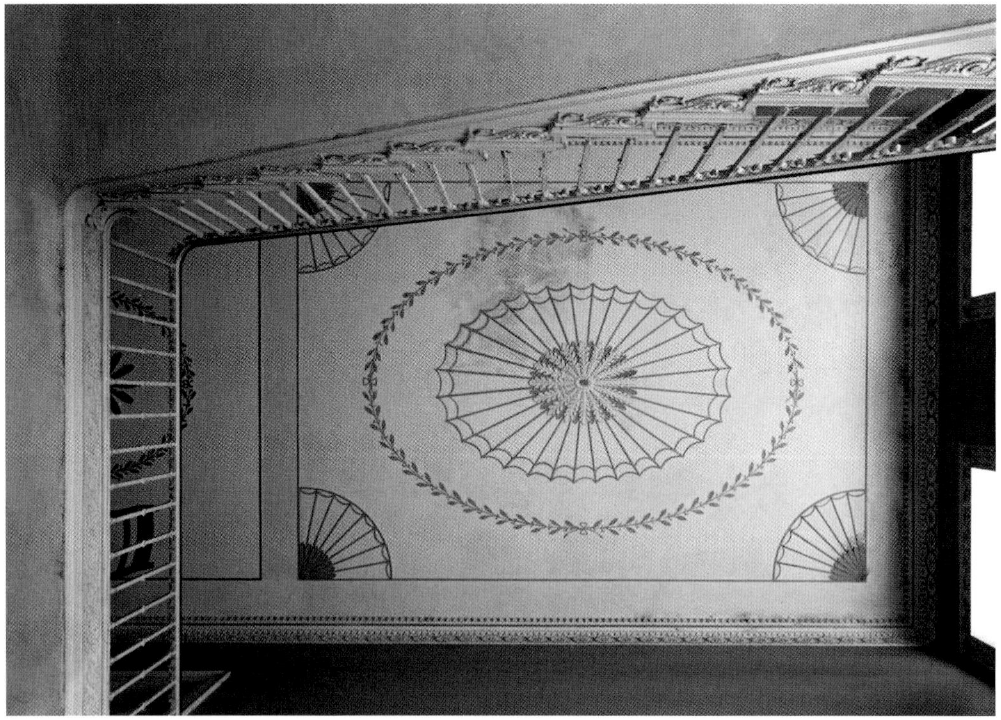

Following Ralph Smyth's death, Glananea was inherited by his son William, who commissioned a new entrance to the demesne from English architect Samuel Woolley. This took the form of a large triumphal arch decorated with Corinthian pilasters as well as Coade stone urns, masks and swags, the whole thing crowned by a unicorn reclining on a pedestal. Ionic colonnades on either side led to curved quadrants that ended in pavilions featuring niches holding classical statues. The erection of this extraordinary confection led its owner to become known locally as 'Smyth with the Gates'. Tiring of the soubriquet, he arranged for the entrance to be dismantled and moved to another property, Rosmead. Thereafter he was called 'Smyth without the Gates'. Today access to the estate is through an altogether more modest set of gates.

At the time of Browne's visit, Glananea was occupied by the last of the family to live there, Abel Edward Smyth. Following his death in 1960 the property was sold. It changed hands more than once over the following decades, but remains a private family house.

Above: Looking up the main staircase
Opposite: A corner of the Drawing Room

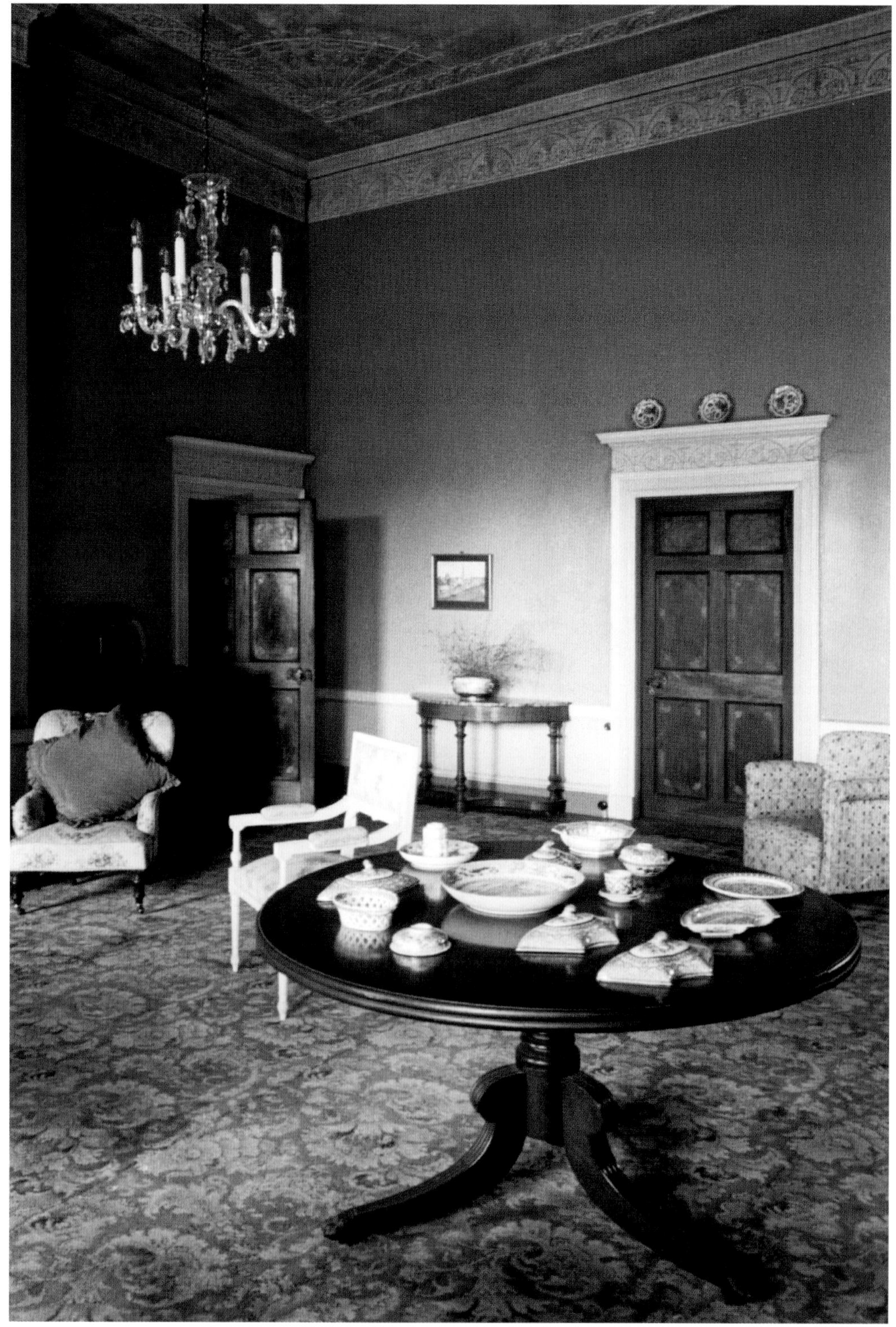